Change Management

A Critical Perspective

Mark Hughes is a Senior Lecturer in Organisational Behaviour in Brighton Business School, at the University of Brighton. Mark teaches change management on MBA programmes and the MA Change Management, and he is a former course leader of the MA Change Management. Mark's work with colleagues and students is focused upon facilitating change in organisations.

The CIPD would like to thank the following members of the CIPD Publishing Editorial Board for their help and advice:

The Chartered Institute of Personnel and Development is the leading publisher of books and reports for personnel and training professionals, students, and all those concerned with the effective management and development of people at work. For details of all our titles, please contact the publishing department:

tel: 020–8612 6204

e-mail: publish@cipd.co.uk

The catalogue of all CIPD titles can be viewed on the CIPD website:

www.cipd.co.uk/bookstore

Change Management

A Critical Perspective

Mark Hughes

Chartered Institute of Personnel and Development

Published by the Chartered Institute of Personnel and Development, CIPD House,
151 The Broadway, London, SW19 1JQ

First published 2006
Reprinted 2007

Typeset by Fakenham Photosetting, Norfolk

Printed in Great Britain by Cromwell Press, Trowbridge, Wiltshire

British Library Cataloguing in Publication Data
A catalogue of this manual is available from the British Library

ISBN-10 1 84398 070 3
ISBN-13 978 1 84398 070 4

Chartered Institute of Personnel and Development
151 The Broadway, Wimbledon, London SW19 1JQ
Tel: 020-8612 6200
E-mail: cipd@cipd.co.uk   Website: www.cipd.co.uk
Incorporated by Royal Charter.   Registered Charity No. 1079797

Contents

List of boxes

Research cases in journals

Acknowledgements

I thank my Mum, Dad and sister (Sheila, Derek and Clair) for all their loving kindness.

I thank Ruth Lake who as the commissioning editor was the catalyst for this particular project. I appreciated her effective support and encouragement throughout the duration of this project. Also, I thank the anonymous reviewers who at different stages of development constructively informed the development of this textbook.

Many colleagues at Brighton Business School have helped me on my journey. Aidan Berry and Tom Bourner helped to make this book possible through their considerable patience and friendly encouragement on earlier writing projects. The Bookmarks writing group (Tom Bourner, Becci Newton, Sue O'Hara and Steve Reeve) I belong to informed and brightened a long journey. Also thanks to Lew Perren for his warm and positive encouragement on this particular project and, really, everyone at Brighton Business School who innocently (and with slight trepidation) asked 'How is the book?' Not forgetting Sue Faulkner, John Lawson, Trix Webber and Marian Whitaker.

Thank you to the postgraduates of the MA Change Management and the MBA programmes: their challenge and enthusiasm for this project was another important motivator. They helped keep me grounded in the real world that exists beyond the university gates. Thank you to John Cormode for his belief in this project and infectious enthusiasm about change management.

I look with envy at previous acknowledgements listing teams of researchers, typists and administrators and wish 'If only ...' In this instance there was just myself and my computer. However, in the summer the sun shone brightly and there was a beautiful sea breeze to cool us both down. Many bands (particularly G.S.Y.B.E and A.S.M.Z) took time out from busy tours to accompany my word processing. In the mornings I had the pleasure of waking to breakfast radio Mithras FM124 with regular wonderful DJs Jo Johnson, Lin Povey and Catherine Matthews – all the news, views, mischief and good humour that you could ever want with your coffee. And in the evenings I enjoyed the tangential musings of Chris Matthews on his Future Sounds of Cornwall show.

Mark Hughes
Brighton

Introduction

CHAPTER 1

INTRODUCING CHANGE MANAGEMENT

This textbook informs understanding about the management of changes regularly occurring inside organisations. These changes may be either planned changes or emergent changes or a hybrid of the two. They are taking place in public, private and voluntary sectors and they may be either beneficial or detrimental to individuals, organisations and society. A motivation for writing this textbook is a belief that change can potentially benefit individuals, organisations and society. For example, the evolution of our hospitals and universities may be attributed to the effective management of change. However, there is much work still to be done in both these types of institutions.

The study of changing organisations can be both fascinating and frustrating. Change has been described as the source of all human progress and all human pain (Page, 1998: 148). The problematic nature of organisational change is slowly being understood and a thorough analysis of organisational change is believed to be a prerequisite of informed change management action. This textbook aims to:

- advance understanding about change management from a critical perspective
- encourage an appreciation of the centrality of individuals in organisational change processes
- provoke debate in terms of the past, present and future understanding of change management.

This chapter introduces major themes of the textbook, starting with a discussion of key terms and concepts. In the discussion of the myths of change management, orthodox thinking is challenged. Three main levels of analysis are pertinent to change management – organisational, group and individual – and each level is introduced in this chapter. A range of academic disciplines inform change management understanding and these are introduced. The pluralism of change management is explained, as well as the development of a critical perspective on change management. Finally, the textbook structure and the chapter structures are introduced. At this stage, the following key terms must be defined, although understanding of each concept will be developed further throughout the textbook:

- change
- organisational change
- individual change
- change management.

Change has many guises, 'transformation, development, metamorphosis, transmutation, evolution, regeneration, innovation, revolution and transition to list but a few' (Stickland, 1998: 14). Although the concept of change is commonly understood, there is no universal definition of what is meant by change. Dawson (1994: 164) suggests that changes in organisations are never clearly defined. In this textbook a broad generic definition of change is favoured as 'any alteration of the status quo...' (Bartol and Martin, 1994: 199). Discussion will frequently focus upon large-scale change. However the definition is broad enough to include the range of changes regularly occurring in organisations. Organisational change may be defined as 'new ways of organising and working...' (Dawson, 2003: 11), raising the question 'What is meant by a work organisation?' Watson (2002: 59) offers the following definition, which is favoured in this textbook:

> *work arrangements involving relationships, understandings and processes in which people are employed, or their services otherwise engaged, to complete tasks undertaken in the organisation's name.*

In considering the concept of individual change a distinction has been made between change and transition (Bridges, 1995: 3). This is between changes which are situational: the new site, the new boss, the new team roles, and the new policy and transition as the psychological process people go through to come to terms with the new situation. The dilemma with such a distinction is that it focuses narrowly upon the psychological processes of change and ignores the organisational and social context of change and how change is managed. In this textbook individual change is concerned with the psychological processes of changing, the changes themselves, and the interplay between individual change and organisational change.

Fincham and Rhodes (2005: 525) offer the following definition of change management:

> *the leadership and direction of the process of organisational transformation – especially with regard to human aspects and overcoming resistance to change.*

The difficulties with this definition are that it may be more effective as a definition of change leadership (discussed further in Chapter 12) and the idea that resistance is something which could/should be overcome may be questioned (discussed further in Chapter 10). Instead, the following definition of change management has been developed for this textbook:

> *attending to organisational change transition processes at organisational, group and individual levels.*

This definition involves all employees in the change process, rather than a single change manager, although the amount of involvement may vary considerably at different hierarchical levels. Also, the definition acknowledges that change may be planned or emergent. 'Attending to' is preferred to 'managing' as an acknowledgement of different approaches to change ranging from education and communication through to explicit and implicit coercion (Kotter and Schlesinger, 1979). In parallel to this definition of change management there will be a requirement for change leadership (see Caldwell, 2003 for an interesting distinction between the two concepts).

The terminology of change is never neutral and even the term 'change management' may be challenged. Clegg and Walsh (2004: 232) believe 'change management' is inappropriate and misleading due to its implementation focus and managerial focus. However, throughout this textbook the processual nature of change is addressed rather than the 'how to' questions of change as implementation, which Clegg and Walsh imply. Also, management does not apply exclusively to senior management – it can equally apply to self-management both personal and professional when dealing with the experience of change. The label 'change management' is favoured for this textbook because it offers a rallying point for anyone interested in organisational change transition processes regardless of their academic discipline/functional background or their hierarchical position.

THE MYTHS OF CHANGE MANAGEMENT

Myths may have beneficial consequences in the context of transforming organisations (Movva, 2003). However, in an academic context myths may lead to misunderstanding change management. Jarrett (2003) has identified seven myths (see also Crom and Bertels, 1999: 162–3 for further common assumptions about managing change). The myths include the belief that change management creates value, that resistance can be overcome, that change agents know best, and that accepted wisdom is to follow the steps. Identifying myths makes tangible the ongoing rethinking of change management taking place both inside organisations and outside organisations.

Myths will be revisited in subsequent chapters (particularly in the *Critical perspective* sections): at this stage it is important not to be overwhelmed by the hyperbole generated around change management. Many of the claims made for change management cannot be substantiated by evidence. For example, stability and continuity will also be evident in organisations even during times of radical change, which challenges the common 'change is the only constant' mantra. The notion that effective change management is about constantly changing regardless of the rationality of such actions is ludicrous:

> *It is important to recognise when not to change as it is to identify when there is a need for change. This is perhaps one of the major myths that pervade the literature on change management – that as changes are inevitable, change initiatives should not be questioned but embraced, as they are ultimately vital to the success of an organisation.*
>
> *(Dawson, 2003: 20)*

The critical scholarship of academics may imply gullible managers and employees believing the myths and misunderstandings which obscure change management understanding. However, although it is impossible to generalise, there is evidence to question such a view. Ezzamel *et al* (1995: 8) in their survey of management practices found that 'managers are rightly sceptical of the evangelical exhortations to change radically, and often show a much greater understanding of the complex implications than do the experts and consultants.' Similarly, Ackroyd and Thompson (1999: 161) acknowledged how aware employees are of the characteristics of culture and change programmes regardless of endorsing the objectives or not. Challenging myths of change management is not a purely academic exercise.

Academics have an obligation to challenge the myths of change management, and one way in which this goal can be achieved is through the advancement of rigorous research-informed theories of change management. Dunphy (1996: 546) argued for the existence of competing theories of change and empirical investigation of the extent to which their claims to achieve their preferred ideals could be substantiated. These aspirations still appear valid today, and this textbook encourages questions about change management rather than offering simplistic answers on how to manage change.

THE CHANGE MANAGEMENT LITERATURE

Dunphy (1996: 545) suggested that 'in the field of organisational change, there is no agreed theory of change and that there is unlikely to be one.' However, the quality of change management literature varies considerably. Dawson (2003: 178) with regret notes that the 'concern in the change management literature remains rooted in a search for key ingredients of "success" in order to sustain competitive advantage.' There are many dangers with searching for key ingredients of success and then making prescriptions about what senior managers should do in other organisations. Such approaches neglect the dynamic nature of change. What worked this year may not work next year, what worked in Organisation A may not work in Organisation B. Success recipes neglect these very different contexts in which organisations operate. A successful change management recipe cannot be transferred to different contexts, however well it is 'spun' by gurus and consultants.

Collins (1998: 35) offers a framework for dividing the organisational change literature into four categories:

- hero-manager reflections and biographies
- guru works
- student-oriented texts
- critical monographs and research studies.

The framework is helpful in beginning to differentiate the competing explanations of change management. This textbook draws particularly upon the last two categories of literature, while pejorative references to popular change literature invariably refer to the first two categories. However, all sources of literature have strengths and weaknesses which may be summarised as follows.

Collins adopts the slightly mocking title of 'hero-manager reflections and biographies' with good reason. Examples of this genre include Iacocca with Novak (1986) and Harvey-Jones (1988). The strengths of such accounts are that they offer insights into senior managers' perceptions of how they lead change. They are often accessible in terms of readability and may offer organisational insights which an outside researcher could not achieve. The weaknesses of these accounts are their often unacknowledged subjectivity and the danger that somebody might mimic such unverified actions.

Guru works is a less precise label, and guru theory is discussed further in Chapter 4. Examples of this genre include Peters and Waterman (1982) and Hammer and Champy (1993). This literature often concentrates on the *how* questions of change management at the expense of the *why* questions. A strength and a weakness of such literature is that it prescribes what to do, rather than encouraging the reader to think and develop. This literature is often presented in an easily digestible manner.

The student-oriented text label applies to this particular textbook and other textbooks books (see, for example, Burnes, 2004a; Carnall, 2003; and Senior and Fleming, 2006). These textbooks represent a body of literature written specifically for students of change management and invariably written by academics teaching and researching change management. A major strength of student-oriented textbooks is that they offer a critical synthesis of the fragmented change management literature in a relatively accessible format. The weakness of such textbooks in terms of Collins's hierarchy would be their research underpinnings, although this is debatable.

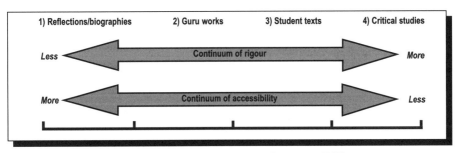

Box 1 – Continuums of literature rigour and accessibility

Critical monographs and research studies are located at the top of the hierarchy which Collins implies, and they are certainly a major source of valid change management knowledge:

> *The authors included under the 'critical' banner are able to stand apart from the so-called needs of management, and so, have the scope and the will to embrace the study of complexity within a well-rooted conceptual and theoretical framework.*
> *(Collins, 1998: 80)*

An example of a critical monograph would include the work of Pettigrew (1985) studying change in ICI longitudinally. The latest research studies as well as previous research may be accessed via academic journals. Again academic journals vary in terms of their accessibility and rigour. Refereed journals are an important source of recent accounts of change research. Their strength is that the papers accepted for publication will have been through some form of review process which is usually specified at the front or the back of the journal. Examples of relevant refereed journals with an explicit change focus include the *Journal of Change Management*, the *Journal of Organizational Change Management* and *Strategic Change*.

The four categories of change management literature may be thought about in terms of the continuums as depicted in Box 1.

The implication here is that a biography may not be rigorous, yet it may be accessible. Although there will be exceptions to these continuums, what can be suggested is that the most rigorous literature is likely to be the least accessible, and vice versa. A research paper in a leading refereed journal may not be the most accessible account of change management, but importantly for the purpose of understanding change management may be the most rigorous.

LEVELS OF ANALYSIS AND CHANGE MANAGEMENT

Daft (1995: 28) suggested that 'four levels of analysis normally characterise organisations.' These are individuals, groups, organisations, and groups of organisations. Writing with specific reference to change, writers have offered classifications of levels.

- individual, group, organisation and wider society (Collins, 1998: 71)
- individual, group and larger system level (Burke, 2002: 83)
- human beings, groups and the organisation (Stacey, 2003: 4)
- individual, group and systems level (Burnes, 2004a: 321).

The references to systems are a reminder of the influence of organisational development (OD) upon change literature. Cummings and Worley (2005: 89) suggest that when organisations are thought of as open systems three levels of diagnosis may be identified:

- *organisational level* – includes the design of the company's strategy, structure and processes
- *group level* – includes group design and such devices for structuring interactions among members as norms and work schedules
- *individual level* – includes ways in which jobs are designed to elicit required task behaviour.

This textbook does not adopt a systems perspective (see Watson, 2002, for a critique of systems orthodoxy). However, the identification and acknowledgement of change at hierarchical levels of organisation, group and the individual does further understanding about change management. The following discussion is organised in terms of organisation, group and individual levels.

Organisational-level discussions are very common in the change management literature. Textbooks such as Carnall (2003) and Balogun and Hope Hailey (2004) explicitly emphasise the adoption of a strategic approach to understanding organisational change. Organisational-level analysis may be particularly fruitful for understanding strategic change, technological change, structural change and cultural change. In this textbook chapters are devoted to each of these important aspects of change management.

Group-level analysis is less prevalent than organisational-level analysis in the change management literature. However, teams are increasingly regarded as the basic units of work organisation (Thompson and McHugh, 2002: 324). In this textbook Chapter 11 is devoted to this level of analysis.

Individual-level analysis is emphasised as making an important contribution to critical understanding about change management in this textbook. However, it is the most challenging and least tangible level of analysis. It is much easier to write and think in terms of how a group or an organisation changes than in terms of the disparate individuals that make up groups and organisations. This caveat highlights the difficulty of a truly individual level of analysis, particularly in a large organisation. The moment you begin to generalise, the level of analysis blurs and the rich diversity of the organisation is lost. Despite such caveats, the literature repeatedly signposts the importance of individual change in organisational change processes (see Box 2).

In Box 2, writers from different academic disciplines and different schools of thought, writing over the past decade, repeatedly acknowledge individual change as an integral ingredient of organisational change processes. The importance of individual-level change in the change management process does not negate the need for organisational- and group-level understanding of change management, but does suggest the need for greater integration of understanding individual-level change into a more sophisticated understanding of change management.

For change to occur in any organisation, each individual must think feel, or do something different. (Duck, 1993: 56)

For organisations to change, people must change. For leaders to help people change, they do not need to understand change – they need to understand people. (Morrison, 1994: 353)

Organisations don't change – people do. Change happens person by person, and you cannot change people: they change themselves. (Quirke, 1995: 106)

Organisations as we know them are the people in them: if the people do not change, there is no organisational change. (Harung, 1997: 194, citing Schneider et al, 1996)

Change in behaviour is considered a primary criterion for effectiveness by organisational development researchers and practioners. (Argyris, 1999: 67)

Change management is about people management. When managing change you manage people. (Paton and McCalaman, 2000: 267)

Organisation change involves, either directly or indirectly, changes in individual behaviour. (Cummings, 2004: 33)

Box 2 – Organisational change involves individual change

Gabriel (2001: 24) warns about the 'holy alliance forged between the manager and the consumer, at the expense of the worker or the employee'. In encouraging an understanding of individuals in organisational change processes, the intention is to encourage a greater appreciation of worker/employee experiences of change. A theme in this textbook is the idea that organisations are reified – meaning that organisations are regarded as 'things'. This shorthand is understandably useful both for organisations and academics. However, the argument is that an organisation will not change without individuals' changing and that we cannot understand how organisations change without understanding individual change as part of the organisational change process.

The above discussion may imply that individualism is being favoured over collectivism, which is not the intention. The position adopted in this textbook is similar to that advanced by Purcell (1987) in his discussion of management styles and employee relations. Individualism and collectivism are not necessarily either/or options. This textbook is not a plea for individualist industrial relations; it does argue for greater understanding of individuals in organisational change processes, while acknowledging the considerable influence of groups, organisations and societies upon individuals.

ACADEMIC DISCIPLINES AND CHANGE MANAGEMENT

Burnes (2004a: 261) has suggested that change management is not a distinct discipline with rigid and clearly defined boundaries, rather that the theory and practice of change management draws on a number of social science disciplines and traditions. Iles and

Sutherland (2001: 12) identify among the difficulties of accessing change management literature the existence of contributions from different academic disciplines. The many references cited in this textbook reflect a broad range of academic disciplines, and all the social sciences potentially have roles to play in informing understanding about change management. However, the following disciplines are believed to be particularly pertinent.

- economics
- strategy
- psychology
- sociology
- management and organisational behaviour.

Discussions about national trends in change management are often informed by economics. A good example is the innovation literature (discussed in Chapter 8). Many of these theories are based upon economics and inform understanding about, for example, trajectories of technological change taking place over time. Economics is most useful explaining organisational-/sectoral-level aspects of change management and least useful explaining groups and individual involvement in change management.

Economics has played an important role in shaping our academic understanding of strategy. Often change management is addressed strategically and change management textbooks may explicitly reflect such an orientation. Again, in terms of levels of analysis, strategy is most useful explaining organisational-level change. A potential shortcoming may be that in focusing at the organisational and sectoral levels, the involvement of groups and individuals may be downplayed.

Fincham and Rhodes (2005: 6) define psychology as a diversified field of study bridging the gap between biology and sociology and focusing upon individuals and the individual's interaction with his or her environment. Psychology is particularly relevant to change management in offering explanations of how individuals respond to change initiatives. For example, do individuals resist change, and if they do resist change, *why* do they resist change? Psychology literature can potentially offer answers to such questions. The limitation of psychology is the inability to locate individuals in the wider social context, although to some extent social psychology has responded to such limitations.

Sociology suggests 'that society consists of a "world out there" existing independently of any one of us' (Fincham and Rhodes, 2005: 10). Sociology and related areas such as social theory have helped encourage a more critical and reflective orientation to understanding change management. Instead of raising questions such as 'How can we manage change?', the agenda has shifted to questions such as 'How does an employee's membership of a wider society influence his or her response to change management initiatives?'

The grouping together of management and organisational behaviour reflects their considerable overlaps. They draw heavily on many of the academic disciplines discussed so far. In this textbook much of the literature reviewing draws upon management and organisational behaviour literature.

Daft (1995: 29) offers a distinction between organisation theory as the sociology of organisations and organisational behaviour as the psychology of organisations. However, in more general terms, management and organisational behaviour comprehensively addresses the three levels of analysis (organisation, group and individual) featured in this textbook.

THE PLURALISM OF CHANGE MANAGEMENT

The above discussion of academic disciplines suggests that a comprehensive understanding of change management will not come from a single discipline. There are as many perspectives on change as people in the organisation affected (Willcocks and Mason, 1987: 21), and Burnes (1996: 11) has emphasised that there is no one best way to manage change. These views suggest the need for pluralism in seeking to understand change management. It may be perceived as antiquated to be advocating pluralist understanding of change management. However 'pluralism in ideas, among people, within organisations, and across industries is a crucial driver of change, even as that very change significantly alters pluralism' (Eisenhardt, 2000: 703).

There is a fit between a pluralist approach to understanding change management and the acknowledgement that specific changes in specific organisations will always be unique. Pettigrew (1990: 269) has effectively articulated this position:

> *Explanations of change are bound to be holistic and multifaceted. Beware of the myth of the singular theory of social or organisational change.*

The need for pluralist approaches to understanding change management is evident elsewhere in the change literature:

> *There can never be a universal theory of organisational change, as change involves a movement to some future state that comprises a context and time that remain unknown.*
>
> *(Dawson, 2003: 11)*

Pettigrew and Dawson in terms of change management caution against adopting universal theories. *The Academy of Management Review* devoted a special issue to change and pluralism, raising concerns that 'pluralism that is so obvious in society at large is often missing from academic theories' (Eisenhardt, 2000: 704). The above discussion provides a rationale for favouring a pluralist approach to understanding change management.

However, in seeking more sophisticated understanding of change management there is a real danger of losing sight of the pioneering theoretical work that has been undertaken and that might still have a role to play in explaining contemporary change. Sorge and Van Witteloostuijn (2004: 1206) believe that many well-established organisation theories, based upon a range of methodologies, combined offer rich insights that are readily applicable to organisational change.

DEVELOPING A CRITICAL PERSPECTIVE ON CHANGE MANAGEMENT

A real concern is beginning to be articulated in the academic literature about the way organisational change and change management is studied (see, for example, Sturdy and Grey, 2003, and Sorge and Van Witteloostuijn, 2004). Academics are accused of not doing enough to deepen understanding about organisational change through critical accounts of change. The previous discussion warned against universal explanations informing understanding about change management, instead favouring pluralism. However, textbooks benefit from having a consistent perspective, while still acknowledging competing explanations of change.

In the case of Collins (1998), he sought to encourage a sociological perspective of organisational change. In the case of Paton and McCalman (2000), their change management textbook sought to guide implementation. And in the case of Burnes (2004a), he adopted a strategic approach to managing change. The adoption of such perspectives ensures continuity in explanations and avoids contradictions, while still maintaining a pluralist approach to change management understanding.

In the context of strategies for change, Darwin *et al* (2002: 121) differentiated Critical Theory from being critical, and writers such as Alvesson and Willmott (1996) have emphasised Critical Theory's being guided by an emancipatory intent. This textbook makes no claims to be a Critical Theory textbook, although a number of critical theorists are cited. Dawson (2003: 167) has argued for the development of a critical reflective awareness when understanding the processes of change, and Collins (2000) refers to a critical-practical perspective when attempting to make sense of management fads and buzzwords. There is a need to be critical of much of what has been written about change management, yet not lose sight of the very real practical challenges of change management (see also Salaman and Asch, 2003: 23). Although this textbook seeks to inform understanding about change management, rather than the practice of change management, the challenges that practitioners face are acknowledged. The meaning of 'critical' in this textbook is the exercise of judgement with specific regard to understanding change management. This textbook privileges evidence-based accounts of change management over anecdotal prescriptions about change management.

The exercise of judgement with regard to taken-for-granted assumptions about change management is beginning to reveal that 'organisational change has an undeniable tendency to produce failure' (Sorge and Van Witteloostuijn, 2004: 1212). Further references are cited, in the *Critical perspective* sections of chapters; in particular, Chapter 15 identifies the prevalence of change management failure and the potential to learn from such failures. The academic implication of literature on change management failure is that rather than assuming that change management succeeds, there is merit in questioning common change management assumptions particularly in terms of asking 'Where is the evidence?'

As well as the failures of change management, there are reasons to be sceptical about much of the acritical change management literature. A benefit of a critical perspective is acknowledging competing approaches, as part of the critiquing process. Resistance to change is a good example of an area where the orthodoxy merits being challenged (see Chapter 10). Perren and Megginson (1996: 24) write about resistance to change as a positive rather than a negative force, suggesting 'reversing the change management literature'. This is an informative way of thinking about the role of critical perspectives in understanding change management. Often the critical perspective is the opposite (or the reverse) position to the orthodoxy. McLoughlin (1999: 145) articulates the rationale for a critical perspective, in his own book, in terms of the metaphor of theatre.

The perspective of this book has not been driven by the perceived needs of the actual or would-be organisational performer for such prescription. Rather, the assumed stance is that of the theatre or cinema critic, perhaps even any member of the audience, keen to sharpen their critical awareness and capacity in order to better understand and explain the action and its context as it is played out before them.

Another potential benefit of adopting a critical perspective towards change management understanding is that an ethical perspective is encouraged, both in terms of acknowledging multiple explanations and critically questioning these explanations. Interest in ethical change management should not be regarded as a new phenomenon. Burnes (2004b: 996) noted that Lewin, as far back as in the 1950s, promoted an ethical and humanist approach to change, and Cobb *et al* (1995: 243) note that 'organisational development has long held an ethical interest in, and commitment to, fairness in planned change efforts.' An ethical perspective begins to speak to the problematic nature of change management. For example, Dawson (2003: 55) found in studies of change he conducted between 1980 and 2002 that it was 'possible to identify "casualties" of change – that is, people who view change negatively and talk of deterioration of their working environment'. Similarly, Weiss (2001: 421) identifies potential ethical dilemmas of change management.

Organisational changes and transformation involve the redistribution of power, information, resources, status, authority, and influence. Therefore, individuals' rights, dignity and privileges can be at risk.

Unfortunately such concerns are not purely speculative. 'The empirical evidence does not support the notion that change brings improvements for all. For many workers, it means working harder with fewer resources and more responsibilities' (Dawson, 2003: 56). Walton and Russell (2004: 143) capture an ongoing tension 'between change management that puts employees' well-being first and change management that serves only business needs'. In encouraging an ethical approach the intention is to challenge crude unitarist assumptions that change is in the best interests of everyone. The perspective developed in this textbook will be that the well-being of the employees is as important as the needs of the organisation/business. Weiss (2001: 421) has identified ethics-related issues that must be considered by those planning or implementing change:

- the rights of individuals affected by the change
- justice to individuals affected by the change
- the fairness of plans, implementation, and methods used in change

These considerations allude to more complex philosophical and theoretical debates underpinning the study of ethics (see Weiss, 2003, for an informative introduction to ethics with specific reference to business).

CHAPTERS AND CHAPTER STRUCTURES

This section briefly introduces the themes of the chapters and the generic chapter structures.

Introducing change management

1 Introduction
2 History and change management

3 Classifying change

4 The causes and contexts of change

The first four chapters introduce change management theories, concepts and perspectives in general. In Chapter 2 the role of history in informing understanding about change management is addressed. Establishing that what is changing is not as straightforward as might be imagined, the change classifications framework featured in Chapter 3 offers clarification. Chapter 4 introduces triggers/drivers of change and the different contexts in which change takes place.

Understanding change management

5 Strategic change

6 Changing organisational forms

7 Cultural change

8 Technological change

The next four chapters look at major aspects of change management – strategy, organisational forms, culture and technology. In each of these areas there are contentious debates around competing explanations of change. In later chapters, areas of change management such as leadership may be applied to strategy, organisational forms, culture and technology.

Individuals, groups and change management

9 Individual and organisational change

10 Resistance to change

11 Group-/team-based change

A theme throughout this textbook is the belief that organisations only change if individuals change. In Chapter 9 theories about individual change are introduced, as well as their relationships with theories of organisational change. Chapter 10 addresses a related theme of resistance to change, which is a common perception of the response of individuals to organisational change. Chapter 11 acknowledges that although organisations are comprised of collections of individuals, these individuals are likely to find themselves working in groups and teams and to be influenced by their membership of groups and teams.

Managing change

12 Leading change

13 Communicating change

14 Control and change

This textbook advances theoretical understanding about change management, rather than addressing the practical challenges of managing change. However, three challenges of leading, communicating and control and change are analysed from a theoretical perspective. In each of these chapters orthodox understanding about leading, communicating and control are explained and critiqued.

Learning about change management

The final two chapters draw upon discussions in earlier chapters. In Chapter 15 the concept of organisational learning is introduced both as a change management concept and as a framework for considering what has been learned from both successes and failures of change management. The final chapter discusses major themes which have emerged in earlier chapters and offers focused conclusions that can be drawn in terms of understanding change management.

This chapter and the final chapter in introducing and concluding the textbook are atypical of the structure of the other 14 chapters. In the other chapters a generic structure has been adopted:

- Learning outcomes
- Introduction section
- Approaches section
- Critical perspective section
- Synopsis
- Discussion questions
- Case study
- Further reading

The *Learning outcomes* offer a focused introduction to what each chapter is seeking to achieve, and the achievement of these learning outcomes are revisited in the chapter *Synopsis*. The *Approaches* section provides an overview of key aspects of change management in terms of debates and theories. The intention in this section is to introduce orthodox explanations of the featured change topic. This is invariably contrasted with the *Critical perspective* which seeks to challenge the orthodoxy. Earlier in this chapter, myths of change management were highlighted and adopting a critical questioning approach to change management is one way of challenging such myths. The discussion questions are another mechanism for encouraging critical thinking. Also, many of the chapters include a *Research cases in journals* section. These discussions signpost research-based cases which have been published in leading academic journals.

All theories have their limitations and the process of questioning theories and concepts introduced in each chapter is believed to deepen understanding about theories and concepts. Another means of deepening understanding about theories and concepts is through their application to a case study change situation, and case studies are included in Chapters 3 to 14. Each case study has been designed with specific reference to the theories and concepts featured in the chapter. Chapters are supported with full Harvard referencing. For anyone who wishes to study a topic in more detail, however, each chapter concludes with a short annotated bibliography of further reading.

History and change management

LEARNING OBJECTIVES

To:

■ introduce major approaches to understanding change management

■ review competing explanations for the origins of the concept of change management

■ question the linearity of change management

■ explain the historiography of change management understanding

■ challenge the underlying managism of change management.

INTRODUCTION

It feels contradictory to write about history and change management in the same sentence, let alone the same chapter. However, historical perspectives offer a means of challenging much of the hyperbole evident in management literature.

> *History is well placed to ask big questions over a long time series and thus act as another counterpoint to the largely ahistorical field of strategic management.*
> *(Pettigrew et al, 2002: 13)*

Thompson and O'Connell Davidson (1995: 17) in critically questioning the rhetoric of turbulent times use the writings of Drucker to illustrate his repeated warnings that we are living through a period of unprecedented change. In a similar manner, Eccles and Nohria (1992: 27) address the question of whether the 1980s and 1990s were truly a time of organisational transformation and discontinuous change as many believe and Drucker implies. They conclude that future business historians may be better placed to make this assessment than are any contemporary writers. 'When one is immersed in the present it is hard to know what is fleeting, what is idiosyncratic, and what is part of more permanent and systemic change.' They are suggesting that understanding change historically rather than as it happens may be more informative.

The above concerns may be summarised in the criticism of change management 'that it is ahistorical and acontextual...' (Cooke, 1999: 97). The contexts of change are explored in Chapter 4. This chapter considers how history informs and misinforms understanding about change management – as Abrahamson (2000: 79) notes, 'Change has been with us forever, and it always will be, but the idea of change itself is changing.'

The challenges of managing change go back much further than the literature featured in this chapter. For example, Morgan (1986: 233) cites Heraclitus writing about change in 500 BC, and Burke (2002: 19) reminds us that 'organisation change is as old as organisations', citing examples of building projects such as the Egyptian pyramids and the Great Wall of China. However, focusing upon the past century is believed to provide an informed understanding of the emerging concept of change management – although Dawson (2003: 11) warns, while acknowledging the emergence of a large body of knowledge about change management over the past 100 years, that he does not believe this work has provided any lasting answers.

UNDERSTANDING CHANGE MANAGEMENT HISTORICALLY

This section introduces major approaches informing understanding about change management and competing explanations of the origins of change management.

Approaches to understanding change management

One approach to understanding change management is the identification of major schools of thought. Burnes (2004a: 262) highlights three schools of thought upon which he believes change management is based:

- the individual perspective school
- the group dynamics school, and
- the open systems school.

This is a good starting point for beginning to understand the range of approaches to understanding change management that exist and is compatible with the levels of analysis discussed in Chapter 1. As the titles suggest, the individual perspective explains change management in terms of individual behaviours, group dynamics emphasise change through groups and teams, and open systems approaches advocate whole organisation interventions. The acknowledgement of schools of thought begins to differentiate theorists and competing explanations of change management. The implication is not that one school of thought is superior to another, but that theorists believe that change management is best understood and explained in a certain way. For example, Chapter 11 focuses on groups and change, and cites Lewin (1951) in terms of his belief in change being best achieved through groups.

Different approaches to understanding change management reflect different academic disciplines again discussed in Chapter 1. In understanding the approaches there are parallels between approaches to management and organisational behaviour in general and change management in particular. Paton and McCalman (2000: 2) regard management and change as synonymous. Hamlin (2001: 44) offers a typical overview of the mainstream theoretical perspectives to understanding organisations. The strength of his classification is the specification of change strategies arising out of each perspective, which may be summarised as follows:

- *structural functionalism*: change structure and functions in order to reduce conflict.
- *human relations*: facilitate change to more readily meet needs of individuals.
- *psychodynamic*: facilitate the individual to realise the implications of defensive behaviour.
- *systems theory*: change will have systematic effects on the other parts of the organisation making up the whole.
- *contingency theory*: change the contingencies within the system to develop the most appropriate management system and structure.

- *action frame of reference*: change the rules which inform behaviour so as to change and transform the meaning of the organisation for the individual.
- *cultural, ethnographic and metaphorical*: change the meaning of the symbols within the culture of the organisation.

Often, theorists are associated with a particular approach. For example, Mayo (1933) is associated with the human relations approach. This approach emerged from studies during the mid-1920s and early 1930s known as the Hawthorne experiments. Mayo is attributed with propagandising the Hawthorne studies although he did not join the team properly until 1928 and was peripheral compared to those who wrote up the detailed research (Thompson and McHugh, 2002: 45). The Hawthorne studies have been influential in terms of the development of organisational behaviour. Criticisms of Mayo and the human relations approach emphasise the uncritical attitude towards economic elites and the 'very shaky' empirical basis of Mayo's assertions (Thompson and McHugh, 2002: 48).

Another means of understanding these different approaches would be in terms of their historical evolution. The earliest writers favoured structural functionalism whereas more contemporary writers have often favoured more cultural, ethnographic and metaphorical approaches. However, it would be inappropriate to believe that the most recent theories are always the most effective theories. A theory may address earlier deficiencies in theorising. At other times previous theoretical advances may be overlooked or misunderstood. This need to respect past theorising may be illustrated with specific reference to the National Health Service (NHS). Iles and Sutherland (2001: 12) in their review of the change literature wrote, 'While some of the challenges facing the NHS are novel, many of them may benefit from the application of concepts that were developed several decades ago.'

Fayol (1916) was an influential classical theorist who shaped the very early development of organisational analysis. Huczynski (1996: 50) identified Fayol as the most popular management writer. His work was not initially widely read, yet he typifies the values and aspirations of classical theorists. One of his major contributions was the classification of activities of organisations in terms of:

- technical,
- commercial,
- financial,
- security,
- accounting and
- managerial.

Fayol also identified 14 general principles of management. In essence his contribution was one of defining and classifying management. Although much of what he wrote about is now taken for granted, his role was fundamental in beginning debates about the classification of management, prompting the question 'What is management?' Watson (2002: 86) critically regards Fayol's lists 'as slogans for the systems-control orthodoxy in organisational and managerial thinking'. The implication here is that something as apparently simple as a classification is not neutral (discussed further in the *Critical perspective* below). However, in terms of this chapter, Fayol is another example of early theorising informing contemporary explanations of change management. Stickland (1998: 29) in his own cataloguing of approaches to change suggests that up to the 1960s the scientific-rational view of change, the human relations view of change and the contingency view of change shaped thinking. More recently, developments such as business process change, organisational development, population ecology and quality approaches have become influential.

There is no consensus list of approaches to change management and it would be possible to challenge any so-called definitive list. However, Stickland (1998: 36) does remind us that approaches to organisational change may be categorised in terms of 'their theoretical contribution at one extreme and practical application on the other'. This practical influence upon change management understanding merits discussion even in a theoretically-orientated textbook. Graetz *et al* (2002: 98) identify the change tools that have been utilised, with varying degrees of success, as part of change management. These include the learning organisation, lean production, total quality management and the high-performance work organisation. This thinking in terms of change tools is useful in that it often reflects the practical application of the more theoretical change approaches discussed earlier, highlighting that as well as an evolution of theories there will have been an evolution of change management tools.

Over the decades, at times change tools have caught the imagination of organisations, although 'this terrain is littered with contributions which, without warning or explanation, abandon the hard ground of research and analysis for the swamp of prescription' (Graetz *et al*, 2002: 98). Burke (2002: 20), acknowledging that scholars have only recently become interested in organisational change, traces important forerunners to the present-day study of organisational change. More recent forerunners are believed to include organisation development (OD), the managerial grid and OD, coercion and confrontation, and management consulting.

The origins of the concept of change management

Because change management draws upon a number of social science disciplines, tracing its origins is difficult (Burnes, 2004a: 261). Equally, given its prevalence it is easy to take change management as an established concept for granted. However, in the first half of the previous century change management was not explicitly discussed.

> *As a formal subject for study and application, change management can be said to have begun some 50 years ago with what has since become known as the planned model of change.*
>
> *(Burnes, 1996: 11)*

In terms of organisational preoccupations with change management, according to Graetz *et al* (2002: 14–15) it was only in the mid-1970s that the highly protected domestic environment with relative security, stability and predictability began to diminish, ending the era of change as familiar, identifiable and incremental. Textbooks explicitly focusing upon change management began to appear in the UK in the 1990s: the first editions of Carnall were published in 1990 and of Burnes in 1992. One of the conundrums of change management is establishing the specific origin of the term 'change management'. Three potential explanations for the origin of change management are discussed below.

This first explanation plausibly suggests that change management can be traced back to the pioneering work of Kurt Lewin, compatible with Burnes' earlier assertion. In *Field Theory in Social Science*, Lewin (1951) introduced one of the most well-known models of the change process, suggesting three stages of change: unfreezing, moving and refreezing. Lewin certainly influenced understanding about change management – but it is debatable whether he originated the specific concept. His interest originally appears to have been around conflict and change in groups rather than in primarily organisational change.

The second explanation for the origins of change management is as an evolution of organisation development (OD). Cummings and Worley (2005: 1) offer the following definition of OD:

> *Organisation development is a systemwide application and transfer of behavioral science knowledge to the planned development, improvement, and reinforcement of the strategies, structures, and processes that lead to organisation effectiveness.*

In this precise definition of OD, Cummings and Worley explicitly note that they are distinguishing OD 'from two related subjects: change management and organisation change...' They trace the origins of OD as emerging from five major stems, comprising the National Training Laboratories, action research, participative management, emphasis upon the quality of work life, and strategic change/organisation transformation. Beckhard (1969) probably coined the term 'organisation development' (OD) (Buchanan and Huczynski, 2004: 578) after which French and Bell (1973) did much to promote and operationalise the concept. Senior and Fleming (2006: 343) offers a positive, even optimistic, perspective on OD:

> *The OD approach to change is, above all, an approach which cares about people and which believes that people at all levels throughout an organisation are, individually and collectively, both the drivers and the engines of change.*

However, Rollinson (2005: 638) highlights contradictions between the humanistic ideals of OD and the ethics of OD, suggesting that it could be regarded as a managerial form of employee manipulation. OD has been a very influential methodology for affecting change in organisations, although criticisms have been raised about OD (see, for example, Dawson, 1994: 16 and Legge, 1995: 13).

A third explanation of the origins of change management may be regarded as a challenge to the claim that change management originated out of OD. Worren *et al* (1999) offer an explanation of the emergence of change management grounded in their research and the literature. Through research with major consulting firms, they identify when change management practices were established in these firms. The following dates are suggested for the five firms featured – 1980s, 1992, 1990, 1993 and 1996 – and lead the authors to declare:

> *Our comparison between traditional OD and change management defined by major consulting firms suggests that change management represents a new approach: There are differences with regard to underlying theory and analytical framework, the role of the change agent, and the preferred intervention strategies.*
> *(Worren et al, 1999: 283)*

Worren *et al* appear to believe that change management was a creation primarily of consulting firms rather than academics, although they do not assert this point. It must be acknowledged that the view that consultancy firms developed change management remains contentious (see Farias and Johnson, 2000, and Hornstein, 2001, for responses to the original paper).

This discussion has addressed an important historical question about the specific origins of the concept of change management. Frustratingly, it is impossible to offer a single answer. Certainly, understanding about change management has been informed by Lewin, OD theorists and management consultants, amongst others.

CRITICAL PERSPECTIVE

This chapter in response to traditionally ahistorical approaches to change management (see Cooke, 1999: 97 and Pettigrew, 2002: 13 for further discussion) has encouraged a more historical orientation to understanding change management. It is an orientation that is favoured throughout this textbook. However, a critical perspective encourages history to be addressed in a critical manner. It is necessary to question the apparent linearity of change management, the historiography of change management and the 'managism' of change management.

Questioning the linearity of change management

Arguing for a historical approach to change management suggests a rather reassuring linear evolution of thinking and understanding about change management. Increasingly, however, linear conceptions of change are being challenged:

> *Organisational change is not linear; if it has any direction, it is very often cyclical. Many current forms of organisational change, although they are described as if they were the very latest in modern thinking, have been around before, often more than once and sometimes very long ago, although often under a different name.*
> *(Salaman and Asch, 2003: 3)*

The implication in this quotation is that history repeats itself. The notion of change as cyclical is informative in terms of understanding change management. A radical new change management initiative, such as business process re-engineering, presented as a break with the past may be understood as revisiting principles of scientific management (Cummings, 2002: 129). Darwin *et al* (2002: 11) raise similar concerns when arguing 'that most, if not all, currently fashionable ideas are reinventions: old wine in new bottles, with packaging and presentation the critical factors.'

However, more radical writers have taken the cyclical nature of change even further than a historic process of reinvention. Burrell (1992) looked at change with specific reference to time, leading him to challenge notions of linearity and chronarchy and to promote the notion of spiral time (depicted pictorially as a coiled serpent). Similarly, Cummings (2002: 180) challenges assumptions about the linearity of change, instead arguing for 'a vision of time not as a straight line but as a spiral, with past, present and future intermingled'. These conceptions of time and change challenge the orthodoxy particularly in terms of planned change and the belief in planned strategic change (discussed further in Chapter 5).

The historiography of change management

Cummings (2002: 9–10) in a radical retelling of management's history argues that management arose at the end of the nineteenth century as a science of efficiency: 'Management tends to take different dimensions and adapt them to fit its prevailing logic or habits, thereby limiting creative thinking.' This is dramatically different from more traditional 'textbook' conceptions of theories of management's development through a process of rigorous empirical work. However, the quotation also warns that there is not a single history of change management but a host of histories. The depiction of management in management and organisational behaviour textbooks may be the dominant version of the historical evolution of management, but it is not the only version. The study of how history is written is referred to as historiography.

Cooke (1999: 81) has devoted a fascinating paper to the historiography of change management arguing that 'change management's very construction has been a political process which has written the left out, and shaped an understanding of the field as technocratic and ideologically neutral.' He (1999: 3) explains how he believes this process works:

> *History, our knowing of the past, is constructed by identifying some of these events as significant, and, by implication, others as not, and by giving these events particular meaning.*

In writing about history and change management, choices about what is written will shape this history and also different interpretations of events will shape this history. This textbook could be analysed in these terms – for example, Chapter 14 focuses upon control and change, and it will be argued that understanding control is integral to understanding change management – yet other change management textbooks do not address control and change.

Cooke (1999: 98) argues persuasively that 'all understanding of management and organisation theory are shaped by historiographical processes.' Such a conclusion could be related to this chapter, this textbook and all literature about change management. The best way to understand Cooke's argument is through examples. Cooke (1999: 83) explains how in the 1984 edition of the classic French and Bell OD textbook the contribution of women such as Mouton, Schindler-Rainman, and Seashore to the development of OD was not acknowledged, whereas in the 1996 edition of the same classic textbook their contribution was acknowledged. The events being written about had not changed between 1984 and 1996, but how this aspect of history was written about had changed. Also, Cooke cites how Lewin's left activism has largely been written out of traditional change management literature. As Burnes (2004b: 979) reminds us: 'For most of his life, Lewin's main preoccupation was the resolution of social conflict and, in particular, the problems of minority or disadvantaged groups.' Yet Burnes (2004b: 995) perceptively notes how Dawson (1994), Kanter *et al* (1992) and Wilson (1992) criticised his work for 'advocating a top-down, management-driven approach to change and ignoring situations requiring bottom-up change'.

Another illustration of historiography is evident in the paper by Wrege and Hodgetts (2000). They analysed the original documents upon which Frederick W. Taylor's famous pig-iron observations of 1899 were based.

Taylor (1911) originated the term 'scientific management', which has been defined as 'works design principles that maximise the amount of discretion over task performance given to managerial experts, who calculate and precisely define how each job is to be carried out' (Watson, 2002: 307).

A major concern with the work of Taylor appears to be his generalised assumptions about human nature. However, scientific management gained legitimacy from the research that underpinned the claims of Taylor. Troublingly, when Wrege and Hodgetts (2000: 1290) retrospectively reviewed the work of Taylor, they found that his observations were erroneous. Taylor and associates had made many mistakes, most importantly simplifying the results of their study and glossing over inconsistencies. Scientific management has been and continues to be very influential in terms of management and organisational behaviour thinking inside organisations, as demonstrated by the rebranding of scientific management as BPR (see Cummings, 2002: 129 and Darwin *et al*, 2002: 25 for further discussion).

The 'managism' of change management

Watson (2002: 53) has written about managism as 'an operating faith that managers themselves sometimes adopt when struggling with the pressures of managing in a complex and fast-changing world'. Watson defines the concept of managism (similar to yet different from 'managerialism') as follows:

> *A belief that there is a distinctive managerial expertise based on a body of objective management knowledge which managers should apply to enable them rationally to design, maintain and drive organisational systems in the same way that expert engineers design, maintain and drive machines.*

The danger in a managist orientation is that in focusing upon the present, the past is neglected. Even remaining at a practical level it becomes difficult to reconcile the existence of managism with fashionable change management initiatives, such as the learning organisation and organisational learning which require reflection upon the past in order to inform management actions. However, the importance of history is much more substantive than this. Again the writings of Watson (2002: 36) are informative:

> *What we are and what we do in the present must always be understood in the light of where we have come from historically. If we don't do this, we will fail to see that the way things are for us in the world is not the only way it can be.*

An appreciation of history highlights the change management choices that are always available. This historical approach is believed to be compatible with the pluralist approach introduced in Chapter 1. Challenging managism may benefit organisations and may be recognised in organisations: 'It is advantageous for leaders to be historians of change in their organisations, learning about positive outcomes and barriers to previous change' (Bruhn 2004: 132–3). This reasoning may be used to challenge the tiring hyperbole of the need for constant change inside organisations. Eccles and Nohria (1992: 4) question notions of newness with specific reference to the past:

> *Yet our experience and research has also led us to the conclusion that a certain scepticism of newness is necessary – that the constant talk about 'new practices for a new age' is short-sighted and may lead us both to misunderstand the past and to ignore what is really important in organisations.*

In a way this criticism may be regarded as an extension of the concerns of Cooke discussed earlier. The concern is that history and theorising about change management is developed from the perspective of the 'knowledgeable' manager. Collins (1998: 160) believed that there were few radical accounts of change to which a management reader could be referred for guidance.

SYNOPSIS

Change management was informed by major schools of thought: these included the individual perspective school, the group dynamics school and the open systems school. Different schools of thought signpost how a theorist may offer different explanations of change management. Major mainstream theoretical perspectives for understanding organisations that may be used to classify change included structural functionalism, human relations, the psychodynamic approach, systems theory, contingency theory, action frame of reference, and cultural, ethnographic and metaphorical approaches.

It is difficult to trace the origins of change management. Textbooks explicitly focusing upon change management began to appear in the UK in the 1990s. Three potentially plausible explanations of the origins of change management were identified. Firstly, change management may be traced back to the pioneering work of Kurt Lewin. Secondly, the origins of change management may be traced back to the evolution of organisation development. A third explanation of the origins of change management relates to when major consulting firms established change management practices.

A historical approach to change management suggests a rather reassuring linear evolution of thinking and understanding. However, organisational change is not linear – it is often cyclical. Radical new change management initiatives, such as business process re-engineering, which are presented as a break with the past may be understood as revisiting principles of scientific management.

The norm is for mainstream textbooks to suggest theories of management developing over time through a process of rigorous empirical work. However, there is not a single history of change management but a host of histories. The study of how history is written is referred to as historiography. History is constructed by identifying some events as significant and others as not significant, and giving these events particular meaning.

Watson defined 'managism' as an operating faith that managers themselves sometimes adopt when struggling with the pressures of managing in a complex and fast-changing world. The danger in a managist orientation is that in focusing upon the present, the past is neglected. An appreciation of history highlighted the change management choices that were always available.

DISCUSSION QUESTIONS

1   What are the potential consequences of adopting an ahistorical approach to understanding change management?

2   In the written history of change management, which groups and roles are likely to have been over-represented and which groups and roles under-represented?

3   Is the history of change management fixed, or does the history itself change over time?

4   Which explanation do you prefer for the origins of change management?

5   Does our understanding of change management benefit or suffer from competing approaches to explaining change management?

6   How does our understanding of change management need to develop in the future?

FURTHER READING

In understanding change management historically there is merit in reading some of the original accounts of the theories discussed in this chapter. Alternatively, the references below signpost historical overviews that would complement reading this chapter.

BURKE W. (2002) *Organization Change: Theory and Practice*, Thousand Oaks, California, Sage Publications.

Burke devotes a chapter in his overview of organisation change to 'A brief history of organisation change'. The chapter emphasises the historical evolution of our thinking about organisation change. There are interesting sections on coercion and confrontation and management consulting. He believes that much can be learned from responses to coercive and confrontational techniques in terms of understanding organisational change.

BURNES B. (2004) *Managing Change*, 4th edition, Harlow, FT/Prentice Hall.

This comprehensive account of change management benefits from a strong sense of history, tracing the origins of contemporary theories. Whereas the norm in other textbooks is to merely acknowledge, for example, the contribution of Lewin, Burnes demonstrates how the theories of Lewin are still relevant to understanding change management today. In essence Burnes acts as an advocate for Lewin.

COOKE B. (1999) Writing the left out of management theory: the historiography of the management of change, *Organization*, Vol.6, No.1, 81–105.

This paper, which has featured in the chapter, is recommended further reading. The reasons for recommendation are that the paper has something to say in that it has a strong storyline. You may not agree with the political perspective of Cooke, but his paper is an effective illustration of how change management writers shape our understanding of change management. The paper is also recommended for offering deeper insights into three major theorists – Kurt Lewin, John Collier and Edgar Schein.

CUMMINGS S. (2002) *Recreating Strategy*, London, Sage Publications.

The innocent title of this book belies the sophistication of the ideas within it. The book is recommended as further reading here for its consistent emphasis upon history. In particular, the author adopts a critical perspective to highlight how history has been misrepresented in developing understanding about organisational behaviour, management and strategy. The tone of the book is critical throughout, and the book has the capacity to provoke alternative thinking about taken-for-granted aspects of organisations. For anyone reading the book selectively there is a very relevant chapter on regenerating change. The only cautionary note would be that the modernist/postmodernist themes are hard work for the uninitiated.

Classifying change

INTRODUCTION

This chapter is concerned with 'the diversity of thinking and activity encompassed by the single term "change"' (Iles and Sutherland, 2001: 14). Chapter 1 introduced many guises of change as 'transformation, development, metamorphosis, transmutation, evolution, regeneration, innovation, revolution and transition ...' (Stickland, 1998: 14). The dilemma of defining change was regarded as not purely academic since changes in organisations are never clearly defined (Dawson, 1994: 164). Organisational change was broadly defined as 'new ways of organising and working ...' (Dawson, 2003: 11). Such definitions accommodate the range of discussions informing a pluralistic understanding of change management. However, there remains a need to be specific about different changes that take place in different organisations. Otherwise, there is a real danger of mimicking the generalised prescriptions and descriptions of change evident in practical change literature.

Organisational change scholars have been concerned that not enough has been done to understand change itself (Stickland, 1998: 9). Yet the dilemma is that searching for the underlying values of change results in different meanings and rationalities (De Caluwe and Vermaak, 2004: 213).

The change classifications framework offered here attempts through a process of questioning to offer a means of classifying specific changes, in the belief that this will deepen understanding and move debates away from generalised discussions about change. The literature underpinning the change classifications framework is discussed in the Understanding section. By way of introduction, however, the change classifications framework questions are specified in Box 3.

Q 1 What is specifically changing?
Q 2 Why is this change taking place?
Q 3 Who made the decision to change?
Q 4 What has been the recent organisational history of change?
Q 5 How is this change being communicated?

Q 6 What is the scale and scope of this change?
Q 7 What are the temporal aspects of this change?
Q 8 Who is managing this change and how is it being managed?
Q 9 What would be a successful outcome of this change?
Q10 Who can influence the success/failure of this change?

Box 3 – The change classifications framework

It is worthwhile considering how other authors have classified change. In the case of Stickland, he focused a fascinating book upon what change actually is. Whereas Collins (1998:34–5) was more sceptical, noting that the 'what is change' narrative can be found in what he perceived as basic textbooks on change. He rejected such an approach in the belief that subsequent accounts can become rather tiresome and repetitive, failing to locate management as an ideology particularly in terms of history, politics and control.

However, the position of Collins, writing in 1998, may be contrasted with recent change textbooks which have attempted to clarify the specific meaning of change. The classifications of Paton and McCalman (2000), Burke (2002), Dawson (2003) and Balogun and Hope Hailey (2004) are summarised in Box 4.

Six key factors associated with successful change classification; role and selection of the problem owner, locating change on the change spectrum, the TROPICS test, force field analysis, success guarantors and managing the triggers. (Paton and McCalman, 2000: 17–18)

Change dimensions characterised in terms of the temporal element, the scale of change, the political dimension and the substantive element of change. (Dawson, 2003: 18)

Scholars and practioners need to identify the following different forms of organisation change:
revolutionary v *evolutionary*
discontinuous v *continuous*
episodic v *continuing flow*
transformational v *transactional*
strategic v *operational*
total system v *local option*   (Burke, 2002: 12)

Development of a change kaleidoscope comprised of the following categories: change path, change start-point, change style, change target, change levers and change roles. (Balogun and Hope Hailey, 2004: 19)

Box 4 – Literature-based change classifications

In each of the forms of classification in Box 4 there are similarities and differences, and although it is possible to see why Collins finds the approach 'tiresome', they do appear pertinent to a more comprehensive understanding about change.

INTRODUCING THE CHANGE CLASSIFICATIONS FRAMEWORK

In this section the rationale for developing the change classifications framework is offered. Each of the ten framework questions are located and explained in terms of relevant change management literature and illustrated in terms of a hypothetical example of a county council experiencing organisational structural change. The framework has primarily been developed to aid academic understanding of change, but has the potential to be used as an analysis tool inside organisations, and this application is discussed further in the final part of this section.

The rationales for developing the change classifications framework

Five rationales may be identified for developing the change classifications framework; these rationales are discussed below.

Firstly, the question 'What is change?' is frustrated by the breadth and occasionally the depth of the change management literature. As discussed in the previous chapter, writers from very different academic disciplines have offered explanations of change management. A consequence of these ongoing discussions is a large, disparate and at times contradictory literature relating to change classifications. The first rationale for developing the framework was to undertake an overview of the change literature in a focused manner in order to create a classification tool.

The second rationale for developing the framework was to move discussion away from change in general to change in particular. It is easy to make rhetorical generalisations about, for example, change being the only constant. However, studying specific changes in specific organisations over time allows more informed judgements about such claims. Understanding specific changes is believed to be compatible with the research informed approach of this textbook.

The third rationale relates to allowing a specific change to be defined in terms of the questions posed. The use by managers of ambiguous rhetoric as part of change management is discussed further in Chapter 13. Through this process of definition it is possible to differentiate changes, which may inform choices about what to study and what not to study.

A fourth rationale for classifying what was known was that this process might make explicit what was not known. Acknowledgement of the unknown is believed to be particularly pertinent to change management in that change involves movement to some future state that comprises a context and time that remain unknown (Dawson, 2003: 11). The framework may be regarded as an audit seeking to identify the unknown as well as the known dimensions of a particular change.

The fifth rationale for developing the framework was the belief that inquisitive questioning may deepen understanding about a change. The advantage of questions over assertions is that they encourage a range of answers, reflecting the complexities, processes and uniqueness of organisational changes. Questions encourage an active rather than a passive engagement with issues arising out of change.

The change classifications framework

The framework is discussed from the perspective of an organisational outsider attempting to understand a change or changes taking place inside an organisation. This understanding may be informed by academic literature, research or experience. Although change may be multidimensional and multiple changes may be taking place, there is believed to be merit in initially understanding specific changes separately. In Chapter 4 it will be emphasised that any understanding of a specific change has to refer to the context of the change both internal and external, as well as in terms of the past, the present and the future. It is recommended that such an analysis of context is undertaken in parallel to answering the ten framework questions.

An illustration of the framework is featured in this chapter, in terms of questions being used to get beneath a newspaper headline 'GREENSHIRES COUNTY COUNCIL IN SHOCK RESTRUCTURING.' Answering the change classification questions provides information informing deeper understanding about this particular ambiguous change. Illustrative answers to each of the questions will be applied to this change, such answers indicated by *Change in Greenshires CC* at the end of each question.

Q1 What is specifically changing?

Although organisations are often depicted as experiencing generalised constant change, this question encourages specification of change. Even if there is a list of interrelated changes taking place, what is changing still needs to be specified if it is to be effectively studied. Dawson (2003: 18) referred to 'the essential nature and content of the change in question', and this is the focus of this first question. Although it may appear to be one of the more straightforward questions, any major change invariably takes place against a backdrop of everyday changes. As Burke (2002: xiii) notes, 'Organisations change all the time, each and every day.' The reasons for change and the scale of change are discussed further in answering subsequent questions. However, the quotation warns that given the prevalence of everyday changes, specifying change requires careful consideration, and this process may be aided by clarification of the scale and scope of change.

Change in Greenshires CC

The specific change involved the removal of one level of management located at the main Council offices in order to create a flatter organisational hierarchy.

Q2 Why is this change taking place?

This question encourages consideration about both explicit and implicit reasons for change, as well as the planned or emergent nature of change. The causes of organisational change are discussed in Chapter 4, and there is likely to be more than one reason why a change takes place. Also, potentially politically expedient reasons may be offered as opposed to actual reasons for change. However, such discussion presupposes that change has been planned.

An important ongoing change management debate relates to the planned or emergent nature of change, and this debate resurfaces throughout this textbook. At this stage it is worthwhile introducing the two positions as they inform the classification of change. The term 'planned change' has been used to differentiate it from changes forced upon an organisation or arising out of accident or impulse (Burnes, 2004a: 267), whereas the main tenets of emergent change have been identified as change as experimentation and adaptation, small-scale incremental changes, managers' fostering and facilitating a climate of change, rather than planning change and emphasis upon information-gathering and analysis (Burnes, 1996: 14). Burnes emphasises that neither approach is right nor wrong but more applicable to particular situations. The implication for questions in this framework is that it would be beneficial to establish if the change appeared to be planned or emergent. It is likely to be easier to answer the classification questions for a planned rather than an emergent change. It is still believed to be beneficial to establish what is known and unknown even about an emergent change.

Change in Greenshires CC

Senior management had become frustrated by what they perceived as excessive bureaucracy in the County Council. They were embarking upon a planned change of de-layering in order to reduce bureaucracy.

Q3 Who made the decision to change?

Identifying the person or persons making a decision to change provides insights into the organisational significance, power and politics of the change. For example, was the decision made by a dominant coalition of senior managers, or perhaps an incoming chief executive wishing to herald a change of direction? Paton and McCalman (2000: 19) write about the problem owners in the context of change suggesting that 'often problem owners identify themselves since they have initiated the change process'. It is acknowledged that according to an emergent approach to change it may prove difficult tracing either the origins of the decision to change or its originator. For example, staff in a public service organisation may have noticed over time that they had developed more of an entrepreneurial orientation reflecting a change in the organisational culture.

The question about who made the decision to change may be related to what Balogun and Hope Hailey (2004: 19) label the change start-point – the concern is with where the change was initiated and developed – for example, bottom-up or top-down change. Notable examples in the change management literature are Beer *et al* (1990: 161) who advocate a bottom-up approach to change, whereas Kotter (1995: 6) advocated a top-down approach.

Change in Greenshires CC

The decision to de-layer the organisation was made by the incoming County Council chief executive in consultation with a team of management consultants.

Q4 What has been the recent organisational history of change?

The recent history of organisational change, as well as being part of the contextualisation of the change, is also part of the classification of the change.

> *What causes change is embedded in the organisation's history up to the present.*
> *(De Caluwe and Vermaak, 2003: 79)*

Similarly, Cummings (2002: 279) suggests that

> *organisations have histories and traditions, and it is difficult to make people forget them. Given this realisation, it may be more fruitful to attempt to work with rather than against the past.*

For example, the experience of total quality management in an organisation may inform subsequent responses (positive or negative) to business process re-engineering. Darwin *et al* (2002: 11) believe that 'most, if not all, currently fashionable ideas are reinventions ...' The implication is that a previous attempt to change a culture, for example, or improve service quality will inform current understanding about cultural change or improving service quality.

Change in Greenshires CC

The last change management initiative in the County Council emphasised improvements in service quality and was believed to have floundered due to bureaucratic practices of middle managers.

Q5 How is this change being communicated?

Wilson (1992: 7) regarded the essence of the managerial task as 'one of establishing some rationality or some predictability out of the seeming chaos that characterises change processes'. In Chapter 13 communicating change will be discussed in detail – however, that discussion may be prefaced as follows. Communication has been defined as 'the transference and understanding of meaning' (Robbins, 2005: 299), certain commentators arguing that 'without effective employee communication, change is impossible and change management fails' (Barrett, 2002: 219). The question focuses upon internal organisational communications and how changes are communicated within organisations. There are a range of variables which influence the nature of such communications. Quirke (1995: 87) suggests that a change communications strategy will be dependent upon the type of change, the degree of urgency, the speed of change and the reactions to the change. Despite such sensible reasoning, during times of change 'the question everyone wants an answer to is, "What is going to happen to me?"' (Balogun and Hope Hailey, 2004: 181). The focus is not solely upon the content of the change message; the communication of change potentially offers insight into power and politics.

Change in Greenshires CC

The announcement about de-layering was made to senior management at an 'Awayday'. Senior managers were required to cascade this information down the organisational hierarchy of the County Council, informing individual managers affected by de-layering in person.

Q6 What is the scale and scope of this change?

Dawson (2003: 18) has differentiated between small incremental change and large-scale radical change. One of the most influential differentiations of organisational change was offered by Dunphy and Stace (1993) in terms of:

- fine-tuning
- incremental adjustment
- modular transformation, and
- corporate transformation.

Evolutionary change focuses on incremental change whereas revolutionary change emphasises radical change. There is a need for caution when classifying the scale of change, because despite potential management claims that they are undertaking radical revolutionary change the tendency is for more incremental evolutionary change (Johnson *et al*, 2005: 27; Burke, 2002: 67). Abrahamson (2000: 79), acknowledging the potential chaos, cynicism and burnout arising out of change, has suggested that 'oscillation between big change and small changes helps ensure dynamic stability in organisations' (see also Romanelli and Tushman, 1994 for a discussion of their punctuated equilibrium model of change). There appears to be a language of large-scale change (see Box 5) evident in academic rhetoric.

Quantum change:
Changing many elements at once instead of piecemeal change (Mintzberg *et al*, 1998: 313, citing Miller and Friesen, 1984)

Transformation:
Massive programmes of comprehensive change to turn around or renew an organisation (as noted by Mintzberg *et al*, 1998: 330)

Turnaround:
Quick dramatic revolution (as noted by Mintzberg *et al*, 1998: 330)

Renewal:
Slower building up of comprehensive change (as noted by Mintzberg *et al*, 1998: 330)

Bold strokes:
Major and rapid changes imposed top-down (Kanter *et al*, 1992)

Long marches:
Small-scale short-term incremental changes leading to longer-term transformation (Kanter *et al*, 1992)

Box 5 – The language of large-scale change

The difficulty of classifying the scale of change becomes apparent in such notions as 'long marches', where apparently small-scale changes may be elements of a larger-scale transformation.

Often the scope of a change is related to the scale of a change, 'scope' referring to who or what will be affected by the change. For example, a large-scale redundancy programme may focus in terms of scope upon either middle management or all employees. An important element of the scope of change is the identification of the level or levels to which the change applies. The scope in terms of individual, group and organisational levels (discussed in Chapter 1) may range from one individual or group being affected to the whole organisation. In terms of enabling change, Bowditch and Buono (2005: 353) have raised interesting questions about scope in terms of whether change should start small and grow or be instituted organisation-wide.

Change in Greenshires CC
The scale of the change was regarded as large in terms of the overall organisational structure. However, the scope focused upon middle management rather than upon the whole workforce of the County Council.

Q7 What are the temporal aspects of this change?

Temporal aspects of change have to be considered in terms of both the timescale and the pace of a particular change. For example, relocating an organisation presents a very tangible timescale, whereas the timescale for a cultural change is much less tangible. Senior management may specify that they want to change a culture over six months, but it is likely to take years to attempt to change attitudes, values and beliefs (discussed further in Chapter 7). In the case of planned change, the timescale – even if it is only a forecast – provides insights into the scale and scope of the change.

As well as the timescale of change, the pace of change merits consideration. Abrahamson (2000: 77) notes proponents of change management arguing for as much change being achieved as quickly as possible. However, he believes that the pace of change is very much dependent upon the particular organisation. There may be difficulties managing change, 'particularly the human aspects of change when the need for change is urgent' (Hayes, 2002: 8). Dynamic stability referred to earlier with reference to Question 6 appears pertinent here, implying that the pace of change may vary over time.

Change in Greenshires CC

The target was for all redundancies in the County Council to be completed within one year, with a further year envisaged for adjusting to the new arrangements.

Q8. Who is managing this change, and how is it being managed?

There are many choices in change management about who is to be responsible for managing a change, how change is to be managed and, according to emergent change approaches, even if change should be managed. Change agents and elements of agency are discussed in Chapter 5 in more detail. Change agents are individuals or groups who help to effect change in an organisation (Johnson *et al*, 2005: 519). Change agent roles include leadership, external facilitation and functional delegation (Balogun and Hope Hailey, 2004: 49). A frequently cited typology of change strategies was developed by Kotter and Schlesinger (1979), which ranges from education and communication through negotiation and agreement to explicit and implicit coercion. This typology suggests options about how to manage change. A more unusual typology has been offered by Mintzberg *et al* (1998: 328–9), who differentiate between planned change, driven change and evolved change:

- *planned change* – programmatic change following set procedures
- *driven change* – an individual or a group ensures that change happens
- *evolved change* – organic change that happens regardless of management.

The evolved change approach reflects the emergent approach to change discussed earlier, suggesting an almost *laissez-faire* approach to change management. As with the other classifications, it is important to remember that organisations and change itself are dynamic, so that although it may be possible to identify how change was managed at one point in time, such an approach to managing change is unlikely to remain static.

Change in Greenshires CC

The management consultants had agreed to act as change agents in terms of carrying out the de-layering in the County Council. However, overall responsibility for the change initiative remained with the chief executive. The de-layering would be managed through a negotiated process involving full consultation with representative bodies.

Q9 What would be a successful outcome of this change?

In Chapter 15 change management successes and failures are reviewed and a tendency for change management initiatives to fail is acknowledged (Kotter, 1995: 59; Guimaraes and Armstrong, 1998: 74; Burke, 2002: 1; De Caluwe and Vermaak, 2004: 197). These findings raise questions about what senior management are seeking to achieve through a change process. Has a successful outcome been specified and communicated, and if so, what will be the criteria for establishing the achievement of the successful outcome? Alternatively, from an emergent change perspective a successful outcome may deliberately not be specified, in order to allow the evolution of change to reflect changes in the environment.

Change in Greenshires CC

The chief executive very publicly stated that once the de-layering was completed, all committee paperwork was to be processed within one week of a committee meeting and fully actioned within one month of a committee meeting.

Q10 Who can influence the success/failure of this change?

Once the nature of a successful outcome of change has been established, this should inform the process of identifying those individuals and groups which could potentially influence the success or failure of a change. Problems have been identified with judging the efficacy of change programmes (Iles and Sutherland, 2001: 13). However, this question speaks to the politics of change emphasised by Dawson (2003: 18) in terms of whether a change is accepted as central and worthwhile or threatening and challenged. An established approach for discussing such influences would be a force-field analysis (see Chapter 4). A major change is likely to generate resistance, defined as 'behaviours acted out by change recipients in order to slow down or terminate organisational change' (Lines, 2004: 198). In Chapter 10 the main focus is resistance to change; at this stage it is worth acknowledging that the existence of resistance may encourage reasoned reflection upon a hastily conceived change. The change agent or change agency may also influence the success or failure of a change depending upon how effectively he, she, it or they undertake the task.

Change in Greenshires CC

Many of the individual managers affected by the change were supportive because of the size of their redundancy payments. The representative bodies were sceptical and critical of de-layering, perceiving it to be a crude cost-cutting exercise.

Classifying change inside organisations

The change classifications framework aims to further academic understanding about change through the classification of specific changes. However, the framework has the potential to inform discussion of change within organisations. De Caluwe and Vermaak (2004: 214) offer a convincing case as to why greater conceptual clarity about change may benefit organisations:

- it facilitates clearer communication between people involved
- it characterises dominant paradigms in groups or organisations as a whole
- it provides a map to deal with possible strategic issues
- it offers change agents a tool for reflection.

The alternative is that organisations adopt a generalised approach to change, possibly using a generic 'off-the-shelf' solution to their change management challenges. The change classification framework helps to emphasise that all changes are unique and must be understood and addressed with reference to their specific dimensions and contexts. Dunphy (1996: 551), in a special issue of *Human Relations* on organisational change, identified three groups amongst the contributors:

- the Analysts (primarily interested in analysing organisational change)

- the Activists (primarily interested in intervening in organisations to produce change)
- the Futurists (primarily interested in discerning the direction of future change).

These groupings, although not mutually exclusive, still appear pertinent to the diverse change management literature today. The target audience for this textbook comprise analysts. However, identification of the three groups signpost time horizons inside organisations. Inside organisations the focus is likely to be activists working in the present. However, there may be organisational benefits both in reviewing past changes and looking forward to future changes. The change classifications framework can be used inside organisations in terms of all three time horizons – past, present and future. The following discussion considers:

- the framework aiding reflection
- the framework aiding project management, and
- the framework aiding forecasting.

The framework aiding reflection
In terms of managing change there is increasingly a need to capture learning from previous change (discussed further in Chapter 15) and for reflection upon change (see Ghaye, 2005). The framework may be used to inform the process of reflecting upon a previous change in terms of either what went right or what went wrong, or both. For example, there may be benefit in reflecting upon either changes that had been poorly defined at the time of implementation or complexities better understood with hindsight. The framework as an aid to reflection could be used at the organisational, group or individual level. For instance, at the organisational level senior management could use the framework as part of a process of critical reflection on a failed change. At the group level a group could reflect upon behaviours and norms displayed with specific reference to the ten questions. At the individual level, individuals could reflect in a similar manner, possibly with a view to developing their own capacity to change. The tense of the questions would have to be adjusted if the framework was used as an aid for reflection as illustrated in Box 6.

Q 1 What specifically changed?
Q 2 Why did this change take place?
Q 3 Who made the decision to change?
Q 4 What had been the recent organisational history of change?
Q 5 How was this change communicated?
Q 6 What was the scale and scope of this change?
Q 7 What were the temporal aspects of this change?
Q 8 Who managed this change, and how was it managed?
Q 9 Was a successful outcome of this change specified?
Q10 Who influenced the success/failure of this change?

Box 6 – Change classification framework as an aid to reflection

The framework aiding project management
The framework may be used as an aid to managing ongoing change. The framework offers a map of a change process which could be used to encourage discussion about issues arising out of the process of change. Again the framework could be used at the organisational, group and individual levels. At all three levels the framework could be used to promote discussion. More importantly, the framework could be used at all three levels to encourage involvement

based upon developing common understandings of specific and unfolding change processes. In terms of the tense of the questions, the original change classifications framework (see Box 3) already poses questions in the present tense.

The framework aiding forecasting

The framework could also be used in a forward-looking manner – although, as Woodward and Hendry (2004: 157) warn, 'in organisations that are undergoing change it is difficult, if not impossible, to define and resolve all eventualities.' In terms of the future, the framework is probably most applicable at the organisational level, but not exclusively applicable at this level. For example, senior management could utilise the framework to enable discussion about scenarios arising out of a future change. In a similar manner, the framework could be used by senior managers to allocate roles and responsibilities arising out of a change. The framework with adjustments to tenses is featured in Box 7.

Q 1 What would specifically change?
Q 2 Why would this change take place?
Q 3 Who would make the decision to change?
Q 4 What has been the recent organisational history of change?
Q 5 How would the change be communicated?
Q 6 What would be the scale and scope of this change?
Q 7 What would be the temporal aspects of this change?
Q 8 Who would manage this change and how would it be managed?
Q 9 What would a successful outcome of this change be?
Q10 Who would be able to influence the success/failure of this change?

Box 7 – Change classification framework as an aid to forecasting

This understanding section has considered the process of classification both in an academic sense and in a practical sense.

SYNOPSIS

The rationales for developing the change classifications framework were that it offered an accessible overview of the classifications literature, moved from the general to the specific, enabled a definition of change, made explicit what was not known, and through inquisitive questioning deepened understanding about change.

The questions that comprise the change classifications frame were listed in Box 3. Each of the ten framework questions was located and explained in terms of relevant change management literature and illustrated in terms of a hypothetical example of a county council going through organisational structural change.

The framework has the potential to inform discussion of change within organisations. The change classifications framework could be used inside organisations in terms of all three time horizons – past, present and future. The framework could aid reflection, project management and forecasting.

DISCUSSION QUESTIONS

1 Collins was sceptical about the 'What is change?' narrative. What do you think was the basis for his scepticism?

2 Are classifications of change likely to be more evident in academic or in organisational explanations of change? Why?

3 In terms of the change classification questions specified, which are going to be the most difficult to answer?

4 What are the implications for change classifications of considering change in terms of the past, present and future?

5 How do you believe senior managers classify organisational changes that they manage?

6 Can you identify any further classifications of change which would develop further the change classifications framework?

Case study – Improving customer service in Merryweather superstore

Case study instructions

The following case study offers an opportunity to apply the change classifications framework to a changing organisation. The change story is told in terms of one individual's experience of organisational change. The fact that Barney is a junior and temporary member of staff does not negate the scale of change being undertaken.

Please read the case study and then address the questions at the end of the case study.

Case study

Each summer Barney – who was studying media studies at university – would work at the large Merryweather superstore outlet in his home town. He did not particularly enjoy the work but found that it supplemented his income during termtime, for which he was grateful. Upon arrival at the store this year he was greeted by the store manager Mr Johnson who, remembering him from previous years, suggested that he start stacking shelves and said that he would speak to him later in the day.

Barney started work quite earnestly, for the manual nature of the job made a change from his academic studies. However, by 10 am he was becoming bored and looked around the store. The layout was similar to last summer's, although he noticed that everything had been rebranded in a rather garish day-glow green. The one major change was at the checkouts: at five of them, staff were serving customers, while at the other five checkouts customers appeared to be serving themselves. This sight perplexed Barney who had been used to shopping at the very security-conscious Cheap and Cheerful superstore near his halls of residence. Barney chuckled to himself as some customers chose to scan their own goods, inserted their debit/credit cards into a machine, and then swiftly left the store. Barney fantasised for a few moments about the potential for students to obtain food and drink very cheaply, and then attempted to more seriously engage with what was going on.

At the 11 am coffee break he caught up with Beryl who had worked at the store for the past decade. Initially, she evaded his question about the new self-service checkouts, choosing instead to moan for five minutes about the new chief executive, Mr Meadows, who had instigated the change. She reckoned he was a callous accountant who would not know a tin of beans if he tripped over one. However, as the break progressed she lightened up and explained that all Merryweather stores were now 50-per-cent self-service, and that the change was believed to have improved customer service and apparently the profits of Merryweather. All the same, she suggested that she remained very sceptical about this fad, and said that her friend Irene – the trade union representative – believed industrial action against the change was imminent. Somebody apparently had mentioned a week on Tuesday. Barney was keen to learn more, but Beryl was evidently tired of the change and started to reminisce about when his mother was a girl.

Barney soldiered on, doing some sweeping until 2 pm when he was given a late lunch break. Because the staff room was empty he started to glance through *Favourable Climate* (the unintentionally amusing internal newspaper of Merryweather superstores). The front page headline was Mr Meadows Serves Himself! The accompanying article explained how over the past 12 months all outlets had been refocused to the new self-service orientation. Mr Meadows was presented as personally managing this significant change himself. Since joining Merryweather 18 months ago he had staked his reputation on the 'Better Service through Self-Service' initiative. As Barney continued to read the internal newspaper it all sounded very positive and Mr Meadows was certainly smiling in all the photographs.

In the afternoon Barney worked in one of the store rooms shifting crates of out-of-date stock. It was a task he hated, but it gave him an opportunity to daydream. Towards the end of the day the store manager Mr Johnson came into the store room looking quite disillusioned. He was clutching some management information reports that should have been returned the previous week. Barney asked about 'Better Service through Self-Service' and for a moment Mr Johnson looked at him blankly. Then, surprisingly, he seemed to open up. He complained that the first he had heard about the initiative was when the new checkouts were being installed. He had subsequently read in the financial pages of his daily newspaper that the chief executive had guaranteed to the shareholders that the new initiative would deliver a 30-per-cent headcount reduction with a corresponding reduction in staff costs. Until recently, very little information had been communicated to Mr Johnson. The previous week, however, he had learned that he was required to interview checkout staff to establish if they would like the opportunity to develop and take on new roles in the store, or would like instead to use the Merryweather redundancy counselling service. Finally, he explained that he could not offer Barney any more temporary work in the future because Beryl and Irene were in the process of being given the opportunity to do the work that he was doing.

Case study questions

1   Drawing upon the case study material, please answer each of the questions in the change classifications framework.

2   In this particular case is it possible to identify any connections between the classifications?

3   In this particular case can you identify any further classifications which would help you to understand this change?

FURTHER READING

BALOGUN J. and HOPE HAILEY V. (2004) *Exploring Strategic Change*, 2nd edition, Harlow, FT/Prentice Hall.

As was acknowledged in the introduction to this chapter, writers often offer some form of change classification in their textbooks. A good example of an alternative framework is the change kaleidoscope developed by Balogun and Hope Hailey (2004: 57): 'The change kaleidoscope is a diagnostic framework which enables change agents to pinpoint key contextual features of their change context.' In understanding change there would be merit in comparing and contrasting this more strategically-oriented framework with the change classifications framework.

BURKE W. (2002) *Organization Change: Theory and Practice*, Thousand Oaks, California, Sage Publications.

This book is recommended because the author has managed to reconcile the theoretical with the practical (many books are either excessively theoretical or excessively practical) – in particular, developing the Burke-Litwin model which has been used in organisations. A number of these real applications are discussed in the book. The book offers chapters on rethinking organisation change, the nature of organisation change, and conceptual models for understanding organisation change, all of which are relevant to discussions in this chapter. The book conveys a strong sense of the author's earnest wish to understand organisational change, regarded as one of the challenges of a lifetime.

BURRELL G. (1992) Back to the future: time and organization, in M.REED and M.HUGHES (eds) *Rethinking Organization: New Directions in Organization Theory and Analysis*, London, Sage Publications.

This chapter is recommended if you are looking for a more philosophically informed critique of traditional approaches to the management of change. Burrell's critique is informed by post-modernism and emphasises the roles of time and space in organisational analysis. The chapter is not an easy read, but Burrell effectively leads the reader into a series of debates which could be explored more deeply from the references he offers if the readers wants to go down this challenging post-modern path.

STICKLAND F. (1998) *The Dynamics of Change*, London, Routledge.

This textbook has a different feel from many of the other textbooks on change. When you read this book you can imagine Stickland trying to make sense of change himself. A strength of this book is its interdisciplinary nature. Particularly relevant to this chapter is Stickland's discussion entitled 'What is this thing, change?'

Causes and contexts of change

INTRODUCTION

This chapter in focusing upon the causes and contexts of change raises important questions relating to understanding change management.

> *Is change within organisations an essentially adaptive activity determined by broader economic and technological imperatives or a consequence of organisation-specific processes of choice and politics?*
>
> *(McLoughlin, 1999: 69)*

This innocent question highlights an ongoing academic debate which has implications for how change is managed. By way of reassurance, Morgan and Sturdy (2000: 7) note that identifying underlying, often hidden, logics of change or motors of change has a long history in ancient and modern philosophy. The differentiation between determinism and voluntarism is helpful in explaining the different philosophical positions which underpin these often contentious debates.

In terms of change management, Hayes (2002: 17) differentiates between deterministic views, which emphasise determining forces outside the organisation limiting the ability of a manager to influence change, and voluntarist views, which emphasise that managers can make an important difference in terms of influencing change. This explanation ripples through the change literature offering both an explanation for how change managers rationalise their actions to themselves and others, and an explanation for different theoretical approaches to understanding and explaining change management.

Any understanding of the causes of change will be closely related to the contexts in which changes take place. Dawson (2003: 46) has identified three determinants that shape change processes:

- context,
- the politics of change, and
- the substance of change.

This framework is favoured in this textbook as constituting a serious yet applicable framework for understanding organisational change. The politics of change is discussed further in Chapter 10 (in terms of resistance) and Chapter 14 (in terms of control). In this chapter, different contexts in which change takes place are discussed, and this chapter is linked to Chapter 3, which was concerned with the substance of change explained in terms of different classifications of change.

In the next section of this chapter, triggers, drivers and tracers of change are discussed. The contribution of Pettigrew is featured, particularly in terms of understanding changes within their own unique contexts, leading to a discussion of external and internal contexts of change. Also, the influence of gurus and consultants as a potential cause of change is reviewed. In the *Critical perspective* section, three approaches to change are introduced in order to demonstrate how the approach to change may determine the way change is explained. The contribution of gurus and consultants introduced in the previous section is critically reviewed.

THE CAUSES AND CONTEXTS OF ORGANISATIONAL CHANGE

Ernecq (1992: 276), in noting a shift in focus of interest 'from external environmental change to internal organisational change', highlighted that the emphasis of study was moving from change and organisations to changes in organisations. In this section the intention is to consider both change and organisations, and change in organisations, although it is sometimes a difficult differentiation to make.

Triggers, drivers and tracers of change

The following discussion introduces popular approaches to explaining how organisational change is believed to take place as a consequence of a series of what are commonly referred to as triggers or drivers. Different authors offer different degrees of sophistication in their specification of triggers and drivers. De Caluwe and Vermaak (2003: 80) eloquently defined a trigger 'as the emotional characteristics that contribute to the emergence of a change idea'.

Tichy (1983: 147) regarded large-scale strategic change as being 'triggered by a large-scale uncertainty – in the form of either a threat or an opportunity'.

Triggering information may be interpreted in different ways, including comparisons between current and past performance, and comparisons between current performance against future projections (1983: 152). Tichy (1983: 153) identified change triggers as including the following: environmental changes, technological changes and changes in people. In this early categorisation of change triggers, the interplay between external and internal factors is evident. More recently, Patton and McCalman (2000: 23) identified potential triggers that included government legislation, advances in process or product technology, changing consumer requirements, expectations or taste, and competitor or supply-chain activities.

Although Dawson (2003: 24) identifies potential triggers of change, he does warn that 'their relative importance remains open to debate.' There is no consensus listing of triggers/drivers of change that would explain all changes in all contexts, and there never will be. Leana and Barry (2000: 753–4) identify forces that drive organisations' pursuit of flexibility and continuous change: adaptability, cost containment, impatient capital markets, control, and competitive advantage. What is different about their account of forces that drive change is their acknowledgement of tension between stability and change as an inevitable part of organisational life. This type of reasoning may be traced back to Lewin (1947) who regarded status quo as being the balance between forces for change and forces for stability, so that change consequently arose out of an increase in the forces for change and a reduction in the forces for stability. Such thinking has been operationalised in the concept of force-field analysis, requiring the sorting of information about a specific change into two lists. The following hypothetical examples illustrate typical forces.

Forces for change	Forces for stability/status quo
Competition	Historical inertia
Government changes	Trade union/Staff association
New senior manager	Organisational culture
IT development	Bureaucratic culture

These forces may be ranked in terms of their perceived power, providing an early indication of the ease or difficulty of a proposed change (see, for example, Senior and Fleming, 2006: 287).

So far this discussion has considered what drives/triggers change. However, there is merit in relating change drivers to change outcomes. The work of Kallio et al (2002) is informative in that they offer an empirically-based attempt to understand matches between change drivers and tracers. The terms 'driver' and 'tracer' have specific meanings in the context of their work. The motives to initiate a change project are called 'drivers', and the results of projects are called 'tracers' (Kallio et al, 2002: 84). Although the norm in the literature is for generalised pronouncements about triggers/drivers of change, it does appear logical to compare motives and results in specific instances.

> It seems to be that sometimes the drivers for starting a change project and tracers of the projects do not match. The results are often more limited in scope than the objectives... The results show that in all cases where the drivers and tracers did not match, the shift was toward lower-level results and tracers.
>
> (2002: 80)

The potential within this approach appears considerable and would offer far greater sophistication than claiming that change is triggered by a list of generalised factors.

The contribution of Pettigrew

In the *Handbook of Strategy and Management* (Pettigrew et al, 2002: 12), major contributions of Pettigrew to understanding strategic change are acknowledged, including:

- the significance of power in shaping strategy outcomes (Pettigrew, 1973, 1977)
- the language of culture in organisational analysis (Pettigrew, 1979)
- a large-scale empirical study of strategic change processes in ICI (Pettigrew, 1985)
- the breaking of dichotomies relating to strategy formulation and implementation and strategy content and process (Pettigrew, 1992)

- combining the content, process and context of strategic change with longitudinal data (Pettigrew and Fenton, 2000).

In terms of change management, Pettigrew has encouraged an appreciation of both the processes of change and the contexts of change. Instead of regarding change as a single event, change is increasingly regarded as a process happening over time – and in the case of major strategic change, typically taking place over many years. In studying change longitudinally and processually there is also a need to study the context in which changes take place. When Pettigrew was developing these ideas, processual/contextualised accounts of change were not the norm: few studies of change allowed the change process to be revealed in a temporal or contextual manner. Pettigrew (1990: 269) defined a contextualist analysis as drawing 'on phenomena at vertical and horizontal levels of analysis and the interconnections between those levels through time'. He (1990: 269) summarised key points of analysing change in a contextualist mode:

- the importance of embeddedness, in terms of interconnected levels of analysis
- the importance of temporal interconnectedness, in terms of past, present and future
- the importance of context and action, in terms of context as the product of action and vice versa
- the importance of causation, in terms of causation as neither linear nor singular.

These key points are pertinent to earlier discussions about drivers/triggers of change. A contextualist analysis of an organisational change is unlikely to explain change in terms of one dominant explanation. Instead, changes in explanations of change over time will be acknowledged, as well as change being explained as a consequence of a range of factors both internal and external.

The contexts of change

Daft (1995: 17) identifies major contextual dimensions that characterise an organisation as size, organisational technology, environment, goals, strategy, and culture. He (1995: 16) acknowledges that 'contextual dimensions can be confusing because they represent both the organisation and the environment as the context in which structural dimensions occur.' Strategy, structure, culture and technology are discussed in subsequent chapters with specific reference to change. At this stage it should be apparent that a range of contextual dimensions help to explain the uniqueness of specific changes in specific situations. The trap to avoid is generalising across organisations and across changes.

RESEARCH CASES IN JOURNALS NO.1 – GLAXO WELLCOME

The authors present an extended case study of change in Glaxo Wellcome, a large pharmaceuticals company. A strength of the case study is that changes in the organisation are analysed with particular reference to the context of the organisation. The authors use their change kaleidoscope in order to facilitate a contextual understanding of the case for readers. In essence it is possible to evaluate the kaleidoscope against the experience of change at Glaxo Wellcome, and the authors offer their own evaluation of the kaleidoscope by way of conclusion to the paper.

Sector: Pharmaceuticals
Research methods: Longitudinal research utilising qualitative and quantitative data.
Authors: Hope Hailey, V. and Balogun, J.
Paper title: Devising context-sensitive approaches to change: the example of Glaxo Wellcome
Journal details: *Long Range Planning*, Vol.35, 2002; pp.153–78

The big 'why' question of change management was posed at the beginning of this chapter. Pettigrew *et al* (1992: 7) point out that 'much of the *why* of change is derived from an analysis of the "inner and outer context".' There are potentially close relationships between the causes of change and the contexts of change. Every organisation has its own unique context, developed over time and developing over time. Even consideration about change in the same organisation over time has to acknowledge that contexts are dynamic.

Dawson (2003: 47) has suggested that we need to think about both internal contexts and external contexts temporally:

> *The contextual dimension refers to both the past and the present external and internal operating environments, as well as to the influence of future projections and expectations on current operating practice.*

The reasoning of Dawson suggests the need to address at least six elements in order to contextualise understanding of any specific organisational change (Box 8):

1 Past internal (inner) organisational environment
2 Past external (outer) organisational environment

3 Present internal (inner) organisational environment
4 Present external (outer) organisational environment

5 Future internal (inner) organisational environment
6 Future external (outer) organisational environment

Box 8 – Understanding internal and external organisational environments

The following discussion is organised around external, internal and future contexts. What is meant by the external and internal context of change? What one writer refers to as a trigger or driver of change, another writer may refer to as the context of change. The difference will tend to be one of emphasis, such that a determinist places more emphasis upon factors triggering or driving change, whereas a voluntarist will emphasise the context in which senior managers make change decisions. As external contextual factors, Dawson (2003: 47) identified the following: 'changes in competitors' strategies, level of international competition, government legislation, changing social expectations, technological innovations and changes in the level of business activity'. In analysing the external environment in which organisations operate, Worthington (2003a: 6) distinguishes between the general or contextual environment and the immediate or operational environment. The general environment includes such macro-environmental factors as:

economic, political, socio-cultural, technological and legal influences on business which affect a wide variety of businesses and which can emanate not only from local and national sources but also from international and supranational developments.

The immediate environment, on the other hand, includes

suppliers, competitors, labour markets, financial institutions and customers, and may also include trading organisations, trade unions and possibly a parent company.

Further elements of the external environment may be considered in terms of the mnemonic LoNG (local, national and global). Organisations' external environments may be differentiated in terms of public and private sector, although increasingly public/private partnerships may complicate such distinctions. The differences between public and private sector contexts raise issues around contextualising change management theories. However, Iles and Sutherland (2001: 18), in their review of change management literature with reference to NHS changes, cite studies (Golembiewski, Proehl and Sink, 1982; Robertson and Seneviratne, 1995) suggesting that knowledge, theories and models developed in the private sector can be transferred to the public sector.

In terms of the internal context Dawson (2003: 47) cites the work of Leavitt (1964) who suggests that internal contextual factors include:

human resources, administrative structures, technology and product or service, as well as an additional category labelled the history and culture of an organisation.

It is unlikely that one model will be applicable to the internal contexts of all organisations. However, the model proposed by Leavitt and adapted by Dawson appears sufficiently generic to apply to the majority of organisations. In Box 9 the factors are restated with an indication of the type of questions that have to be answered to understand the internal context for change.

Human resources What are the skills, abilities, attitudes, values and beliefs of the employees?
Administrative structure What is the structural form of the organisation, and what are the implications of this form for: leadership, authority, responsibility, and communications?
Product or service What products and/or services does the organisation provide?
Technology What technology is used to deliver the product and/or service?
History and culture What is the history of the organisation, and what cultures are evident within the organisation?

Box 9 – Understanding the internal context

The questions in Box 9 could be answered with regard to the past, present and future. What were the skills and abilities of employees? What are the skills and abilities of employees? What skills and abilities will be required of employees in the future? In such questioning a more dynamic approach to understanding change emerges as encouraged by both Pettigrew and Dawson.

In terms of developing tools and approaches to anticipate the nature and extent of future changes in context, strategy has made a major contribution (discussed in Chapter 5). Popular tools include PESTLE analysis, Porter's model, scenario-writing and SWOT analysis.

PESTLE analysis – analyses potential changes in the political, economic, social, technological, legal and ethical environment

Porter's model – an analysis of competition based upon five basic forces: current competition, potential competition, the threat of substitute products, the power of buyers, and the power of suppliers

Scenario-writing – an attempt to paint pictures of the future in terms of best-case, worst-case and most-likely-case predictions

SWOT analysis – an analysis in terms of the internal strengths and weaknesses of an organisation and the external opportunities and threats to an organisation.

Box 10 – Environmental analysis tools

Inevitable concerns arise with any forward-looking analysis of the environment. Worthington (2003b: 473) identifies limitations including: dependency upon the process of information-gathering and evaluation, unanticipated events occurring, senior management avoiding their responsibilities, and the analysis becoming an end in itself. Dawson (2003: 179), who himself advocated including the future as an element of contextualising change, is quite philosophical about the outcome of such an endeavour:

> *The essential unforeseeable character of change means that the process cannot be predicted and that outcomes are often only understood in retrospect.*

But this does not negate the need for some form of consideration of the future context – however speculative.

Gurus and consultants as catalysts of change

This chapter has identified drivers and triggers of change both internal and external to organisations. However, the external expertise of change management gurus and large consultancy firms may act as another impetus to senior management embarking upon change management initiatives.

> *Management gurus create a climate of expectations about organisational change; they may prepare the ground for consultants as the live actors in firms, and many have advanced to gurudom through the ranks of consultancy (particularly the high-profile strategy consultancies like McKinsey).*
>
> *(Fincham and Evans, 1999: 34)*

The management guru and fashion phenomenon received little serious attention from academics until recently (Jackson, 2001: 8). There is now an emergent literature (see, for example, Huczynski, 1996; Jackson, 2001; Clark and Fincham, 2002) offering a commentary upon the influence of gurus and consultants. Management consultants and the large global consulting organisations emerged in the 1990s as expressions of managerialism and globalisation of economic activity (Wright, 2005: 467). Huczynski (1996: 38) in his comprehensive account of management gurus offered a definition of guru theory as seeking 'to help managers build strong business systems which can successfully compete in their chosen market segment'. He (1996: 46) distinguished three sub-schools of guru theory:

- the Academic guru school (eg Porter and Mintzberg)
- the Consultant guru school (eg Drucker and Peters and Waterman)
- the Hero-Manager guru school (eg Trump and Iacocca).

The ingredients of guru success are believed to include an understanding of the world of work, an intellectual focus which enhances the status of management, and a practical appeal and application (Collins, 2000: 105–6).

Consultants often have the task of operationalising the ideas of gurus – for example, in terms of quality, leadership or culture. However, in this applied orientation there are tensions around helping organisations and making explicit their knowledge base. Sorge and Van Witteloostuijn (2004: 1222) warn that consultants have no 'incentive to make this judgement explicit, let alone public, for anyone could acquire and use it if they did, which is not in their interest'. In this quotation tensions become apparent between the business interests of consultants and the wider interests of society. Sharing knowledge could be beneficial to the development of both the public sector and the private sector, and such issues are explored in the *Critical perspective*.

Wright (2005: 469–70) in his review of *Critical Consulting* (Clark and Finchman, 2002), while acknowledging the merits of analysing the micro-dynamics of consultant-client relations, argues for a more macro-level analysis of the outcomes of consultancy:

> *Consultants in many cases provide a valuable service for their management clients often in both an ideological sense (as highlighted by Salaman) as well as more fundamental business outcomes (reduced costs, greater efficiency, new insights and techniques).*

In this quotation Wright (2005) is cautioning against the fashion of critiquing the 'soft target' of consultants. Also, Jackson (2001: 179) concludes his rhetorical critique of management gurus arguing that we can learn from their rhetoric in order to make academic accounts more plausible to practising managers. The message here appears to be that at the very least gurus, and by association, consultants, have been more effective in communicating about change with organisations than academics.

CRITICAL PERSPECTIVE

The explanations offered in the earlier section for organisational change and the depictions of contexts are very plausible and may be regarded as the orthodoxy. In a practical sense the clarification and articulation of rationales for change are important ingredients of the change management process. However, in terms of the goal of this textbook to understand change management, some of this orthodoxy is questionable – particularly notions of change that is independently triggered by factors beyond the control of senior management. For example, Collins (2000: 43) argues that the environment does not force change upon actors, but rather that actors work within a context and act to shape this context. The following critical perspective on the causes and contexts of organisational change is organised around four challenges:

- the managerialism in explanations of change
- the need to appreciate the political shaping of change
- the need to appreciate the social shaping of change
- the shortcomings of guru-/consultancy-driven change.

The following discussion elaborates upon each of these challenges. The first three sub-sections are organised around academic approaches to organisational change highlighted by Morgan and Sturdy (2000).

Managerialist approaches to explaining change

Managerialist approaches to change offer prescriptions and techniques 'whereby managers can and should engineer change and control' (Morgan and Sturdy, 2000: 8). Specific examples of this type of literature include Peters and Waterman (1982) and Hammer and Champy (1993), although managerialism is implicit in much of the change management literature. Interest in recent decades in cultural change and leading change are often informed by managerialist approaches (see Chapters 7 and 12 for further discussion). Morgan and Sturdy (2000: 14) highlight three features of managerialist approaches, summarised as follows: little evidence of top-down approaches to change being successful, weak analysis of how and why organisations change, and theories informed by and having become part of the language of many managers and consultants.

What are the implications of the above discussion for this chapter and this textbook? Earlier discussions about causes and contexts can be seen as reflecting a managerialist tradition in change management writing likely to dominate the literature for the foreseeable future. De Caluwe and Vermaak (2004: 197) regard the dominant way of talking about change being in terms of planning and contingency approaches, although in functional terms managerialist approaches may be failing to deliver successful change management. Managerialist approaches deliver a reassuring rationality that organisations effectively respond to internal and/or external triggers, and in this way senior managers successfully – even heroically – manage change.

Political approaches to explaining change

Another concern with managerialist approaches is that they offer few insights into the organisational politics of change. Dawson (2003: 20) emphasises that 'it is important to reflect critically on the need and reasons for change, and to take into account the concerns of others...' The political approach conceptualises 'organisational change in terms of competing interest groups' (Morgan and Sturdy, 2000: 15). There is an emphasis upon the temporal dimension of change, as well as the external and internal contexts of the change process. The writings of Pettigrew featured in the earlier section offer good examples of this type of approach to change management. Morgan and Sturdy (2000: 17) explain how the political approach to organisational change, rather than being seen as a rejection of managerialist approaches, 'promotes more sophisticated "cultural engineering"'. Although there may be factors that trigger change, the emphasis upon these factors may change through the actions and interpretations of different interest groups. (The politics of change is discussed further in Chapter 10.)

Social approaches to explaining change

Morgan and Sturdy (2000: 8) define these approaches in terms of an examination of 'how management practices and knowledges are constructed and reproduced in particular institutional and social settings'. It is acknowledged that the approach draws upon different streams of literature which can sometimes be in conflict and sometimes complementary: Marxist approaches, psychodynamic approaches, organisational culture, meaning and identity approaches, institutional theory and genealogical and discourse approaches. Institutional theory is a form of social approach which is pertinent to concerns in this chapter, offering an alternative yet persuasive explanation for why organisations implement change management programmes. This theory suggests that organisational decision-makers under conditions of uncertainty are forced into action resembling the lead taken by others in the field (Grint, 1998: 143). DiMaggio and Powell (1991) were influential in identifying three mechanisms within an institutionalist approach to organisations.

- *coercive isomorphism*: resources secured through demonstrating conformity with key power-holders expectations
- *mimetic isomorphism*: copying supposedly successful organisations as an organisational response to uncertainty
- *normative isomorphism*: standardized views transferred across different organisational contexts as a consequence of the professionalisation of management functions.

Although managerialist and political approaches are the norm in terms of explaining why and how organisations change, social approaches appear to offer more sophisticated forms of analysing change management. Against this backdrop the identification of triggers or drivers of change becomes less clear-cut: 'their relative importance remains open to debate' (Dawson, 2003: 24).

Critically reviewing the contribution of gurus and consultants

There is a need to critically review the contribution of gurus and consultants to change management processes, particularly given their high profile. Tichy (1983: 291) cited a beautifully mischievous quotation from Kaplan (1964): 'I have found that if you give a little boy a hammer, he will find that everything needs pounding.' A cynic might argue that a major outcome of the gurus' and consultants' prescriptions to change is that they are in the business of manufacturing the hammers, regardless of the organisational need for hammers (or, coincidentally, Hammer).

More recently, Sorge and Van Witteloostuijn (2004: 1207) have critically warned of organisational change becoming the *raison d'être* of the consultancy and management professions: 'the involvement of consultants is self-sustaining once it has set in.' Although they do not offer empirical evidence to support this view, the implications are troubling that change is being driven/triggered not so much by any interplay of internal and external factors but in order to serve the financial interests of large management consultancies. Salaman and Asch (2003: 22) neatly articulate the conundrum managers must face when attempting to choose between the practical prescriptions of consultants and the more evidence-based criticisms of change management fads and fashions offered by academics:

> *Consultants try to sell them packages, beautifully presented, forcefully marketed, clearly stated in persuasive language, which promise radical dramatic organisational transformation... On the other hand, academic commentators – Cassandra-like – warn against too easy acceptance, noting numerous problems with the advice and recommendations on offer, pointing out inconsistencies, contradictions and simplifications.*

The temptation to criticise the contribution of gurus and consultants is very strong, and the criticisms have been very strong. For example, Jackson (2001: 16) highlights some of the labels given to gurus' work: 'intellectual wallpaper', 'business pornography', 'shameless narcissism', 'behavioural fast food' and 'commonsensical in the extreme'. However, he does believe that they have influenced organisational life and academic research. Sorge and Van Witteloostuijn (2004: 1223) 'plead for an evidence-based consultancy'. The consequences of change management initiatives for individuals, groups, organisations and society are considerable. These stakeholders merit change management based upon reliable and valid evidence.

SYNOPSIS

Change was believed to take place as a consequence of a series of what were commonly referred to as triggers or drivers, different authors offering different degrees of sophistication in their specification of triggers and drivers.

Change triggers included government legislation, advances in technology, changing consumer requirements, and an acquisition or merger.

Pettigrew encouraged an appreciation of both the process and context of change. Instead of regarding change as a single event, change was regarded as a process happening over time. In studying change longitudinally and processually there was also a need to study the context in which changes take place. The key points of analysing change in a contextualist mode were: the importance of embeddedness, the importance of temporal interconnectedness, and the importance of context.

Major contextual dimensions that characterise an organisation were size, technology, environment, goals, strategy and culture. There was a need to think about both internal and external contexts temporally. According to Dawson, context refers to both the past and the present external and internal operating environments, as well as to the influence of future projections and expectations on current operating practice.

The external expertise of change management gurus and large consultancy firms may act as another impetus to senior management to embark upon change management initiatives.

Managerialist approaches to change were concerned with offering prescriptions and techniques. Political approaches to explaining change conceptualises organisational change in terms of competing interest groups with an emphasis upon the temporal dimension of change, as well as the external and internal contexts of the change process. Social approaches to explaining change examine how management practices and knowledges are constructed and reproduced in particular institutional and social settings.

Change may be driven/triggered not so much by any interplay of internal and external factors as by the financial interests of the large management consultancies. Managers increasingly face the conundrum of having to choose between the practical prescriptions of consultants and the more evidence-based criticisms of change management fads and fashions offered by academics.

DISCUSSION QUESTIONS

1 Are internal or external factors more influential in causing organisational change?

2 In what ways do the contexts in which organisations operate change over time?

3 Why is there no consensus about the causes of organisational change?

4 What would trigger an organisation to stop changing?

5 What are the implications of this chapter for how you might design a change management research project?

6 Why has the change management guru-generated literature proved so popular?

Case study – Changing times at Factory Bank

A brief history of Factory Bank

The origins of Factory Bank can be traced back as far as the late eighteenth century. The Bank began in Yorkshire serving two functions – financing developments in the new industrial towns and acting as a savings bank mainly for the factory workers. In the nineteenth century the Bank grew from being a regional bank into being a large national bank. This process was facilitated through a series of mergers with smaller banks. Despite the mergers and acquisitions, Factory Bank still had a disproportionate number of branches in the north. The Bank was regarded as being a steady if uninspiring institution. The following discussion of Factory Bank is structured around three time horizons reflecting the past, the present and the future of Factory Bank.

Factory Bank (the 1990s)

The 1990s were a challenging decade for Factory Bank: employee numbers were reduced from 100,000 to 60,000. The Bank had always had a different culture from other clearing banks' due to its unique historical origins and the fact that it was the only bank to have worker representatives on the Board. In the early 1990s when other clearing banks began implementing cost-cutting strategies, Factory Bank had bucked this trend with their provocative 'Caring for Customers not Conning Customers' campaign. This had initially won them customers but had alienated them in relations with the other clearing banks. Despite the appearance of fierce competition amongst the clearing banks, they still cooperated closely and the campaign proved costly in terms of strategic alliances. However, one of the major catalysts for change was the increasing prominence in the marketplace of the building societies. The major building societies targeted the same demographic groups as Factory Bank, and by the mid-1990s there was talk of crisis. The costs of the building societies were a fraction of Factory Bank's, and throughout the Bank there was a realisation that the Bank would struggle to survive in its current form. In summary, the Bank abandoned its regional structure that had served it so well in previous decades. The goal of survival was used as the rationale for removing the worker representatives from the Board, who were replaced by representatives of the institutions who had become major investors in Factory Bank. Despite this investment or because of this investment, Factory Bank embarked upon a radical cost-cutting programme involving branch closures and compulsory redundancies.

There was industrial action and strikes closed the branches for a week – the first time in the history of Factory Bank. Many employees became bitter and disillusioned and voluntarily left the Bank. However, the financial press were delighted with progress, and when Factory Bank declared record profits, the headlines announced that 'Factory Bank Comes of Age'.

Factory Bank (today)

The current chief executive of Factory Bank is the charismatic Tony Wilson. He used to be a television company executive and was deliberately brought into Factory Bank to introduce greater financial realism into the operation. It was he who personally oversaw the refurbishment of branches and the rebranding of Factory Bank products with his New Order campaign. Competition for financial services was fierce with the recent entry into the market of retail stores. He had engineered a very lucrative partnership arrangement with Merryweather superstores whereby Factory Bank provided them with financial services products which were promoted using the Merryweather superstores brand. Also, Factory Bank had purchased a regional building society in the south-east which helped rectify a discrepancy in its branch network.

The industrial action in the 1990s left a legacy of poor industrial relations, although the banking union had benefited from increased membership. Tony Wilson was reputed to have said at a banker's dinner: 'I do not care about the commitment of the workforce as long as they work hard for their salaries.' This had become an urban myth, but what was real was the staff share ownership scheme that he had aggressively promoted. This had resulted in 20 per cent of shares in Factory Bank being owned by employees – a sizeable proportion for any bank.

Factory Bank (the next decade)

Nobody can predict the future with certainty, but the following offers a flavour of the forecasts about the next decade that the Bank has been working on.

The diversification of delivery channels is expected to continue to gather momentum. Whereas in the 1990s the majority of financial services were delivered via the branch networks, increasingly telephone banking and Internet banking have been becoming the norm. The branches are being repositioned as sales outlets rather than service outlets. However, it is privately envisaged that the branch network will have to be considerably reduced. What was once an asset has become a huge liability in terms of costs to the bank.

The competition from the retail sector will continue to grow, but more troublingly is the increasing threat of global competition. The Internet has made it possible for traditionally loyal customers to invest their savings with overseas financial service providers at far better rates of interest.

The joint arrangements with Merryweather superstores will have worked very well, leading to a series of joint ventures with other, smaller retailers. There is even speculation that Factory Bank might rename itself Retail Bank to draw a line under its industrial past and signpost the retail future.

Case study questions

1   In terms of the past, present and future of Factory Bank, what potential drivers of change may be identified?

2   How might the past, present and future context of Factory Bank help or hinder change management inside the bank?

FURTHER READING

ACKROYD S. (2002) *The Organization of Business: Applying organizational theory to contemporary change*, Oxford, Oxford University Press.

This textbook by Ackroyd is recommended for anyone who seeks an accessible macroeconomic analysis of organisational changes. The organisational theory emphasis offers an effective counterbalance to the organisational-behaviour emphasis of this textbook. Ackroyd relates change to theories of institutions and industrial policy in an unusual and thought-provoking textbook.

CAPON C. (2004) *Understanding Organisational Context: Inside and outside organisations*, 2nd edition, Harlow, FT/Prentice Hall.

Capon devotes a very accessible textbook to furthering understanding about organisational context. The strength of the book is that it brings together many of the functional areas of business which are often treated independently in academic settings. The textbook offers a systematic and thoughtful approach to understanding the contexts in which organisations operate.

DAWSON P. (2003) *Understanding Organizational Change: The contemporary experience of people at work*, London, Sage Publications.

In explaining the contexts of change, this chapter has encouraged the use of frameworks developed by Dawson. The approach to change that Dawson advocates can be seen as a development over time of his writings in the early 1990s. The book is recommended here for anyone who wishes to read further about processual/contextualised approaches to change. In particular, the book benefits from a series of research-based case studies which illustrate different experiences of change.

PETTIGREW A. M. (1990) Longitudinal field research on change theory and practice, *Organization Science*, Vol.1, No.3; pp.267–92.

Many of the references to Pettigrew would be relevant further reading to support debates featured in this chapter. However, this particular paper has been chosen because it presents a tacit account of how Pettigrew and his colleagues undertook research into change. Often discussions of research methods in academic journals offer sanitised accounts of how research was conducted. This paper conversely benefits from the disclosures, particularly in terms of the thinking behind the research methods.

Strategic change

CHAPTER 5

LEARNING OBJECTIVES

To:

- review the meanings and theories of strategic change

- consider the paradox of revolutionary and evolutionary change

- contrast planned and emergent change

- understand the role of change agency in the change management process

- identify strategic change tools

- critically question the concept of strategic change

- evaluate the case for and against mergers and acquisitions.

INTRODUCTION

This chapter addresses relationships between two large and sometimes contradictory bodies of literature – strategy and change. There is no consensus with regard either to effectively managing change or to theoretically explaining change. In a similar manner there is no consensus about either undertaking or explaining strategic management. As Whittington (2001: 2) warns, 'There is not much agreement about strategy.'

A strategic change perspective has been utilised effectively in change management textbooks such as Burnes (2004a) and Balogun and Hope Hailey (2004). In this textbook there is a greater emphasis upon individual and organisational change as components of change management. However, focusing upon a strategic change perspective in this chapter furthers understanding about change management. Earlier assertions (see Box 2 in Chapter 1) about the importance of individual change as part of organisational change implicitly criticise more strategic approaches to change management, implying that in attempting to manage 'the big picture' managers lose sight of individual members of an organisation. Equally, strategists are suspicious that approaches to change management may over-emphasise the role of the individual. For example, Wilson (1992: 2), in advocating a strategic approach to change, criticises the 'rather individualistic, psychological explanations of resistance to change' in the organisational behaviour literature.

In the Approaches section, the different meanings of 'strategic change' are explained, as well as evolutionary and revolutionary and planned and emergent approaches to change. The concept of change agency is considered, as are examples of strategic change management tools a change agent might use. In the *Critical perspective*, strategic change is critically questioned and mergers and acquisitions are critically reviewed as examples of strategic change in practice.

APPROACHES TO STRATEGIC CHANGE
The meanings and theories of strategic change

Examples of strategic changes include 'reorganisation, a diversification move, a shift in core technology, a business process redesign and product portfolio reshuffle ...' (De Wit and Meyer, 2004: 164), raising the question 'What do we mean by strategic change?' De Wit and Meyer (2004: 163), in acknowledging the pervasive nature of change, emphasise that not all change is strategic and that much is operational, defining 'strategic change' in the following terms:

> *Strategic changes have an impact on the way the firm does business (its business system) and on the way the organisation has been configured (its organisational system). In short, while operational changes are necessary to maintain the business and organisational systems, strategic changes are directed at renewing them.*

Defining strategic change is contentious, and consequently a prerequisite is to establish the meaning of 'strategy'. Five definitions of 'strategy' have been offered – as a plan, a ploy, a pattern, a position and a perspective (Mintzberg, 1998). One way to conceive of strategy is in terms of the metaphor of a war. Generals employ their different strategies in order to win the war. 'In the common parlance, strategy refers to the tactics on which wars are won or lost, and this same militaristic image tends to suffuse much of the discourse on business strategy' (Eccles and Nohria, 1992: 87). Such a conception fits with Mintzberg's definition reflecting strategy as a plan. The traditional and rational approach to strategy as a plan first took hold in the 1960s and 1970s (Graetz *et al*, 2002: 53) and in many ways has been the orthodoxy particularly within business (see Pettigrew *et al*, 2002 for a concise overview of the historical evolution of strategy). However, in recent decades understanding of strategy has benefited from a critical academic questioning of the concept. Whittington (2001: 2) identifies four generic approaches to strategy:

- classical
- evolutionary
- processual, and
- systemic.

The classical approach relates to traditional views of strategy, with an emphasis upon the drawing up of strategic plans by senior managers for others to implement. The evolutionary approach emphasises the responding of senior managers to markets, placing less emphasis upon the process of planning. The theoretical foundations of the evolutionary approach are rooted in population ecology. The processual approach challenges both the rationality of strategic planning and the supposed efficacy of markets in favour of an emergent approach that acknowledges political compromise influenced by cultures and subcultures. The systemic approach suggests that social systems shape strategic goals and processes so that strategies reflect both organisational and societal interests. This typology offers a more sophisticated understanding of strategy and competing strategic change theories. For example, the following discussion by Hayes (2002: 58) illustrates the classical approach and the processual approach to strategic change:

> *A change strategy is essentially a plan to make things happen. It needs to address all of the things that have to be done to bring about the change. When developing a strategy, change managers need to attend to each step in the change process and to the way the overall process is to be managed.*

53

The dilemma becomes one of selecting which approaches to strategy are most appropriate to explaining the narrower subset of strategic change. Mintzberg *et al* (1998: 302) offer a way out of this dilemma. In a comprehensive overview of the competing schools of thought on strategic management, the penultimate chapter is devoted to the configuration school explanations of strategy formation as a process of transformation. This school is different from other schools in offering the possibility of reconciliation in terms of integrating the messages of other schools.

RESEARCH CASES IN JOURNALS NO.2 – NOVOTEL

This longitudinal case study focuses upon the international hotel chain between 1992 and 1995. The authors in particular address the rejuvenation side of the renewal strategy. The case is informative in terms of the detail offered and because the researchers were able to interview members of the top management team about strategic aspects of the case study. The authors are also able to offer prescriptions derived from the case about how to orchestrate the change process. These include assessing the four parameters that influence the speed of change and politics of the project and designing and controlling the dynamics of the change process over time.

Sector: Hotels
Research methods: In-depth interviews and documentary research.
Authors: Calori, R., Baden-Fuller, C. and Hunt, B.
Paper title: Managing change at Novotel: back to the future
Journal details: *Long Range Planning*, Vol.33, 2000; pp.779–804

The paradox of revolutionary and evolutionary change

De Wit and Meyer (2004: 170) introduce this paradox in their discussion of strategic change with reference to the struggle managers face in choosing their approach to strategic change:

> *On the one hand, they usually realise that to fundamentally transform the organisation a break with the past is needed... On the other hand, they also recognise the value of continuity, building on past experiences, investments and loyalties.*

De Wit and Meyer (2004: 170) acknowledge a tendency amongst commentators to depict revolutionary change as strategic and evolutionary change as operational. However, Burke (2002: 67) suggests that 'more than 95 per cent of organisational changes are evolutionary', and Burnes (2004a: 267) highlights the artificiality of the evolutionary/revolutionary distinction when he discusses how an evolutionary change may be a component of a revolutionary change. It is informative to note that 'no consensus has yet developed within the field of strategic management on how to balance revolution and evolution...' (De Wit and Meyer, 2004: 182).

Planned change and emergent change

Another ongoing strategic change debate relates to whether strategic changes are planned or emergent, mirroring larger debates about the planned or emergent nature of strategy. Strategy 'emerges constantly in a firm as different people respond to and reinterpret their sense of the organisation's identity and purpose' (Eccles and Nohria, 1992: 87). Genus (1998: 4) poses the question 'How deliberately planned (or plannable) is fundamental change, as exemplified by major restructuring, re-engineering or total quality programmes?'

The concept of planned change was developed by Kurt Lewin in the early 1950s. Burnes (1996: 12) believes that 'There must also be an appreciation of the states that an organisation must pass through in order to move from an unsatisfactory present state to a more desired future state.' De Caluwe and Vermaak (2003: 70–3), noting that 'the literature is full of all sorts of definitions of planned change', offer their own definition of planned change, which includes realising intended outcomes by going through a sequence of phases or steps while the change process is monitored and guided by change agents. The origins of step/stage models so prominent in the change management literature are evident in planned change approaches. Many of the models that prescribe an approach to change management are deeply rooted in this planned change tradition. Wilson (1992: 27) captures the potential of such approaches in the following caricature:

In the extreme, planned change strategies would be those processes in which there was a smooth transition from some previously articulated strategic vision towards a future desired state (such as an envisaged portfolio of potentially successful products and services).

The irony in such a caricature relates to the realism of such aspirations. Again a classical approach to strategy is evident – the change process is simultaneously bold and reassuring. Yet in recent decades the planned approach to change has been challenged.

Burnes (1996: 13) depicts the emergent model of change as a response to criticisms of planned change. The emergent model of change views change as being unpredictable, as a process shaped by inter-relationships with a range of variables. Change is seen as bottom-up rather than top-down, and as an open-ended and continuous process of adaptation to changing conditions (Burnes, 1996: 13). In terms of Whittington's earlier typology, the emergent model of change may be understood as a processualist approach to strategic change. Burnes (1996: 16), in concluding his review of planned and emergent approaches to change, writes:

Rather than seeing the argument between the planned and emergent approaches to change as a clash of two fundamentally opposing systems of ideas, they can be better viewed as approaches which seek to address different situational variables (contingencies).

There does appear to be merit in avoiding a polarised distinction between planned change and emergent change. It is conceivable that senior management will commence a change management initiative in planned change mode and then move into a more emergent mode, or vice versa.

Change agents and agency

Internal and external change agents play a number of different roles in change processes such that change normally involves a plurality of actors or players (Buchanan and Badham, 1999: 23). De Caluwe and Vermaak (2003: 255) regard the role of the change agent as 'possibly one of the most important factors in effecting change'. Johnson *et al* (2005: 519) define a change agent as 'the individual or group that helps effect strategic change in an organisation'. The concept of change agency is sometimes favoured over change agent in order to signpost that a group rather than a single individual is overseeing the change process (Buchanan and Badham, 1999: 23). An important ingredient in change agency is change leadership (discussed in Chapter 12). Change agency may come from within an organisation or from outside in terms of a new chief executive, new management, consultants or a stakeholder network (Johnson *et al*, 2005: 522).

Paton and McCalman (2000) devote a chapter to what they call the objective outsider as change agent. They offer a persuasive argument for utilising external expertise as part of the change process. There is an inevitable functionalism about discussions of change agency, the task of effectively managing change overshadowing more theoretical discussions about change agency.

Strategic change tools

Adopting a voluntarist approach over a determinist approach to change agency suggests the need for strategic change tools in order to effect changes. Similarly, change tools fit with a planned rather than an emergent approach to change. Randall (2004: 35), in writing about what he describes as 'the tradition of interventional change in organisations described as organisational development', regards OD as a movement which utilises a series of tools and techniques as part of its approach to change management. Strategic change tools are still utilised today, as evidenced by the Organising for Success research programme (CIPD, 2004: 6) for which the questionnaire survey revealed that:

> *Across large and small organisations, and in both private and public sectors, there is a fairly standard set of reorganising tools that must be mastered, but success comes from artfully selecting and adapting these tools according to the specifics of the situation.*

Diagnostic models are regarded as part of the change agent's toolkit and the accumulation of diagnostic tools by change agents is seen as an important part of their ongoing professionalisation (De Caluwe and Vermaak, 2003: 159). In Chapter 4 there was discussion about tools that might be utilised as part of an environmental analysis. De Caluwe and Vermaak (2003: 159) identify a range of different diagnostic tools which may be applied at different organisational levels: these include the Eisenhower principle, the fishbone diagram, the balanced scorecard and environmental analysis.

As well as diagnostic strategic change tools, there are intervention tools. 'Interventions can be conceived in all kinds of sizes, scopes and depths' (De Caluwe and Vermaak, 2003: 150). Popular strategic change tools include force-field analysis, the balanced scorecard, scenario-planning and strategic surface assumption-testing.

Although strategic change tools play a significant role in the practice of change management, it is worthwhile sounding a note of caution. The danger with generic tools as advocated as part of the classical approach to strategy is that they will not suit all situations. Iles and Sutherland (2001: 19) raise this issue with particular reference to work on organisational change in the NHS:

> *No single method, strategy or tool will fit all problems or situations that arise. Managers in the NHS need to be adept at diagnosing organisational situations and skilled at choosing those tools that are best suited to the particular circumstances that confront them.*

This warning appears applicable to all sectors, highlighting why issues around change agency discussed earlier are so important – how the tools are used is as important as which tools are used.

CRITICAL PERSPECTIVE

The following critical perspective on strategic change is organised around two challenges:

- strategic change has been over-emphasised
- mergers and acquisitions fail to deliver their promised benefits.

The following discussion elaborates upon each of these challenges.

Questioning strategic change

Pettigrew *et al* (2002) in their *Handbook of Strategy and Management* offer an informed overview of the strengths and limitations of the field. This discussion draws very selectively upon their overview in order to raise questions about strategy. One concern in reviewing the strategy literature is the apparent lack of reflexivity (see also Whipp, 1996). An explanation for this lack of reflexivity centres on the divide between theory and practice – specifically the need to meet the expectations of the various stakeholders interested in the subject (Pettigrew *et al*, 2002: 11). The suggestion here is that there is a creative tension between critical theorising involving reflection which would advance a theoretical understanding of strategy and practical requirements made of strategy by senior managers in organisations.

Pettigrew *et al* (2002: 7), in terms of the history of strategic management, acknowledge that the subject draws upon other disciplines and sub-fields of management, but that 'there has been a consistent reaching out to the theoretical apparatus of economics.' This emphasis upon economics is informative in suggesting preferences and biases built into strategic management. Individual-level analysis has been emphasised in this textbook. The economics orientation of strategy may explain why individuals appear to be acknowledged in change literature yet not adequately addressed in strategic approaches to change management. Even differentiation between organisations may be challenging in terms of economic analyses:

> *Economic theory is unable to distinguish effectively between firms, except through glib generalities about comparative efficiency of the firm's production function.*
> *(Pavitt and Steinmueller, 2002: 345)*

It is unlikely that economic theories or, by association, strategy can address the diversity of individuals that comprise contemporary organisations. Whittington (2001: 99) acknowledges that organisations are, literally, mindless:

> *They have no unity and collectively they are rather stupid. Yet the notion of 'strategy' implies that all the multitudinous individuals who make up an organisation can be united around the effective pursuit of a coherent goal.*

The quotation offers an explanation for the potential assumption that organisations change as part of strategic change processes without explaining how individuals change as part of such processes. The questioning so far has arisen within strategy debates. However, some writers have been critical of the broader concept of strategy. Pettigrew *et al* (2002: 14) note that 'mainstream strategy research and writing is a particular target for the critical management theorist.' Sorge and Van Witteloostuijn (2004: 1213), in a polemical attack on what they regard as the nonsense of organisational change, criticise popular notions of strategic change, amongst other things. They create an argument challenging the preoccupation of strategists with radical change: 'Strategies and structures need credibility, consistency, and legitimacy in order to mobilise people.' The contradiction of strategic change is that

> *strategy itself is not about change at all, but about continuity – whether as deliberate plan to establish patterns of behavior or as emergent pattern by which such patterns get established.*
>
> *(Mintzberg et al, 1998: 302)*

However, Sorge and Van Witteloostuijn's (2004: 1213) main target is the perceived preoccupation of strategists with an increasing rate of environmental change:

> *Empirically, we have not seen any demonstration that the rate of environmental change has uniformly increased across the board over a longer time span... It is an unsubstantiated myth so far shamefully tolerated or cultivated by scholars.*

Understanding about strategic change is being shaped by a series of critical debates among academics about the meanings, explanations and prescriptions of strategy. There have been periodic cries for a unifying paradigm in strategic management. 'One has not appeared, it is unlikely to do so, and it would be creatively destructive if it did arrive' (Pettigrew *et al*, 2002: 11).

Critically reviewing mergers and acquisitions

Gaughan (2002) mapped out five waves of mergers and acquisitions activity, the first wave taking place between 1897 and 1904. In recent years senior managers appear to have favoured mergers and acquisitions as a means of gaining scale and global scope. However, this raises the question 'Have mergers and acquisitions delivered what senior managers expected?' DiGeorgio (2002 and 2003) reviewed what is known and not known about mergers and acquisitions with specific reference to change management, and his work will be drawn upon as the first part of this critical review.

DiGeorgio (2002: 135) reviewed relevant literature as well as drawing upon his own experience as a consultant working on mergers and acquisitions. He highlights the overview of previous studies undertaken by LaJoux (1998):

> *LaJoux cites 15 major studies of the success or failure of acquisitions. For the studies reporting failure rates, the rate ranged from 40 per cent to 80 per cent, with the exception of one study done in 1965, which reported a 16 per cent failure rate.*

The reasons mergers and acquisitions do not work include: inadequate due diligence by the acquirer or merger partner, lack of compelling strategic rationale, and unrealistic expectations of possible synergies (Zweig, 1995). There are a number of challenges which a merger/acquisition will raise.

DiGeorgio (2003: 261) notes that managers in the acquired companies invariably have significant negative feelings that need to be overcome.

Another challenge is the problematic nature of cultural change (discussed further in Chapter 7). As well as acknowledging the problematic nature of mergers and acquisitions, DiGeorgio (2002 and 2003) cites Cisco systems and GE Capital as case examples of companies which appear to have been successful in their merger and acquisition activity. DiGeorgio (2003: 273) believes that 'the answers lie in a very systematic approach to both selection and integration, and not just a systematic approach on paper, but one that gets executed.' Sorge and Van Witteloostuijn (2004: 1205) in a more scholarly paper highlight:

> *A well-established finding after decades of in-depth work is that a strikingly high incidence of overly popular merger and acquisition strategies is associated with failure.*

They also cite Copeland *et al* (1993) who found that '61 per cent of their sample of acquiring firms in the 1980s have not even been successful in recovering the capital cost of their acquisitions.' The irony is that despite the overwhelming empirical evidence senior managers until recently continued to pursue mergers and acquisitions.

SYNOPSIS

The pervasive nature of change was acknowledged, but it was emphasised that not all change was strategic and that much was operational. De Wit and Meyer defined strategic change as having an impact on the way a firm does business and on the way the organisation was configured. Four generic approaches to strategy – classical, evolutionary, processual and systemic – were discussed.

Evolutionary change focused upon incremental change whereas revolutionary change emphasised radical change. Commentators tended to depict strategic change as revolutionary, yet it was suggested that more than 95 per cent of organisational changes were evolutionary.

Ongoing debate related to whether strategic changes were planned or emergent, mirroring larger debates about the planned or emergent nature of strategy and change. Planned change included realising intended outcomes by going through a sequence of phases or steps while the change process was monitored and guided by change agents. The planned approach to change had attracted critics. The emergent model of change depicted change as being unpredictable, a process shaped by inter-relationships with a range of variables – change was seen as bottom-up rather than top-down, and as an open-ended and continuous process of adaptation to changing conditions.

Internal and external change agents played different roles in change processes. A change agent was the individual or group that helped effect strategic change in an organisation; the concept of change agency was favoured rather than change agent, signposting that a group rather than a single individual was overseeing the change process.

The use of change tools fits with a planned rather than an emergent approach to change. There was a fairly standard set of reorganising tools that had to be mastered. These tools included diagnostic models and intervention tools regarded as part of the change agent's toolkit. Examples of tools included the Eisenhower principle, the fishbone diagram, the balanced scorecard and environmental analysis.

In reviewing the strategy literature there was an apparent lack of reflexivity. The emphasis upon economics suggested preferences and biases built into strategic management. The economics orientation of strategy may explain why individuals were acknowledged yet not adequately addressed in strategic change. It was unlikely that economic theories or, by association, strategy could address the diversity of individuals that comprise contemporary organisations.

Senior managers favoured mergers and acquisitions as a means of gaining scale and scope in the new global economy, begging the question 'Have mergers and acquisitions delivered what senior managers expected?' LaJoux cited 15 major studies of the success or failure of acquisitions. For the studies reporting failure rates, the rate ranged from 40 per cent to 80 per cent, with the exception of one study done in 1965, which reported a 16 per cent failure rate. Sorge and Van Witteloostuijn highlighted elements in the financial press noting the disappointing average performance of mergers and acquisitions.

DISCUSSION QUESTIONS

1 What are the advantages and disadvantages of adopting a strategic approach to change management?

2 As an employee would you prefer to work in an organisation which favoured a planned approach or which preferred an emergent approach to change?

3 Which is the more vital ingredient in a successful change – change agency or change tools?

4 What would be the disadvantages of favouring a single academic approach to strategic change?

5 Is it possible for a strategic change perspective to accommodate the diversity of individuals that comprise an organisation?

6 Why have mergers and acquisitions remained popular if the empirical evidence suggests they invariably fail?

Case study – Strategic change at Higson's Plastic Parts

Higson's Plastic Parts (HPP) is a family firm established over 60 years ago, and has one factory that employs 320 people in roles ranging from production to administration. The company moulds specialised plastic parts for a range of large organisations that manufacture cars, buses, lorries and trains. The business was for long successfully run by Walter Higson, who passed away 10 years ago, but has since been jointly run by the Higson brothers Charlie and Bobby, who succeeded their father. Over the past decade the brothers have repeatedly clashed over the strategic direction of the business, which may account for why a once prosperous business is now in financial difficulties. At the suggestion of a friend they have engaged a business consultant who has agreed amongst other things to act as a mediator between the two brothers.

She spent her first day with the brothers touring the site and meeting many of the long-serving staff. She had also had a chance to 'eyeball' the accounts and talk with the sales and marketing team. Also, towards the end of the day she had an opportunity to talk with each of the brothers independently of each other and together as a pair. After what had been a long yet productive day she sat down to write up her notes.

In order to orientate herself she started by sketching out a simple SWOT analysis. HPP had been very successful and appeared to be a respected supplier of plastic parts. The workforce was very skilled, loyal and committed to HPP. However, in terms of weaknesses, HPP was no longer operating as a profitable business and was reliant upon cash reserves that had been accumulated in more profitable times. Sales and marketing staff saw opportunities to diversify into new lines of business which had not existed in the past. Also, it was believed that the workforce was very flexible and would be prepared to work differently to secure the long-term future of the business. The threats were the most troubling part of the analysis. HPP was reliant upon five major contracts which were renewed annually. The plant that had been an asset in the past was becoming obsolete and would need replacing with the latest advanced manufacturing technology in the near future. However, the biggest threat was now from Asia, where the competition was increasingly able to produce plastic parts at far lower costs.

The consultant's discussions with Charlie and Bobby was hard work because they appeared to favour very different positions, particularly in terms of ways forward. At times they contradicted each other, and at times they even contradicted themselves. She doodled 'Strategic change at Higsons over the next five years?'

Charlie was the more assertive of the two brothers and the keener to remember his father's ways of working. His father had schooled him in the use of the Plan. The Plan involved the manipulation of a series of fairly simple sales and costs ratios which had helped to determine the rate at which the business had grown in the past. Inside HPP the Plan had been the secret ingredient that had given the business its competitive advantage. Every six months the Plan was recalculated and heads of the functional areas of the business would wait with anticipation for their budget forecasts. Information would then be cascaded down throughout the organisation, to such an extent that shopfloor employees looked to the Plan as a barometer of how the business was doing. At one point Charlie had asserted that 'The Plan has served us well in the past, it serves us well in the present, and it will serve us well in the future.' Despite this he was now in search of a Plan B that would not replace the Plan but would complement it. In particular, he was interested in the development of more sophisticated financial models that would help with more effective business planning. When challenged about the threat of competition from Asia, he retorted that their absence at the Plastic Mouldings Traders Association conference had been rather conspicuous. In terms of the next five years the Plan suggested that the time was not right in terms of sales and costs to invest in expensive technology. However, when the time was right his preference would be to bring in a consultant to carefully manage the change he envisaged. He favoured a five-stage approach to change which had worked effectively 15 years ago when the new production line was introduced. In the short term, though, it was important to consolidate the strengths of the business.

Bobby was initially reticent to talk, appearing to live in his brother's shadow. However, with encouragement he began to talk very freely about his hopes and even dreams for HPP. He was disparaging about the Plan, questioning its relevance and its predictive capabilities. He mumbled that what his father had taught him was not the importance of numbers but the importance of people. 'People make our products, people sell our products, and people buy our products – that's *my* plan.' He explained that every day he would tour the site talking to employees. His brother thought he was time-wasting, but he would always respond that he was listening to the business talking. He was popular with employees and was beginning to hear concerns from employees about the likelihood of future generations' working at HPP. He had deliberately located his office alongside the sales and marketing office. The recurrent message from that office was that there were many requests for small plastic mouldings, but that reluctantly they had to turn away this business because the company was concentrating upon large production runs. His fact-finding trip to Taiwan had left him anxious. He had seen the new highly automated factories and knew that HPP would be unable to compete and – more troublingly – could no longer afford the investment in advanced manufacturing technology in order to compete. He explained that for some months he had been in a deep depression but that the solution had emerged out of an informal discussion with staff in the canteen the previous month.

They had been asking for advice on how they could set up their own businesses in order to serve the lucrative and expanding small-production-run market. At this point he began to see a very different future for HPP. Parts of the manufacturing site could be sold to employees who would operate independently of HPP but still gain the benefits of being on a single site, possibly subcontracting personnel and sales functions back to HPP. These businesses would be less susceptible to overseas competition and the existing technology would be an asset rather than a liability, in terms of small-scale production runs. He believed there was an urgency, but was also interested in getting into a serious dialogue with their five main clients, believing other options might arise out of such discussions.

Case study questions

1 Evaluate the visions of Charlie and Bobby in terms of their strengths and weaknesses.

2 Which of the brothers is more likely to favour change agency and change tools, and why?

3 If you were the consultant, what advice would you give to the brothers about strategic change in Higsons?

FURTHER READING

AMBROSINI V., with JOHNSON G. and SCHOLES K. (1998) *Exploring Techniques of Analysis and Evaluation in Strategic Management*, Harlow, FT/Prentice Hall.

This edited collection of readings offers guidance on the tools and techniques of strategy. The book is intended for both students and practising managers. The intention is that the book should be used in a practical rather than a conceptual manner. One of the strengths of the book is that the tools and techniques believed to be popularly understood are dealt with in more depth by the individual chapter authors than in a standard textbook. For example, Gerry Johnson offers a chapter on cultural mapping and Kevan Scholes offers a chapter on stakeholder mapping.

DE CALUWE L. and VERMAAK H. (2003) *Learning to Change: A guide for organization change agents*, London, Sage Publications.

As the title suggests, this book is concerned with informing the practice of change management. There are many discussions in the book that are pertinent to this chapter, including chapters on planned change and change agency. However, of particular interest are the chapters on diagnostic models and interventions. In each of these chapters the authors catalogue a wide range of strategic change tools and discuss how they could be used in a change context.

PETTIGREW A., THOMAS H. and WHITTINGTON R. (eds) (2002) *Handbook of Strategy and Management*, London, Sage Publications.

The volume of strategy literature and the volume of many strategy textbooks can be daunting for anyone outside this specialism. However, this handbook edited by respected academics in the strategy and management field offers an informative collection of readings, giving a flavour of the many debates that shape thinking about strategy and management.

STACEY R. D. (2003) *Strategic Management and Organisational Dynamics: The challenge of complexity*, 4th edition, Harlow, FT/Prentice Hall.

Stacey offers a thought-provoking systemic perspective on the twin themes of this chapter. What is intriguing about his textbook is his skilful ability to adopt a strategic perspective while emphasising that knowledge of individuals and their capacities is an important element in our understanding of change management. Throughout the textbook the emphasis is upon understanding what managers do rather than prescribing what they should do. Stacey is able to offer sophisticated philosophically-grounded rationales for his approach.

Changing organisational forms

LEARNING OBJECTIVES

To:

- highlight the historical emphasis on organisational structure

- evaluate contributions to understanding organisational structures

- review organisational structural change choices

- critique functional/contingency approaches

- acknowledge changes in processes and boundaries

- critically review downsizing.

INTRODUCTION

Understanding how organisational forms are changing is closely related to other change management topics such as strategy, culture and technology. However, this change management topic is hampered by academics and senior managers who seek out 'ideal types' of organisation which may never exist:

> *There is a great deal of variation in organisational forms. It is not helpful to think of the main task of organisation studies as being to identify the one new and distinctive organisational type that fits most observable examples.*
>
> *(Ackroyd, 2002: 169)*

In Chapter 4 the importance of internal and external contexts was emphasised, in view of the fact that these contexts are part of the explanation of the diversity of organisational forms. However, organisational forms are also influenced by managerial choices and power relations. In the first half of this chapter an overview of orthodox thinking about organisational structure is offered. In the second half this orthodoxy is questioned in favour of an acknowledgement of new forms of organising.

APPROACHES TO ORGANISATIONAL STRUCTURE

Historical perspective on organisational structure

Oxman and Smith (2003: 77) note that Alfred Sloan and others in the 1920s articulated

> *a doctrine that came to be known as 'the three Ss' – having crafted a strategy, senior managers must find a structure to fit it and align the two with supporting systems ...*

This was to become the established logic for senior managers and academics over many decades, and is still popular today in certain quarters. Interest in organisational structures predates interest in change management. Leavitt (1965) regarded organisations as consisting of four elements – task or mission, structure, technology, and people. He believed that a change in one would have consequences for the others.

There are close links between debates in this chapter and debates about strategic change in the previous chapter. Oxman and Smith (2003: 80) have suggested that 'companies have shifted their change management focus from the anatomical to the physiological' in a manner similar to the De Wit and Meyer discussion in the previous chapter. The shift from the anatomical (structure) to the physiological (processes) is discussed further later in this chapter.

Explaining and understanding organisational structure is not solely an academic pursuit. Urwick (1947) regarded a deficient organisational structure as illogical, cruel, wasteful and inefficient. As well as being detrimental to the interests of senior management, working in an organisation with a deficient structure has consequences for individuals in terms of their experience of work.

Theorising organisational structure

Functional/contingency approaches have been influential in shaping thinking about organisational structure. Understanding organisational structure is presented as an ongoing academic riddle, echoing debates within change management relating to the potential 'fit' between structure and variables such as strategy, environment, technology and size. These explanations often place different emphases upon different variables. In order to explain organisational structure it is worthwhile reviewing four early contributions to debates about organisational structure.

At the beginning of the twentieth century the writings of both Taylor and Fayol in attempting to explain and classify management began an ongoing process of prescribing organisational structures. Many management and organisational behaviour writers have since contributed to understanding organisational structures. This section selectively focuses upon four significant contributions to our understanding of organisational structure:

- Weber: bureaucratic structures
- Burns and Stalker: mechanistic and organic structures
- Miles and Snow: fit between strategy and structure
- Mintzberg: five structural stereotypes.

An enduring conceptualisation of organisational structure is as a bureaucracy. Weber (1947), a German sociologist, through translations of his writing gave impetus to understanding organisations as bureaucracies and appreciating structuralist approaches to organisational behaviour. He identified three types of authority in organisations – rational-legal, traditional and charismatic – and an 'ideal type' of bureaucracy which had the following defining characteristics: specialisation, hierarchy, rules, impersonality, appointment, progression, exclusivity, segregation and accurate written records. Many of these organisational attributes are still evident in organisations today. In reviewing the contribution of Weber it is important to acknowledge that he established the agenda for discussing organisational structure (Dunkerley, 2001: 98). His continuing contribution has been to encourage consideration about authority and rationality with regard to organisational structure.

The structuralist approach of Weber may be contrasted with the contingency approach advocated by Burns and Stalker (1961), whose research was based upon Scottish manufacturing firms. Their findings highlighted two types of organisation structure which appeared to be responses to the environment in which the firms operated – these were mechanistic and organic structures. Mechanistic organisations include a clear definition of jobs, standardised policies and procedures governing organisational decision-making and rewards determined by adhering to supervisory instructions. Organic structures include decreased emphasis upon formal job descriptions and a view of the formal organisation that is fluid and changeable. Burns and Stalker were able to argue from their research that the adoption of a mechanistic or an organic organisation structure suited specific markets. In this classification the origins of debates about the merits of 'flat' versus 'tall' organisations become apparent. The mechanistic organisation structure suggests a tall structure, whereas the organic organisation structure suggests a flat structure.

Both the work of Miles and Snow (1984) and Mintzberg (1983) offer a more strategic perspective in terms of the perceived fit between organisational structures and the environment in which they operate. Miles and Snow (1984), tracing the evolution of organisational structures from the 1800s through to contemporary times, identified the following patterns of strategy-structure linkage: defender strategies, prospector strategies, analyser strategies and reactor strategies. Defenders were concerned with stable domains and sustaining a prominent position in narrow markets. Prospectors, on the other hand, sought to exploit new options – they were open to new opportunities and innovation. Analysers were a hybrid of defenders and prospectors, seeking to maximise profits and minimise risk through both routinised work as well as new work. Reactors were regarded as unstable, in failing to achieve an appropriate defending, prospecting or analysing strategy. The danger was that reactors reacted to change in inappropriate ways.

In a similar manner, Mintzberg (1983) identified five organisational forms, as well as the prime co-ordinating mechanism for each form:

- the simple structure – direct supervision
- the machine bureaucracy – standardisation of work processes
- the professional bureaucracy – standardisation of skills
- the divisionalised form – standardisation of outputs
- the 'adhocracy' – mutual adjustment.

Each of the four contributions discussed in this chapter was influential in furthering understanding about organisational structure.

Organisational choices and structures

Reviewing earlier contributions to understanding organisational structure and reviewing structures, it is easy to believe that structures are determined by forces beyond the control of senior managers. However, organisational structures are a consequence of senior management choices and these choices are themselves influenced by a range of factors. Bowditch and Buono (2005: 275) identified four main factors that influence decisions about organisational structure:

- the environment
- the size of the organisation

- the organisation's dominant technology, and
- the organisation's strategy.

The dilemmas faced by senior managers include choices about centralisation versus decentralisation, control versus commitment and change versus stability (Carnall, 2003: 58). Although senior managers are likely to be influenced by such considerations, there are a range of questions that have to be addressed in order to design or redesign an organisational structure. The complexity of choices about organisational structure that have to be made are further complicated when senior managers adopt a hybrid structure within an organisation.

Johnson *et al* (2005: 397–410) identify the following organisational structures: the simple structure, the functional structure, the multidivisional structure, the holding company structure, the matrix structure, team-based structures, project-based structures and intermediate structures. (These structures are well documented in strategy, management and organisational behaviour textbooks – see, for example, Buchanan and Huczynski, 2004.) Such structures must be regarded as templates because they are unlikely ever to correspond exactly with actual organisations. In considering organisational structures, the unique context of a particular organisation may influence the structure, so the type of questions that have to be addressed are:

- What is the nature of the environment in which the organisation operates?
- What type of technology does the organisation use?
- What is the size of the organisation?
- What are the organisational goals?

Inevitably, organisational structures are likely to be intermediate structures – few organisations adopt pure structural types. This might explain why commentators have begun to criticise the over-emphasis upon organisational structure in orthodox accounts of management and organisational behaviour.

CRITICAL PERSPECTIVE

Managing change and organising are dynamic processes, and an understanding of such processes should be dynamic in a similar manner.

> *Commentators are in agreement that a new form of organisation is emerging which differs from its classical predecessors... Exactly what shape (or shapes) the new form will take is still not clear.*
>
> *(Buchanan and Huczynski, 2004: 537)*

This quotation highlights the dilemma that although organisational forms are changing, probably only with hindsight will it be possible to assert the new forms that have emerged. The following critical perspective on changing organisational forms is organised around three challenges:

- the limitations of orthodox emphasis upon organisational structures
- acknowledgment that processes and boundaries are changing as well as structures
- questioning the perceived benefits of downsizing.

The following discussion elaborates upon each of these challenges.

Critique of functional/contingency approaches

Functional/contingency writing about organisational structure has been influential in shaping senior management thinking as well as academic thinking. Eccles and Nohria (1992: 117) have warned that historically, proposals about structure have claimed to provide a 'best' way of dealing with the problem of structure. The theorists cited earlier in this chapter illustrate such functional thinking. Consequently, any critique challenges an orthodoxy that has developed over time. However, in the context of a change management textbook it is necessary to consider the dynamic nature of changing organisational forms rather than the static nature of organisational structures. Johnson *et al* (2005: 396) regard views about designing organisations as changing, raising two issues:

- a static concept of formal structure is less and less appropriate
- informal relationships and processes are vital to generating and sharing in-depth knowledge.

The following discussion draws together criticisms of functional/contingency explanations of organisational structure.

Ackroyd (2002: 72) effectively challenges assumptions of functional and contingency writing in two ways. Firstly, organisational structures are not simply functional. Secondly, organisational structures are not simply a consequence of adapting to an external environment. Organisation structures must take account of functions (eg finance and personnel). However, there is a danger of privileging these functions over other factors. Structural change may perversely be regarded as responding to the need to be seen to be changing – changing in a way that is tangible for stakeholders.

Oxman and Smith (2003: 77) remind us of Michael Hammer's disparaging yet helpful reference to 'the widespread malady of structuritis'. Issuing a new organisational chart may be perceived as a proactive response to an organisational problem, and may offer the hope of making an organisation more effective. However, the counterpoint is that an organisation may need to change processes rather than structure. Mechanisms of control and power may be designed into what is presented as an apparently neutral organisation structure.

> *Structures institutionalise inequalities and therefore any conflicts and tensions that arise from this. The structure is not likely to be optimally functional for this reason.*
> *(Ackroyd, 2002: 72)*

The concern of critics is that orthodox accounts of organisational structure underplay managerial objectives which are designed into organisations. This apparent neutrality is magnified through traditional contingency preoccupations with the 'fit' between organisational structures and external environments in which organisations operate. However, Ackroyd (2002: 72) argues that 'far from passively adapting, organisations commonly shape (or enact) their environments.'

This critique has so far emphasised academic concerns with orthodox emphasis upon organisational structure. However, there are signs that senior management is beginning to question 'restructuring as the first tool employed to effect organisational change' (Oxman and Smith, 2003: 80). In a thought-provoking paper Oxman and Smith question the limits of structural change, citing short case examples from BP plc, Duke Power and W. L. Gore to illustrate how change is now being achieved in ways other than structural change. They conclude:

Whilst structure is clearly still part of the equation, strategists are now being forced to change their image of 'organisation' from that of a static photograph of boxes and lines to a dynamic movie depicting a continuous flow of internal and external responsiveness.

(Oxman and Smith, 2003: 82)

One potential explanation of the apparent rejection of structural change prescriptions is that a simplistic view of organisational structure and functioning can oversell its promises, exchanging one set of problems for another (Salaman and Asch, 2003: 9). There does appear to have been a shift from organising around structure to organising around processes and social and relational dimensions (Graetz *et al*, 2002: 140). Watson (2002) favours a process-relational perspective on structure which looks at processes and practices. Ackroyd (2002: 74) meanwhile suggests that 'the structure of an organisation is what emerges from the ongoing relationships between people in the organisation.'

Changing structures, changing processes, and changing boundaries

De Wit and Meyer (2004: 166) draw upon Bartlett and Ghoshal (1995) in explaining the corporate body using an analogy with the human body. They suggest how 'the organisational system can be divided into its anatomy (structure), physiology (processes) and psychology (culture).' Similarly, Salaman and Asch (2003: 36) identify three aspects of organisations – organisation structures, organisational systems and processes and organisational cultures – noting that these factors in combination produce the capability of the organisation. They (2003: 25) believe that attempts to change organisations are concerned with links between strategy and capability, and identify three central variables as organisational or business environment, business strategy, and organisational capability.

Whereas earlier sections encouraged consideration of structural choices that senior managers made in the past, structural change may have less influence in the future. Weiss (2001: 338) draws upon the work of Keidel (1994) in order to explain three approaches to organisational design. These are restructuring, re-engineering and rethinking. Restructuring is regarded as the most fundamental approach to organisational redesign and involves the reconfiguring of organisational units through initiatives such as downsizing. Re-engineering dramatically attempts to change business processes in works systems through initiatives such as business process re-engineering. Rethinking encourages groups and individuals to redesign thinking and mindsets through initiatives such as the learning organisation.

The INNFORM research project gave impetus to new thinking about innovative forms of organising for the twenty-first century. The research involved an international survey of new forms of organising in Europe between 1992 and 1996. Led by Andrew Pettigrew (1999: 3) working in collaboration with scholars from foremost European universities, the research highlighted evolutionary rather than revolutionary change. Yet key features included changes in:

- structure – decentralising, de-layering and project forms of organising
- processes – investment in information technology (IT), horizontal and vertical communications, and new human resources practices
- boundaries – downscoping, outsourcing and strategic alliances.

RESEARCH CASES IN JOURNALS NO.3 – WAIT (AUSTRALIAN FE INSTITUTION)

The authors offer a longitudinal research-based case study of the William Angliss Institute of Technical and Further Education (WAIT). A strength of this case study is that it tells a story of change over a decade from 1992 to 2002. The retirement of the Director of 20 years was an opportunity for this Australian institute to embark upon a 'seismic shake-up'. The authors were able to interview the senior managers in 1996, 2002 and 2004, enabling them to gain strategic insights into the processes of change over time. However, of particular relevance to this chapter is the applicability of the case in terms of new forms of organising as identified by the INNFORM study. The authors discuss how radical change at WAIT was attempted over a decade through changes to structures, changes to processes and changes to boundaries.

Sector: Further education (Australia)
Research methods: Semi-structured interviews and document analysis.
Authors: Graetz, F. and Smith, A.
Paper title: Organizing forms in change management: the role of structures, processes and boundaries in a longitudinal case analysis
Journal details: *Journal of Change Management*, Vol.5, No.3, 2005, pp.311–28

Structural change was discussed earlier in this chapter; technological change as an example of changes in processes will be discussed in Chapter 8. In the following discussion outsourcing and strategic alliances are featured as examples of boundary changes.

Child (2005: 179) offers the following definition of outsourcing:

> *Outsourcing normally refers to the farming out of activities that were previously performed in-house and which, quite possibly, are still performed by some organisations in the same sector.*

In the 1990s there appeared to be an increase in outsourcing which the INNFORM project was able to quantify. Between 1992 and 1996, 65 per cent of firms claimed an increase in outsourcing (Pettigrew, 1999: 3). Child (2005: 186) has identified a range of potential managerial benefits of outsourcing which may explain the increase in outsourcing. Such benefits include:

- enabling a concentration on what organisations do best
- enabling the selection and utilisation of the best expertise available
- removing operational headaches and bottlenecks
- assisting downsizing and de-layering.

However, Child (2005: 189) also identifies potential organisational problems that arise with outsourcing, which include: unreliability of suppliers, loss of employee morale and communication problems. Child (2005: 222) offers the following definition of a strategic alliance:

> *An 'alliance' is any medium- to long-term co-operative relationship between organisations, normally between firms... Alliances are often termed 'strategic'*

because they are normally formed to help the partner firms realise their strategic objectives on the basis that this can be done better in co-operation than alone.

The INNFORM survey evidence revealed that 65 per cent of firms claimed the formation of long-term alliances between 1992 and 1996 (Pettigrew, 1999: 3). Child (2005: 228) has identified potential organisational challenges posed by alliances as: achieving trust, managerial role conflict, clashes between partner cultures, and control.

The implication of the above is that organisations may be changing from bureaucratic organisations to post-bureaucratic organisations. As Clegg *et al* (2005: 93) suggest 'We now live in post-bureaucratic times, where a concern with efficiency predominates over issues of equity or justice.' However, as this chapter has warned, it is quite difficult to assert precisely how organising is changing. Salaman and Asch (2003: 3) have even suggested that 'the pattern of organisational restructuring could well soon show a return to earlier patterns.' It is certainly likely that senior managers are choosing a mix of classic and new forms, and that organising is dependent upon both internal and external contexts of organisations.

Critically reviewing downsizing

The frequency of organisational restructuring implies that restructuring benefits have been hard to achieve or fleeting when achieved (Oxman and Smith, 2003: 78). Against this backdrop, downsizing has been one of the more dramatic forms of organisational change. The following discussion addresses the meaning/terminology, rationales and consequences of downsizing.

Attempting to define a rhetorical term such as 'downsizing' can be challenging in that the terminology can be deliberately ambiguous. However, establishing a clear definition begins the process of understanding the concept:

> *Downsizing is carried out by making process modifications that cut staffing needs and working out systemic change that can support the streamlined organisation.*
> *(Nutt, 2004: 1086)*

Immediately, the definition suggests links with business process re-engineering. Also, outsourcing maybe undertaken alongside downsizing, and Lewin and Johnston (2000: 47) have specified the goals that managers must determine in terms of what tasks should be accomplished in-house, what tasks should be accomplished through strategic partnerships, and what tasks should be contracted out (outsourced) to third-party specialists.

In exploring the etymology of downsizing, Collins (2000: 287) describes 'downsizing' as a euphemistic form of phrasing, drawing parallels with the terminology used to express our sympathies when someone has died. Ironically, the term 'downsizing' was originally developed by the Detroit automobile industry in order to encapsulate reductions in car size and engine capacity in the early 1970s. The term 'survivor syndrome' used to describe those left behind after downsizing was borrowed from studies of the Nazi holocaust. Griggs and Hyland (2003: 178) note that survivors of downsizing 'are left to carry their own workloads as well as the workloads of their departed colleagues'. Employees are significant stakeholders in any organisation. Any attempt to change the form of an organisation raises ethical issues. Weiss (2001: 341–2) highlights the type of questions that have to be answered, which include:

■ What happens to employees' professional identity when a company or parts of an organisation are outsourced or networked?

- What happens to trust and loyalty between employee and management when downsizing and streamlining occur?

- Who manages the obligations of the organisation to its stakeholders as organisations become more free-standing, networked, and dispersed through the use of information technologies?

There is simple business logic to downsizing in terms of making money through either cutting costs or raising revenues. Downsizing is an attempt to make money through the former route, which may explain why 'stock markets have tended to reward downsizing announcements...' (Sorge and Van Witteloostuijn, 2004: 1211). However, Nutt (2004: 1086), in tracing the roots of downsizing to 'cutback management' ideas popularized by Levine (1978, 1980), illustrates the public sector rather than the private sector origins of this concept.

Collins (2000: 309) believes that initially, management academics and management gurus were up-beat about downsizing and the prospects for corporate transformation via large-scale restructuring. However, Sorge and Witteloostuijn (2004: 1210), basing their views upon reviews of research studies, are more sceptical:

> *Even the direct positive effects of downsizing (a decrease in spending and an increase in productivity) are reported by only 46 per cent and 22 per cent of the firms, respectively. Even worse, increased product quality, improved innovativeness, and technological progress hardly occur at all.*

Sorge and Witteloostuijn (2004) cite similar findings from the Society of Human Resource Management in 1990 and the American Management Association in 1998. More recent evidence of downsizing failing to achieve its goals has been cited by Nutt (2004) (see also Littler *et al*, 2003; McKinley *et al*, 2000; and Shah, 2000). What is interesting about these and other critical findings is that they challenge notions of downsizing as a 'bitter pill' which will benefit organisations in the longer term.

Collins (2000: 309) notes that 'right-sizing' has taken over as management's preferred concept and practice of restructuring. Much of the critical literature cited above serves an important function in questioning assumptions upon which downsizing is based, yet does little to offer an alternative. Nutt (2004: 1085), after reviewing empirical evidence of failures of both business process re-engineering and downsizing, suggests de-development as an alternative to downsizing, which 'is done by orchestrating a gradual letting go of some organised complexity using a process called "devolution".' He regards de-development as an alternative for organisations with limited resources which are declining in the face of turbulence. But Nutt concedes that more work is required on what appears to be an interesting and more ethical alternative to downsizing.

SYNOPSIS

Interest in organisational structures predated interest in change management. Since the 1920s, there had been the view that having crafted a strategy, senior managers must find a structure to fit it and align the two with supporting systems. In more recent times senior managers have shifted their focus from structure to processes.

Many writers contributed to understanding organisational structures. Four contributions to understanding of organisational structure were focused upon: Weber in terms of bureaucratic structures, Burns and Stalker in terms of mechanistic and organic structures, Miles and Snow in terms of the fit between strategy and structure, and Mintzberg in terms of five structural stereotypes.

Senior managers are likely to be influenced by a range of questions which have to be addressed in order to design or redesign an organisational structure. These questions were: What is the nature of the environment in which the organisation operates? What type of technology does the organisation use? What is the size of the organisation? What are the organisational goals?

Functional/contingency writing about organisational structure was influential in shaping senior management thinking as well as academic thinking. However, Ackroyd challenged assumptions of functional and contingency writing in two ways. Firstly, organisational structures are not simply functional. Secondly, organisational structures are not simply a consequence of adapting to an external environment. Mechanisms of control and power may be designed into what is presented as an apparently neutral organisation structure. The concern of critics was that orthodox accounts of organisational structure underplay managerial objectives which are designed into organisations.

Three organisational design dimensions of structure, process and boundaries with key indicators of change were identified. In a similar manner, Keidel explained three approaches to organisational design: these were restructuring, re-engineering and rethinking. The terminology of new organisational forms was acknowledged to be quite daunting. Child (2005), under the heading new network forms, identified four new network forms – outsourcing, virtual organisations, strategic alliances and organising across boundaries.

Downsizing was one of the more dramatic forms of organisational structural change. Nutt suggested that downsizing was carried out by making process modifications, cutting staffing needs and working out systemic change.

'Downsizing' was described as a euphemistic form of phrasing. Reviews of research studies warned that every downsizing objective had been reached only by a minority of organisations and then in almost the complete absence of any increased product quality, any improved innovativeness, and any technological progress.

DISCUSSION QUESTIONS

1 Do senior managers change organisational forms, or are organisational forms changed by the environment?

2 Is it possible for an organisation to remain successful over time without a change of organisational form?

3 Who is responsible for a deficient organisational structure?

4 Will a universal optimum organisational form ever be discovered?

5 How do you believe individuals employed in an organisation will respond to downsizing?

6 How could organisational structure be represented without using the traditional organisational chart?

Case study – New organisational forms at the University of Midchester

The University of Midchester successfully delivers a mix of research, teaching and scholarship benefiting students, clients and the wider community. The vice chancellor for the past five years has been the charismatic and strident Professor Hope Sandoval. Professor Sandoval, whose background was as a senior academic at Harvard Business School, has enjoyed the challenge of running a large academic institution and has been supported by a very capable senior management team. Once a week this senior management team have met with Professor Sandoval to discuss strategic and operational matters. At these meetings there has been a standing item entitled 'twenty-first-century university', which entails an ongoing discussion about correctly positioning the university for the challenges of the twenty-first century. For these discussions, the need to bring together the work of the separate faculties of IT and business have been identified as a priority.

The university has ten faculties, each faculty comprised of a number of academic departments. Each faculty is led by a Dean, beneath whom Heads of Department head up individual departments. The focus has been upon the Faculty of IT and the Faculty of Business. Each faculty has approximately 400 staff (a mix of academics and administrators) and each faculty has approximately 4,000 students, who include part-time and full-time students – undergraduates and postgraduates. Bringing these two areas together was believed to be beneficial and would be appropriate to an increasingly competitive higher education environment. A closer relationship would allow the university to offer more business courses with IT and more IT courses with business. Also, there were potential commercial benefits to bringing together IT and business in terms of the research services the university offered. The financial environment was very influential in terms of senior management thinking. Although the University of Midchester was financially successful, the senior management team was aware that many universities were in debt and wanted to avoid such a situation by being proactive. As a consequence of discussions at the previous week's meeting Professor Sandoval had been tasked with sketching out ways forward for bringing the two faculties together. She presented her ideas to the senior management team as Plans A, B and C. She believed each plan had merit, and was keen for an informed evaluation of each plan.

Plan A

The obvious choice was to merge the two faculties into a single faculty under the provisional title of the Faculty of Business and Information Technology. There would be cost savings in terms of one fewer Dean's salary and one fewer faculty administration team. It was envisaged that the small number of staff affected would be offered alternative positions or generous redundancy packages. For staff and students in the two faculties the impact of the merger would be minimal. Current staff and students would continue as normal. However, in the future opportunities were envisaged in terms of new courses and new research. One potential obstruction to merging the two faculties was that they were based on two different parts of the campus.

Plan B

This involved the two faculties' maintaining their existing structures but radically changing their processes, as would be enabled through IT. Committees overseeing, for example, academic quality and research strategy would become joint faculty committees with an equal representation of members from each faculty. In a similar manner, heads of department from both faculties would meet together on a regular basis. Communications and report structures would become more collaborative, involving joint reports on key strategic partnerships. The cost savings of a single faculty office would not be achieved, but estimates suggested that the joint working proposed would be less costly than Plan A. Students and staff would experience no disruption under the new arrangements, although again potential developments in terms of new courses and research were envisaged. One potential hurdle was the increased levels of bureaucracy. Staff already moaned about the amount of paperwork and there was a danger of increasing the number of committees under the joint arrangements.

Plan C

The most radical proposal was the closure of the Faculty of IT, and for the subcontracting of specialised IT expertise to a neighbouring university with which the University already had many collaborative arrangements. In the plans it was acknowledged that the consequences for staff would have to be managed and that some staff would join an expanded Faculty of Business whereas others might be offered opportunities to join the neighbouring university. The thinking behind this was that Midchester was unable to attract IT students like the neighbouring university, and that collaboration was believed to be a better long-term arrangement than competition. The neighbouring university did not have a business faculty – which was another argument in favour of Plan C. Although student places on courses would be safeguarded, this was the most disruptive option for staff and students. The biggest hurdle to Plan C would be the anticipated industrial action that would arise.

Case study questions

1   Evaluate each plan in terms of its strengths and weaknesses; ensure that you consider the perspectives of different stakeholders in any change.

2   How does thinking about this change as being a senior management choice inform understanding about this change?

FURTHER READING

CHILD J. (2005) *Organization: Contemporary principles and practices*, Oxford, Blackwell.

Child is a respected theorist who has influenced thinking about management and organisational behaviour over many decades. This textbook is recommended because emerging organisational forms are highlighted rather than historic organisational structures being emphasised.

GRAETZ F., RIMMER M., LAWRENCE A. and SMITH A. (2002) *Managing Organisational Change*, Chichester, John Wiley & Sons.

Graetz *et al* devote an informative chapter to new forms of organising. In this chapter they discuss the INNFORM project with specific reference to change management. More generally, this textbook offers interesting alternative perspectives on organisational change debates.

JOHNSON G., SCHOLES K. and WHITTINGTON R. (2005) *Exploring Corporate Strategy*, 7th edition, Harlow, FT/Prentice Hall.

The chapter 'Organising for success' offers an accessible overview of organisational structure from a strategic perspective. In choosing the title of their chapter Johnson *et al* acknowledge their interest in the verb 'organising' rather than in the noun 'organisation'. Cataloguing the many different structural designs, they offer theoretical frameworks to explain changes in organisational structures.

THORNHILL A., LEWIS P., MILLMORE M. and SAUNDERS M. (2000) *Managing Change: A human resource strategy approach*, Harlow, FT/Prentice Hall.

Thornhill *et al* in their chapter on downsizing and the management of change offer an interesting overview of downsizing which benefits from their human resources approach to managing change. The chapter uses two case studies to illustrate the human consequences of downsizing initiatives. The chapter also maintains a clear focus upon downsizing as part of a broader approach to managing change.

Cultural change

CHAPTER 7

LEARNING OBJECTIVES

To:

■ clarify the meaning and review explanations of organisational culture

■ consider approaches to managing cultural change

■ assess culture as an impediment to organisational change

■ question the feasibility of changing organisational culture

■ challenge the ethics of cultural change

■ critically review the case of total quality management.

INTRODUCTION

This chapter focuses upon organisational culture, sometimes referred to as corporate culture, and the plausibility of changing such cultures. It is concerned with organisational cultures rather than national cultures (see Hoftstede, 1991, for an influential study of national cultures). Mintzberg *et al* (1998: 272) identify the Scandinavian Institutes for Administrative Research, formed in 1965, as undertaking the earliest pioneering academic work into culture. However, culture was not a dominant issue in management literature outside Scandinavia prior to 1980 (Willmott, 1993: 515; Mintzberg *et al*, 1998: 264; Watson, 2002: 239). In the 1980s the impetus for engaging with culture was the perceived benefits arising out of managing culture. Benefits managers perceived as arising out of an appropriate culture included effective control, normative order, the promotion of innovation, strategy formulation and implementation, and employee commitment (Hodgetts, 1991). Similarly, Brown (1998: 89) identified potential functions of culture as including conflict reduction, co-ordination and control, reduction of uncertainty, motivation, and competitive advantage. However, many academics have been sceptical that culture can deliver what it promises: 'Research on organisational culture has sometimes been dismissed as a dead end, as unrelated to mainstream theory, or as a fad that has failed to deliver on its promises' (Frost *et al*, 1991: 7).

This chapter addresses the apparent contradiction between the popular appeal of cultural change and academic scepticism. The *Approaches* section of this chapter clarifies the meaning of culture and introduces theoretical explanations of and practical prescriptions for changing cultures. Critical commentators have made major contributions to understanding cultural change, although their work has not been as well publicised as the more prescriptive literature. Collins (2000: 117) even argues that 'most management writers seem either to ignore or to be unaware of the conceptual and methodological critiques made of cultural management…' In the *Critical perspective* section, culture is considered a potential impediment to change, in terms of its feasibility and the ethics of cultural change. Total quality management is critically reviewed as a change management initiative which placed emphasis upon cultural change.

APPROACHES TO CULTURAL CHANGE

An understanding of organisational culture that has been informed by anthropology and organisational sociology may be traced to at least four different sources: 'climate research, national cultures, human resource management, and from a conviction that approaches which emphasise the rational and structural nature of organisation cannot offer a full explanation of organisational behaviour' (Brown, 1998: 2).

The meanings and theories of culture

The success (in terms of book sales) of *In Search of Excellence* (Peters and Waterman, 1982) lent impetus to managerial interest in cultural change because the potential benefits of successfully managing cultural change appeared to be considerable. The timing for a new form of change initiative was also right, earlier change initiatives tending to focus upon strategy and structure. Another motivation for interest in culture appears to have been economic. 'It was Western observation of the Japanese "economic miracle" which arguably stimulated most interest in culture in organisations' (Dawson, 1996: 146; see also Burnes, 2004a: 169). However, as well as the economic challenge of Japan, further influential factors included 'a resurgence of economic neo-liberalism and the reassertion of managerial prerogative in the governance of employee values' (Willmott, 1993: 517).

Salaman (1997: 248), while regarding culturalist explanations of Japanese success as one-sided and partial ,believes that such explanations helped to give birth to the corporate culture movement. In the absence of any consensus definition of culture (Jones *et al*, 2005: 363), the following definition of 'culture' is offered:

> *The pattern of beliefs, values and learned ways of coping with experience that have developed during the course of an organisation's history, and which tend to be manifested in its material arrangements and in the behaviours of its members.*
> *(Brown, 1998: 293)*

Organisational culture has been commonly conceptualised as dynamic, multifaceted and layered (Ogbonna and Wilkinson, 2003: 1153). Studies of culture either benefit or suffer (depending upon your perspective) from the existence of imprecisely defined classifications. Two common classifications are in terms of *strong* versus *weak* cultures and *culture* versus *climate*. A strong culture is believed to enable an organisation to achieve excellent performance and was originally associated with the writings of Deal and Kennedy (1982). Brown (1998: 226) suggests that 'strong' is usually used as a synonym for consistency, suggesting that strong cultures are understood as being consistent cultures. However, he (1998: 230) is sceptical about assertions that have been made about strong cultures.

Another classification is between culture and climate, 'climate' defined as a context 'concerned with the current atmosphere within an organisation' (McKenna, 2000: 471). The differentiation between climate and culture is in terms of time horizons – culture is concerned with the long term whereas climate is concerned more with the short term. It is possible for the climate in an organisation to change a number of times within a single year. Changes may relate, for example, to the performance of the organisation or the environment in which the organisation operates. The focus of this chapter is upon culture rather than climate. However, for anyone interested in differentiating culture and climate, Rickards (1999: 102) cautions 'We are some way from a consensus that climate and culture are distinct phenomena.'

One way to begin to understand culture is in terms of identifying observable artifacts such as the physical layout of organisations, the technology and language used, the symbols an organisation employs, and the rules, systems procedures and programmes. The cultural web (Johnson *et al*, 2005: 201) offers a framework for understanding cultures of specific organisations in terms of seven elements: the paradigm, the power structures, organisational structures, control systems, routines, and rituals, stories and symbols.

Popular commentaries about culture are discussed below in terms of the contributions of Harrison (1972), Peters and Waterman (1982), Deal and Kennedy (1982) and Schein (1992).

Harrison (1972), writing as early as 1972, identified four main types of organisational culture. However, as Brown (1998: 66) notes, it was Handy (1978) who reworked and promoted Harrison's ideas, describing the four cultures using simple pictograms and making reference to Greek mythology.

> Power culture (spider's web) – emphasis upon a single power source
> Role culture (Greek temple) – emphasis upon rules, procedures and job descriptions
> Task culture (lattice) – emphasis upon expertise rather than position or charisma
> Person culture (cluster) – emphasis upon the individual as part of a collective

Box 11 – Handy's four organisational cultures

In Box 11 the four cultures are specified in terms of how they may be represented and what they place emphasis upon. This classification is believed to have been influential in shaping the way culture scholars, students and practitioners understood how organisations work (Brown, 1998: 66).

Peters and Waterman (1982) in *In Search of Excellence* highlighted the relationship between organisational culture and performance, based upon their studies of (at the time) successful companies which included IBM, Boeing, Walt Disney and McDonald's. Attributes of excellent companies included bias for action, closeness to the customer, autonomy and entrepreneurship, and productivity through people. The plausibility in what Peters and Waterman were proposing captured the imagination of many. However, although their writings proved popular with senior managers in organisations, they have been heavily criticised by academics. Guest (1992) offered a comprehensive critique neatly summarised in the title of his chapter 'Right enough to be dangerously wrong'. His methodological concerns major upon the choice of successful companies upon which to base the study and the questionable nature of the data collection techniques adopted within the study.

Deal and Kennedy (1982) identified four general corporate culture types based upon the degree of risk and speed of feedback characteristic of a given industry. In Box 12 the culture types are identified with illustrative examples.

> Tough-guy, macho culture (example: surgeons)
> Work-hard/play-hard culture (example: McDonald's)
> Bet-your-company (example: aircraft manufacture)
> Process-culture (example: public sector organisations)

Box 12 – Deal and Kennedy culture types

Senior and Fleming (2006: 157) in summarising the limitations of the typology (see Box 12) regards the typology as dated and difficult to fit complex organisations into the neat types offered. Schein (1992) offered one of the more useful contributions to our understanding about culture in advocating a deeper understanding of culture in terms of visible artifacts, espoused values (what ought to be done) and the basic underlying assumptions (invisible). This simple framework is useful in differentiating between deep and shallow cultural change. What is interesting is that changing artifacts is more visible and may receive more attention than changing basic underlying assumptions.

Managing cultural change

According to Burnes (2004a: 169) the case for culture was best summed up by Deal and Kennedy (1982) who argued 'that culture, rather than structure, strategy or politics, is the prime mover in organisations'. It is easy to challenge Deal and Kennedy with the benefit of over 20 years' hindsight, although in mitigation at the time the appeal of what cultural change appeared to offer was considerable. Salaman (1997: 261) identifies three explanations for the appeal of culture to managers. Firstly, cultural projects tap into and appeal to the values and feelings of managers. Secondly, the way ideas are presented in cultural projects appeals to managers. Thirdly, cultural projects offer managers dramatic and heroic status. In terms of quantifying the appeal of cultural change to managers, Ogbonna and Wilkinson (2003: 1153) cite an IRS *Employment Trends* (1997) survey concluding that 94 per cent of organisations experienced planned cultural change in 1997.

In the *Critical perspective* section the case of total quality management will be critically reviewed as an illustration of cultural change. However, as Salaman and Asch (2003: 11) remind us, all current programmes of organisational change (360-degree feedback, competence systems, performance appraisal and BPR, etc) have a cultural change element. They attempt 'to change the way employees think and feel about their work and its purposes and priorities'. In this discussion the focus is upon explicit management attempts to change cultures. Any attempt at managed cultural change needs to acknowledge that cultures 'unfold over the years without conscious design, a result of the many policies and decisions that have accumulated over time' (Conner, 1998: 169). The dilemma here is that although cultures may have changed in the past without conscious design, the new goal is to manage cultural change through conscious design.

Morgan and Sturdy (2000: 10) although not advocates for such an approach, map out the ingredients of a cultural change programme.

> *First, identify the current shared values and norms of the organisation; second, state what the culture should be; third, identify the gap between the two and develop a plan to close it.*

There are dangers with generalised cultural change management recipes – however, in view of their proliferation, they merit discussion. Sathe (1985) identified five points at which managers seeking to create cultural change must intervene: behaviour, justifying behaviour changes, using cultural communications, hiring, and socialisation and removal of deviants.

The process whereby an individual is introduced to a culture is referred to as socialisation. Socialisation is often most evident upon joining an organisation, but is an ongoing process. Socialisation varies from organisation to organisation and can be either explicit or implicit. However, the dilemma that cultural change invariably has to address centres on changing the way existing employees think and feel about their work. Cultural change prescriptions are often couched in terms of guidelines. The guidelines offered by Weiss (2001: 368) are typical of guidelines offered and include beginning with a clear vision, the senior management actively committed to the new values, and needs and cultural change supported in all organisation systems.

A danger with such prescriptions on how to manage cultural change is that they are not based upon research and have not been tested through research. In essence, they are sensible suggestions which any informed person could make. Smith (2003) is positive about the potential of cultural change, yet uses research to further understanding about cultural change. His research was based upon questionnaire responses from 210 North American managers who had been asked to describe a major change effort by their organisation to improve its performance. His findings are informative, particularly when set against the backdrop of perceived difficulties of achieving cultural change:

> *Only 19 per cent of the culture change efforts surveyed in this study attained breakthrough or near-breakthrough success. One key to successful change is to recognise the crucial role of the middle rank of leadership at the department, division or business unit level.*
>
> *(Smith, 2003: 259)*

The findings of Smith quantify the difficulties of achieving successful cultural change. However, in the *Critical perspective* section the whole premise of cultural change will be challenged.

CRITICAL PERSPECTIVE

At a practical level it is revealing that there was a wave of populist cultural change literature in the 1980s and early 1990s, yet the popularity of this literature was not sustained. The following critical perspective on cultural change is organised around four challenges:

- culture may impede change management
- it may not be feasible for management to change a culture
- the implications for individuals of cultural change may be unethical
- total quality management did not deliver the changes it promised.

The following discussion elaborates upon each of these challenges.

Culture as an impediment to change

Quirke (1995: 105) in his functionalist account of communicating change offers a beautifully acidic aside about culture: 'The force of the culture is for the status quo; culture is the means by which we bring stability to the threat of change.'

Managing cultures and managing change both gained prominence in the 1980s onwards, suggesting a mutual compatibility. However, commentators have questioned the potentially contradictory nature of culture and change.

Dysfunctional aspects of culture especially relevant to strong cultures have been identified – culture as a barrier to change, culture as a barrier to diversity, and culture as a barrier to mergers and acquisitions (Robbins, 2005: 491). For example, a strong culture may be a barrier to diversity such that managers do not seek out and hire individuals from different backgrounds: 'A multicultural organisation not only has a diverse cultural workforce but also values diversity'(Weiss, 2001: 362). It is difficult to reconcile strong unifying cultures with diverse workplaces. According to Mintzberg *et al* (1998: 281) culture can discourage necessary change in favouring the management of consistency. In emphasising tradition and consensus a kind of stagnation is encouraged.

Flynn and Chatman (2001: 235) have explored the apparent paradox by which cultural strength purportedly limits individual creativity. However, the innovation literature lacks 'an agreed-upon theoretical model that explains the conditions under which innovation is most likely to occur' (Flynn and Chatman, 2001: 247). They suggest that further research might focus on the role of organisational culture in the innovation process. Yet in drawing conclusions they do question the culture-innovation paradox, arguing that 'Instead, the paradox misnomer stems from a conceptual misunderstanding about culture strength and content – two concepts that are clearly unique...' (Flynn and Chatman, 2001: 247). Although a strong culture may be an impediment to organisational change, the work of Flynn and Chapman suggests the need for caution when making connections between these poorly defined concepts.

The feasibility of cultural change

Ogbonna and Wilkinson (2003: 1154), in acknowledging widespread controversy amongst academics about cultural change, identify three broad positions. Functionalists view culture as an organisational variable, subject to the control of management like any other organisational variables. This for a time influential perspective was evident in the writings of Peters and Waterman and Deal and Kennedy on culture. A second perspective may be regarded as a half-way house, suggesting some scope for cultural manipulation. The third perspective, which most critical researchers frequently argue, is 'that the assumption that organisations can achieve planned cultural change is both intellectually flawed and practically impossible' (Ogbonna and Wilkinson, 2003: 1154). It is this third perspective that is used as the basis for questioning the feasibility of cultural change.

RESEARCH CASES IN JOURNALS NO.4 – STAR GROCERY RETAILER

The authors in their case study of grocery retailing explore the impact of culture change on one group of employees – middle managers. The case study organisation referred to as STAR employed over 100,000 employees at the beginning of the research in 1996. As this chapter has warned, culture can be an area of study in which serious ambiguity can hamper effective organisational research. However, the strengths of this case study published in a leading management journal are the effective development of the context for the case and level of access to managers working in STAR. The authors are able to offer verbatim quotations from managers, highlighting perceptions of the cultural change taking place. The authors believed that middle managers might potentially have more readily identified with the espoused values of a cultural change programme. However, they found that changes in managerial behaviour related more to surveillance, direct control and the threat of sanctions rather than to any transformation of managerial values.

Sector: Retail
Research methods: Interviews, documents and analysis of trends.
Authors: Ogbonna, E and Wilkinson, B.
Paper title: The false promise of organizational culture change: a case study of middle managers in grocery retailing
Journal details: *Journal of Management Studies*, Vol.40, No.5, 2003, pp.1151–78

Salaman and Asch (2003: 13) raise doubts about the grounds of the gurus' claims and their efficacy with regard to cultural change. Their five doubts may be summarised as follows.

Firstly, organisational culture may prove to be more useful as an explanation of organisational behaviour than as a prescription on how to change an organisation. The excessive marketing of cultural change prescriptions appears to have increased this problem. As Dawson (1996: 162) reminds us, culture caught the imagination and appeared to promise the basis for a universally applicable recipe for success.

Secondly, the concepts of culture and cultural change – despite excessive populist writing – remain confused and poorly defined. 'Conceptually it is so fuzzy that it is unlikely to be able to deliver success in these terms' (Dawson, 1996: 162). A concern with the concept of culture relates to assumptions about organisations as excessively consensual and unitary (Salaman and Asch, 2003: 14). Despite considerable writing about culture, Mintzberg et al (1998: 280) criticised the conceptual vagueness of the cultural school.

Thirdly, it is difficult to reconcile the long-term time horizons of cultural change with the short-term time horizons of organisations. Organisational cultures do change over time, but this process takes place over years and even decades rather than days and months.

Fourthly, doubts have been expressed that senior management can change a culture. Many of these criticisms focus upon the difficulties of changing attitudes, values and beliefs. Individuals' values are not open to short-term manipulation (Dawson, 1996: 152). Intriguingly even Deal and Kennedy (1999: 35) challenge the myth that cultural change can be managed, acknowledging the difficulties of changing culture and the time it takes to change cultures:

> *There must be a million consultants promising to help 'change the cultures' of companies. Many of these consultants are even making a reasonable living from the practice. What a lot of bollocks.*

Fifthly, cultural change initiatives are more likely to influence official as opposed to unofficial versions of an organisation. Watson (2002: 229) defines official aspects of the organisation as all the rules, activities and values formally sanctioned by management. The unofficial aspects are defined as 'the rules, activities and values that people at all levels in the organisation develop but which do not have formal managerial sanction'. In terms of considering the feasibility of changing a culture, senior management may have a perception of the culture of an organisation which differs from the perception of employees.

Salaman (1997: 252) argues that the dream of corporate culture books and consultants was the promise 'to be able to manage staff without their knowing or resenting this control; to get workers to accept managerial goals, authority and decisions so that they don't need managing or controlling...'

The above discussion of the feasibility of cultural change encourages a view of cultural change as another flawed fad. However, Salaman (1997: 268) warns against such a view, arguing that although corporate culture programmes have not delivered the compliant and conformist individuals suggested by more prescriptive literature, they have re-engineered the psychological contract between employee and employer. Individuals' sense-making and the construction of meaning are likely to have been impacted upon by corporate culture programmes.

The ethics of cultural change

Willmott (1993: 528) warns that 'advocates of corporate culture would like to persuade and assure us that their prescriptions are morally benign.' However, because organisations are comprised of individuals, any attempt to change an organisational culture raises ethical concerns relating to changes in individual attitudes, values and beliefs.

> *Our heads are full of knowledge, ideas and images, not only about our society but also about our work – and these ideas, images and values provide us with shared frameworks, assumptions and moralities which we use to define and make sense of our work and employment.*
>
> *(Salaman, 1997: 237)*

The essence of cultural change programmes, however they are promoted, is to change what is inside our heads, usually without requesting our explicit consent. Watson (2002: 267) asks 'What right do managers have to engage with the deeper beliefs and conceptions of right and wrong held by organisational employees?' Brown (1998: 104) has identified three areas where culture and ethics overlap. Firstly, organisations are developing their own ethical codes. There may be overlaps between tangible statements in an ethical code and the intangibility of an organisational culture. Secondly, ethical choices may be implied by the values and assumptions that exist within an organisation. Thirdly, there may be a morally dubious third-order control function over individuals – this may take the form of power being exercised over individuals without individuals' realising.

Critically reviewing total quality management

Cultural change aspirations are very evident in total quality management (TQM), portrayed as a change management initiative 'whose success depends entirely on the attitudes and behaviour of the employees' (Kelemen *et al*, 2000: 156). In a manner similar to the appeal to senior management of cultural change, TQM can be traced back to Japan's search for quality improvements. There are different varieties of TQM, but three of the major quality gurus were Deming, Crosby and Juran (Collins, 2000: 189).

Dawson (2003: 148) regards quality management as being at the forefront of change initiatives over the last 20 years, peaking in terms of organisational popularity in the late 1980s and early 1990s. Total quality management may be defined as follows:

> *Policies, processes and tools designed to ensure that products (and, more recently, services) are 'built right first time', have become subsumed within the catch-all title Total Quality Management (TQM).*
>
> *(Collins, 2000: 175)*

The three core principles of TQM have been defined as customer orientation, process orientation and continuous improvement (Wilkinson *et al*, 1997).

Redman and Grieves (1999: 46) cite empirical evidence suggesting that between 70 per cent and 90 per cent of TQM programmes fail. Based upon their analysis of the literature on TQM failure five main clusters of explanations were identified:

> *a lack of integration between quality management and everyday business practices; difficulties in winning managerial commitment; problems of adapting HR practices to support TQM; the effects of recession and restructuring; and the broad somewhat 'catch-all' category of poor implementation.*
>
> *(Redman and Grieves, 1999)*

The authors offer a research-based case study of Metco illustrating many of these shortcomings (see also Wilkinson *et al*, 1998, and Collins, 2000, for thorough overviews of the empirical literature relating to TQM failure). In a manner similar to earlier discussions of culture, TQM appears to have suffered from problems of definition. 'In spite of the commonsense pronouncements of the gurus, the central elements of TQM – quality and management – do not have singular and stable meanings' (Collins, 2000: 198).

A dilemma in attempting to evaluate the impact of change management initiatives relates to the convergence/divergence of the different change management initiatives to which organisations have been exposed. Kelemen *et al* (2000: 154) have questioned the belief promoted by Hammer and Champy (1993) that business process re-engineering (BPR) and TQM are fundamentally different philosophies of organisation. 'In reality, BPR and TQM practices can draw on similar resources and, in certain settings, be interrelated to the extent that their complex, programmatic effects are difficult, if not impossible, to separate.' This finding complicates our understanding of the rhetorical claims made for TQM. History may reveal that the most important role of TQM was not in terms of quality management but rather as a precursor to subsequent change initiatives such as BPR.

SYNOPSIS

Culturalist explanations of Japanese success helped to give birth to the corporate culture movement. Culture was defined as the pattern of beliefs, values and learned ways of coping with experience that developed during the course of an organisation's history, and which tend to be manifested in its material arrangements and in the behaviours of its members. Major classifications identified were in terms of *strong* versus *weak* cultures and *culture* versus *climate*. Popular commentaries about culture by Harrison, Peters and Waterman, Deal and Kennedy, and Schein were discussed.

All current programmes of organisational change were recognised as having a common cultural element in attempting to change the way employees think and feel about their work. Attempts at managed cultural change need to acknowledge that cultures unfold over the years without conscious design. Although cultures have changed in the past without conscious design, the new goal was to manage cultural change through conscious design. The ingredients of a cultural change programme would be to identify the current shared values and norms of the organisation; state what the culture should be; identify the gap between the two; and develop a plan to close it. Managing cultures and managing change gained prominence in the 1980s onwards suggesting a mutual compatibility. However, commentators questioned the contradictory nature of culture and change. Dysfunctional aspects of culture especially relevant to strong cultures were identified – culture as a barrier to change, culture as a barrier to diversity, and culture as a barrier to mergers and acquisitions.

Doubts about the feasibility of cultural change were raised. Organisational culture may prove to be more useful as an explanation than as a prescription. The concepts of culture and cultural change remain confused and poorly defined. It was difficult to reconcile long-term time horizons of cultural change with the short-term time horizons of organisations. Doubts were expressed that senior management can change a culture. Cultural change initiatives were more likely to influence official as opposed to unofficial versions of an organisation.

Any attempt to change an organisational culture raises ethical questions relating to changing individuals' attitudes, values and beliefs. The essence of cultural change programmes, however they were promoted, was to change what was inside our heads, usually without requesting our explicit consent.

Cultural change aspirations were very evident in total quality management (TQM). TQM was defined as policies, processes and tools designed to ensure that products (and, more recently, services) are 'built right first time'. Three core principles of TQM were customer orientation, process orientation and continuous improvement. Redman and Grieves cited empirical evidence which suggested that between 70 per cent and 90 per cent of TQM programmes fail.

DISCUSSION QUESTIONS

1 Which is easier to change – an organisational culture or an organisational climate? And why?

2 In what ways can change management be considered to be a form of cultural change?

3 Why has the notion of cultural change been described as arrogant?

4 How may a culture impede or enhance attempts to change an organisation?

5 How do you believe attempts to manage quality such as TQM help to change an organisational culture?

6 What do you believe the future holds for our understanding of culture and our attempts to manage cultural change?

Case study – Cultural change in Merrydown Building Society

The origins of Merrydown Building Society (MBS) can be traced back to the beginning of the last century. MBS developed through a series of mergers into being a respected if not high-profile regional building society. The Society employs 1,000 staff, of which 500 staff work part-time. Staff work either at one of the 80 branches or at Head Office. The Society is able to provide customers with a range of financial services from deposit accounts through to loans and mortgages. It is proud to have remained a mutual building society despite overtures from a number of large financial services institutions. Although the Building Society has experienced mergers and has recently changed the fascias of all the branches, in other ways little has changed in MBS. Their logo 'Community Banking: Banking on the Community' has remained the same for as long as anyone can remember.

Against this backdrop of quiet inertia Patrick Fitzgerald has joined MBS as the new chief executive.

Mr Fitzgerald was deliberately head-hunted by the board of MBS from a senior management position in one of the high street banks. The board had impressed upon Mr Fitzgerald that mutual status was not negotiable, but that MBS was ready for 'some radical change'. The board never expanded upon what they had in mind by this last phrase, but it was apparent that part of Mr Fitzgerald's role would be to act as a change agent. Upon his arrival, in a short message to staff he announced he would spend the first 100 days visiting every branch and meeting as many staff as possible. He was true to his word, and at the end of a gruelling schedule he felt well prepared to report to the board.

As they had anticipated, he confirmed their suspicions. Everything he had seen and heard suggested that MBS was flourishing. There was a low turnover of staff and high levels of staff commitment were apparent. Staff really did believe that they were providing a service to the community, which had been repeatedly demonstrated by the actions of staff, particularly in the branches. He had been unable to access any marketing information because there was no marketing department as such. However, the impression gained was of a loyal elderly customer base who felt assured when they deposited their savings with MBS. There had been a few rumblings from customers about the new branch fascias. In having a content workforce and a content customer base, Mr Fitzgerald as chief executive could have been regarded as being in an enviable position. However, Mr Fitzgerald was very troubled by what he had learned.

The finance function at the head office was antiquated yet very competent. They showed him forecast information which suggested that MBS would be experiencing large and growing deficits within two more years. When he explored the reasons for the deficits, it was very apparent that costs were escalating but revenues were static. In particular, staff costs were proving to be a large drain upon resources and the rents on the high street premises were making many of the branches uneconomic to run. On the revenues side the Building Society gained from its large deposit base, but in potentially profitable areas – such as the provision of credit facilities – business was weak. This troubling report did not surprise the board. Mr Fitzgerald's recommendations did, however, surprise the board.

He warned that there needed to be a dramatic cultural change if MBS was to survive, and he advised that even if there was cultural change he could not guarantee the survival of MBS. In order to 'wake up' the building society he recommended the immediate announcement of plans to close eight branches (10 per cent of the branch network). The rationale for these closures would be presented to staff as vital cost-cutting and part of a wider project referred to internally as Project Phoenix.

Project Phoenix aimed to encourage a sales culture while maintaining the high-quality customer service that typified MBS. All branch managers would be required to attend the Sales Through Service management development workshops. These workshops would be deliberately challenging, and at the end of the workshop each branch manager would be required to sign a promise to deliver sales at a specified amount. Any branch manager who failed to sign the promise would be offered career counselling. A less intense version of Sales Through Service would be cascaded through MBS to the effect that all employees would be required to make a verbal pledge to deliver sales, on every day of every week of every year. Again, if the pledge was not made, staff would be encouraged to rethink their future with MBS. The Phoenix facilitators would visit branches at six-monthly intervals to check that the new attitudes, values and beliefs had been adopted through a series of questionnaires and interviews. The facilitators would also ensure that sales targets had been exceeded. All the data would be gathered to establish the six-monthly branch grading that might be 'Sales Competent', 'Sales Confusion' or 'Sales Incompetent'. An urban myth was deliberately spread throughout the branches that any branch graded as 'Sales Incompetent' would be top of the list in the next anticipated wave of closures.

The board was shellshocked at the end of the presentation. Three board members walked out of the room mumbling that this was the death of the Society as they knew it. The remaining members were more philosophical, arguing for an evolution rather than a revolution. They argued quite persuasively that the change would be too radical for both staff and customers. Certain board members felt uneasy with a sales culture that they saw as contradicting the long-established service culture MBS had developed. However, Mr Fitzgerald was adamant that either the board adopted Project Phoenix or he would resign because he was otherwise unable to envisage a future for MBS.

Case study questions

1 Explain what is being proposed, with reference to theories of cultural change.

2 How are employees being socialised into new ways of thinking and behaving?

3 What would be the impediments to achieving this cultural change?

4 How could this cultural change be managed differently?

FURTHER READING

BROWN A. (1998) *Organisational Culture*, 2nd edition, London, FT/Pitman Publishing.

Brown achieves an effective and respectful balance between the theoretical and more empirically-based approaches to culture and organisational applicability in terms of case examples. The book benefits from being exclusively focused upon culture, which is frequently dealt with as a mere chapter in more generalist management and organisational behaviour textbooks.

COLLINS D. (2000) *Management Fads and Buzzwords: Critical-practical perspectives*, London, Routledge.

In reviewing some of the major management fads and buzzwords, Collins devotes a chapter to culture. The book seeks a balance between the need for critical questioning of concepts and the practicalities of management, and the chapter reflects this perspective. The strength of the chapter is the extensive review of culture literature upon which the chapter is based. Collins highlights the almost evangelical assertions of the gurus to manage culture and employs his own effective rhetoric to denounce most of the claims made for culture.

DEAL T. E. and KENNEDY A. A. (1999) *The New Corporate Cultures: Revitalizing the workplace after downsizing, mergers and re-engineering*, London, Orion Business.

This book is not an update of the authors' earlier work, *Corporate Cultures*, but rather a review of major changes – such as downsizing, re-engineering, outsourcing and mergers

– which took place in the 1980s and 1990s. As the title suggests, the theme running through the book is still corporate culture. The book benefits from a being reflective account of culture, with the feel of looking back after the culture 'party' has finished. It does include supporting references, although it is at the accessible end of the accessibility–rigour continuum.

SALAMAN G. (1997) Culturing production, in P. DU GAY (ed.) *Production of Culture/Cultures of Production*, London, Sage Publications in association with the Open University.

Salaman in this book contributes a chapter about culture with specific reference to work organisations. The chapter is critical of corporate culture and questions many of the popular premises about managing cultural change. Most usefully, the book encourages the reader to think about contemporary debates in terms of relevant social theories.

Technological change

INTRODUCTION

There is an understandable tendency in the change management literature to leave the coverage of technological change to separate specialist technology textbooks. The major drawback of such an approach is that organisational change and technological change are dealt with as if they exist in separate silos. Such a differentiation is believed no longer to be sustainable (see, for example, Watson, 2003: 183). In the latest editions of organisational behaviour textbooks (Buchanan and Huczynski, 2004, and Mullins, 2005), a chapter is dedicated to technology, and there is now a similar case for engaging with technological change as part of understanding change management.

In reviewing major debates relating to technological change, the caveat is that contradictions and competing explanations evident in the organisational change literature are mirrored in the technological change literature. There is a plethora of insights regarding technological change in the literature of economics, sociology and psychology (Stein, 1995: 38). This chapter consequently very selectively introduces technological change debates pertinent to change management. The challenges of managing technological change are considerable. Pavitt and Steinmueller (2002: 351) identify three dimensions which have seen increasing demands on technology management:

- the range of fields of knowledge, and related products, components and systems to master, combine and exploit

- the variety of possible market applications to identify, assess and exploit, and

- the need to match technological opportunities with market needs through appropriate organisational structures and practices.

Modern technologies have been described as both 'exhilarating and frightening' (Taras and

Bennett, 2002: 335). It is easy to regard technology as a recent phenomenon, but 'technology' in various forms has existed throughout human history as a human response to the environment (Hatcher, 2002: 138). An evolution of technological labels over time is evident: 'computing machinery, electronic data-processing, computer information processing, information systems, management information systems and information technology' (Orlikowski and Barley, 2001: 152).

The *Approaches* section of this chapter begins with a discussion of the meanings of technology, which is a precursor for four competing explanations of technological change. One popular explanation of technological change is in terms of innovation theory. This section also addresses the practicalities of introducing and adopting new technology. In the *Critical perspective*, social approaches to technological change are considered, as well as relationships between technology and organisation. The section concludes with a critical review of business process re-engineering (BPR) which emphasises technology-enabled change.

APPROACHES TO TECHNOLOGICAL CHANGE
The meanings of 'technology'

Although 'technology' is an everyday term, exploring the meaning of 'technology' reveals subtle differences. Scarborough and Corbett (1992: 3) suggested that

> *technology is often presented as part of a spectrum which ranges from hardware at one extreme to social and organisational structures at the other.*

This is a useful starting point for considering competing meanings and avoids the trap of thinking about technology only in terms of hardware. Another way to understand the meaning of 'technology' is in terms of metaphors. McLoughlin (1999: 26) highlighted how technology has been explained in terms of a machine, an organism and an information-processing brain. The question remains 'What is technology?' Grint and Woolgar (1997: 7) note that 'The term "technology" derives from the original Greek *tekhnē*, meaning "art" or "skill".' In studying technology it becomes apparent that the definition of 'technology' is closely related to the competing explanations of technology. Grint and Woolgar (1997: 8) review a range of definitions of 'technology', and amongst them cite a definition by Kaplinsky (1984):

> *Technology refers to the general material content or process, such as microelectronics; technique refers to the way in which the general technology is developed for a specific purpose often in conjunction with other technologies or work processes.*

In the absence of a universal consensus definition of technology, this definition is favoured for this chapter. In terms of understanding change management, both 'technology' and 'technique' appear relevant.

Theories of technological change

There is a need for caution when theorising about technological change. 'The analytical base for making confident predictions about the future organisational implications of ICTs is a flimsy one' (Pavitt and Steinmueller, 2002: 346). McLoughlin and Clark (1994) have offered four competing explanations of technological change (see also Wilkinson, 1983) effectively illustrating different emphases of different theories. The following discussion introduces influential theorists associated with each explanation.

- Woodward (1958) – the contingency approach
- Child (1972) – the strategic choice approach
- Braverman (1974) – the labour process approach
- Piore and Sabel (1984) – the flexible specialisation thesis.

Woodward (1958) concluded from research undertaken in south-east Essex that there was a relationship between the type of technology used and organisation structure. She argued that specific forms of organisation structure were suited to particular production systems. The implication of the research was that technology determines work and organisation structure. Grint (1998: 330) defines technological determinism as 'the assumption that technology determines – that is, leads directly to – a particular form of society or organisation'. The notion of determinism is a central feature of contingency approaches to change which emphasise that variables such as the environment determine change within particular organisations. The pioneering work of Woodward has often been criticised as being technologically determinist, although Grint (1998) notes that Woodward's later work (1965) shifted towards a middle zone between social and technological determinism.

Child (1972) introduced the concept of strategic choice 'as a means of emphasising the role of managerial choice, rather than technology, in shaping work and organisation' (McLoughlin and Clark, 1994: 56). In understanding strategic choice, earlier discussions in Chapters 4 and 5 are again relevant. Child put emphasis on 'restoring the significance of the internal environment, and particularly the degree of discretion available to power-holders and decision-makers...' (Thompson and McHugh, 2002: 63). As with all approaches to technological change Child's work has been influential, but equally his approach has drawn criticisms. Thompson and McHugh (2002: 64) warn that 'There is a good deal of ambiguity as to whether Child's work has sought to modify or supplement contingency and systems theory or significantly depart from it.'

Braverman (1974) in *Labour and Monopoly Capital* offered a Marxist explanation of how workplace changes increased managerial control and deskilled employees. The contribution of Braverman was in offering an academic challenge to the scientific management of Taylorism which had (and continues to have) an influence upon the organisation of work. Braverman was able to illustrate his thesis through examples of workplace deskilling of groups such as bank clerks and their experiences of the introduction of new technology. His work has been influential in explaining the human consequences of capitalist-driven technological change in the workplace. However, Collins (1998: 163) acknowledges that a vast number of criticisms of Braverman's analysis have been published – in particular, he was criticised for romanticising notions of skill and craft.

Piore and Sabel (1984) applied and extended the idea of 'flexible specialisation', as originated by the regulation school of French social theorists (McLoughlin and Clark, 1994: 48). Flexible specialisation has been defined as:

> *An approach to employment and work organisation which offers customised products to diversified markets, building trust and co-operative relationships both with employees, who use advanced technologies in a craft way, and other organisations within a business district and its associated community.*
>
> *(Watson, 2003: 68)*

In respect of criticisms of the flexible specialisation thesis, McLoughlin and Clark (1994: 52) believe that criticisms have been of two types: those that reject the argument that a radical break with past practices has occurred, and those broadly sympathetic to the argument but requiring conceptual refinement.

There is merit in each of the four explanations of technological change offered here, and different theorists continue to work to develop more sophisticated explanations while acknowledging early pioneering work. What can be asserted is that there is no consensus explanation of technological change, and there never is likely to be.

Innovation and technological change

'Innovation' and 'organisational change' have been described as the buzzwords of the last 20 years (King and Anderson, 2002: 2). However, there is a broad range of different types of innovation. Francis and Bessant (2005) have identified innovations in terms of products, processes, positions and paradigms. Tidd *et al* (2005: 66), on the other hand, define innovation as 'a process of turning opportunity into new ideas and of putting these into widely used practice.'

This change management textbook could have been written from an innovation perspective. However, there would be difficulties in reconciling an innovation approach to change while emphasising the centrality of individual members of organisations in the processes of organisational change. This becomes particularly apparent in Thompson and McHugh's (2002: 254) discussions about change agents or change champions in relation to innovation:

> *While key individuals are important, this way of looking at things separates individuals from their context and neglects other participants. The latter are only brought into the picture as potential 'resistors to change' with a predisposition to be hostile to novelty.*

Although an innovation approach is believed not to be compatible with the change management focus of this textbook, in seeking to understand technological change in this chapter, innovation approaches merit further discussion. An innovation perspective to technological change encourages an understanding of technology adoption as evolutionary. Innovation is regarded as a key 'milestone' in the process beginning with the invention of a new product, process or system and concluding with the diffusion of an artifact within a specified population of 'users' (McLoughlin, 1999: 32).

Tidd *et al* (2005: 169), acknowledging criticisms of technological determinism aimed at innovation theories, argue that 'pure technological development does have its own internal logic, which helps define where firms will find innovative opportunities.' A vast number of different factors have been identified as facilitators or inhibitors of innovation, including people, structure, climate and culture and environment (King and Anderson, 2002: 125). In understanding technological trajectories, innovation theorists (Tidd *et al*, 2005:170–1) have identified the following differences:

- the size of innovating firms
- the type of product made
- the objectives of innovation
- the sources of innovation (eg the supplier of equipment)
- the locus of in-house innovation (eg an R&D laboratory).

The dilemma that emerges from acknowledging this difference is that it is dangerous to generalise, yet equally problematic to say that every organisation is different. One effective response has been to identify five major technological trajectories: supplier-dominated, scale-intensive, science-based, information-intensive and specialised suppliers (Tidd *et al*, 2005: 172). The strength of the development of these trajectories is that they are based upon a systematic analysis of more than 2,000 significant innovations in the UK, as well as upon reading historical and case material. They offer a more sophisticated account of the trajectories of technological change than the triggers/drivers of change evident in Chapter 4.

Adopting new technology

The appeal of technology may be motivated by what Haddad (2002: 55) has described as 'techno-lust' rather than rational analysis. Similarly, Johnson *et al* (2005: 478) warn that technological developments can distract senior management from considerations about overall strategy and the specific role of technological developments in specific strategies. In terms of acquiring new technology, Haddad (2002: 57) identifies the following range of underlying broad goals: efficiency, cost, product/service quality, flexibility, health and safety, quality of working life, and market share/public sector accountability. Preece (2005: 674) offers clarification on how 'new' technology refers to technology which is new to a particular organisation, rather than always being new in a temporal sense. He (1995: 7) developed a framework which identified two phases and seven stages of new technology adoption and introduction:

- *Adoption phase*:

    Stage 1 – initiation

    Stage 2 – progression and feasibility

    Stage 3 – investment decision

    Stage 4 – planning and systems design.

- *Introduction phase*:

    Stage 5 – installation/introduction

    Stage 6 – operationalisation, and

    Stage 7 – post-operationalisation evaluation.

Preece (2005: 674) offers caveats that the implication of the framework is not that the adoption process is always rational or systematic, or that all organisations have to go through all stages. In a manner similar to organisational change being understood as a process, so the framework developed by Preece encourages a processual approach to understanding technological change.

Another practicality of managing technological change is a consideration of potential responses to technological change, particularly inside the organisation. Haddad (2002: 69) highlights difficulties in planning the introduction of technological changes. There may be a senior management tendency to focus on the acquisition and installation of the equipment or software, at the expense of identifying and eliminating organisational barriers to technology.

RESEARCH CASES IN JOURNALS NO.5 – ATC (AIR TRAFFIC)

ATC was the name used to refer to the case study organisation which operated in the air traffic sector. The role of ATC was to control the arrivals and departures of aircraft at several small and large airports. There were demands on the organisation to become more commercialised, yet with reduced resources. The technological focus of the case study was the implementation of a new radar and work system in ATC. In particular, the case study highlights problems with the implementation of the new Central Management Function. The research for the case study was undertaken between 1993 and 2001 with the permission of the ATC directors. The case study indicated omissions in the planning of technical change and the neglect of worker concerns during implementation.

Sector: Air traffic
Research methods: Interviews, observations, attendance at meetings and documentary analysis.
Author: Hallier, J.
Paper title: Embellishing the past: middle manager identity and informality in the implementation of new technology
Journal details: *New Technology, Work and Employment*, Vol.19, No.1, 2004, pp.43–62

CRITICAL PERSPECTIVE

This critical perspective questions orthodox thinking about technological change, although even the process of questioning technological change feels heretical when set against popular notions of technology as something neutral and determining its own future. However, as Rosenbrock (1989: x) has warned, 'People should not be subordinate to machines; machines should be subordinate to people.' The following critical perspective on technological change is organised around three challenges:

- the influence of social factors upon technological change has been underplayed
- relationships between technology and organisation have been misrepresented
- business process re-engineering has not delivered the radical changes promised.

The following discussion elaborates upon each of these challenges.

Social approaches to technological change

An awkward question emerges from earlier discussions of technological change – is technology the force that shapes society, or does society shape technology (Hatcher, 2002: 138)? A similar question was asked of organisational change in Chapter 4, and was answered in terms of differences between voluntarist and determinist emphases upon the environment. As earlier discussions demonstrated, no universal explanation for technological change exists – only a series of competing explanations instead. The following discussion draws upon the writings of Grint and Woolgar (1997) who have highlighted theories of technology:

- socio-technical systems
- the social shaping approach

- socio-technical alignments
- actor-network theory
- anti-essentialism.

Whereas large bodies of literature exist in support of each of these five positions, the intention here is to briefly summarise each position as one critical alternative to more orthodox explanations of technological change (contingency, strategic choice, labour process and flexible specialisation) introduced earlier in this chapter.

The socio-technical systems approach is the best-known and closest to orthodoxy of these sociologically-oriented approaches to technological change. The approach focuses upon links between the technical system of production and the social system of work. Trist and Bamforth (1951) are cited as major proponents of this approach. Trist, a social psychologist, and Bamforth, an ex-miner, studied the advent of mechanisation in the mining industry. They were influential in developing the concept of the working group, which they regarded as an interdependent socio-technical system.

The social shaping approach is another sociologically-oriented approach to explaining technological change. This approach rejects notions that technology has impacts and natural trajectories (McLoughlin, 1999: 123). Technological development is explained in terms of social, political and economic interests giving rise and direction to invention, design, implementation and use. The social shaping approach challenges the neutrality of technology as depicted in innovation accounts of technological change.

Grint and Woolgar (1997: 25) explain the socio-technical alignments approach as a more ambitious macro-approach which considers the significance of the alignment between technology and society. Those in control of society may legitimate technological change through a rhetoric which denies human choice – 'There is no alternative' – or through a rhetoric which equates 'common sense' with technological progress (Grint and Woolgar, 1997: 26). Actor-network theory may be regarded as ostensibly similar to the alignment approach.

Finally, Grint and Woolgar (1997: 32) introduce the anti-essentialist approach in the following terms:

> *Hence, what a machine is, what it will do, what its effects will be, are the upshot of specific readings of the text rather than arising directly from the essence of an unmediated or self-explanatory technology.*

As Grint and Woolgar (1997: 32) move deeper into social theory, the academic rhetoric of technological change can appear increasingly obtuse. Yet within their arguments there is something eminently plausible. When they write 'Technology does not speak for itself but has to be spoken for' (1997: 32), the computer being used to word-process this textbook springs to mind as an illustration. The choice to buy this particular computer was informed by reading about different computers, and using this computer was informed by manuals and tutorials (increasingly online). Grint and Woolgar (1997: 32) believe that 'we need to attend closely to the process of interpretation rather than assuming that we are persuaded by the effectiveness of the technology.'

The pattern evident in the theories cited in this chapter reflects a shift from technological determinism towards social determinism, which may crudely be equated to a shift from economic explanations to social theory explanations. It would be wrong to assume that this chapter reflects an evolution of theorising about technological change. Innovation approaches to technological change continue to be very relevant and prevalent, although their relevance to change management could be challenged.

Technology and organisations

The ambitious aspiration of this chapter has been to bring together technological change and organisational change, two areas of study often approached independently. Orlikowski and Barley (2001: 145) have offered a very persuasive case for why research on information technology and research on organisations can learn from each other:

> *Transformations currently occurring in the nature of work and organising cannot be understood without considering both the technological changes and the institutional contexts that are reshaping economic and organisational activity.*

Whereas organisational studies are dedicated to social aspects of organising, and information technology studies are dedicated to technical aspects of organising, there are believed to be benefits in cross-fertilisation. Orlikowski and Barley (2001: 148) review potential benefits of such cross-fertilisation. One dimension they consider is materialism versus agency:

> *The legacy of treating technology as a material cause, of abstracting away from the specifics of a design, and of ignoring the role of human agency in the process of technological change extends well beyond early contingency and strategic choice theories.*

The danger with perceiving technological change as all-pervasive is that theories may be no longer required to have sophistication, describing an inevitable process of diffusion, happening regardless of human intervention. The concern with technological determinism is that human behaviour may be regarded as being largely determined by, rather than having influence over, technology (Grint and Woolgar, 1997: 7). Earlier, the contribution of innovation theories to understanding technological change was acknowledged. The dilemma with innovation models is that 'models and theories growing out of economics are weak in coping with the internal organisational dimensions of technological change...' (Pavitt and Steinmueller, 2002: 346). In this textbook a middle position is favoured. Grint and Woolgar (1997: 14) clarify this middle ground, although not favouring this position themselves:

> *The resulting model portrayed itself as one which avoided extreme determinism of either kind in favour of a conceptual apparatus that included many different elements: technology, people, organisations, genders, interest groups and many others besides.*

There is believed to be expediency in drawing upon different academic disciplines to explain technological change, rather than excessive reliance upon economics or social theory (see Stein, 1995, for further discussion).

Critically reviewing business process re-engineering

This critical review considers business process re-engineering (BPR) as a case example of a change management initiative seeking radical change through both technological and organisational change. BPR as a strategy was at its most influential in the early 1990s. It appeared to offer a radical solution to the competitive environment in which organisations operated. The bestselling book *Re-engineering the Corporation* (Hammer and Champy, 1993) gave impetus to the BPR movement in the 1990s. Morgan and Sturdy (2000: 12) regard managerial interest in restructuring organisational processes and activities as a response to perceived limitations of large-scale and incremental cultural change programmes. In the provocatively titled paper 'Reengineering work: don't automate – obliterate', Hammer (1990: 104) argued for re-engineering as follows:

> *We should 're-engineer' our businesses: use the power of modern information technology to radically redesign our business processes in order to achieve dramatic improvements in their performance.*

As with many change management initiatives, re-engineering was ill-defined (Jones, 1994: 354). Kallio *et al* (2002: 83) differentiate between strategic projects – such as business re-engineering and business process structuring – and operational projects – such as business process re-engineering, business process automation and information infrastructure revision. BPR may be differentiated from other recipes for business transformation in terms of three key features:

- a shift in organisational emphasis from function to process
- a belief in entrepreneurialism
- an emphasis upon the use of information communication technologies (Knights and Willmott, 2000: 3).

One explanation for the adoption of BPR is in terms of the rhetoric employed by its originators Hammer and Champy (1993). However, academics (Jones, 1994; Willmott, 1995; and Grint and Case, 1998) have all been troubled by the violent language used by proponents of BPR. Grint and Case (1998) in their paper offer many examples of this rhetoric taken from the writings of Hammer *et al*. They cite Hammer and Stanton (1995: 183) writing in their handbook as follows: 'However, those who are deliberately trying to obstruct the re-engineering effort … need the back of the hand.' Aligned with this reliance on violent rhetoric is the ambiguity of the re-engineering concept.

Although BPR definitely caught the imagination of organisations in the early 1990s, it has been challenged for failing to deliver the radical changes it promised. As early as 1994 there were warnings that 'given BPR's focus on business processes, it is remarkable how little attention is given by BPR to human dimensions of organising' (Willmott, 1994: 35). And Grint and Willcocks (1995: 99) warned that:

> *The claims are as immodest as the reliable data is difficult to find. In reality, many projects seem to disappoint. Hammer and Champy themselves estimated a 50–70 per cent failure rate for radical-breakthrough high-risk projects...*

Jackson (2001: 74–5) vividly captures the rise and fall of business process re-engineering through a selection of headlines in popular business journals.

- Re-engineering, the Hot New Management Tool (in *Fortune*, August, 1993)
- Hammer Defends Re-engineering (in the *Economist*, November, 1994)
- Business Process Re-engineering RIP (in *People Management*, May 1996).

Collins (2000: 264) effectively summarises concerns with BPR as follows:

- the terminology is imprecise and ambiguous
- mechanisms for initiating and maintaining BPR are ill-defined
- evidence of successes are anecdotal and involve sweeping generalisations
- BPR is a euphemism for large-scale redundancies.

SYNOPSIS

Technology may be regarded as part of a spectrum ranging from hardware to social and organisational structures. Different explanations of technological change utilised different metaphors – for example, technology as a brain. In studying technology it was apparent that the definition of technology was closely related to explanations of technology.

Four competing explanations of technological change were promoted by Woodward, Child, Braverman and Piore and Sabel. Woodward concluded that there was a relationship between the type of technology used and organisation structure. Child introduced strategic choice as a means of emphasising the role of managerial choice, rather than technology, in shaping work and organisation. Braverman offered a Marxist explanation of how workplace changes increased managerial control and deskilled employees. Piore and Sabel demonstrated how flexible specialisation represented an approach to employment and work organisation offering customised products using advanced technologies in a craft way.

There was a broad range of different types of innovation in terms of products, processes, positions and paradigms. An innovation perspective to technological change was believed to encourage an understanding of technology adoption as evolutionary.

In terms of acquiring new technology, broad goals – efficiency, cost, product/service quality, flexibility, health and safety, quality of working life and market share/public sector accountability – were identified. Preece developed a framework which identified two phases and seven stages of new technology adoption and introduction.

Social approaches allowed an understanding of technology in very different ways. Grint and Woolgar identified five alternative theories of technology: socio-technical systems, the social shaping approach, socio-technical alignments, actor-network theory and anti-essentialism.

Transformations in the nature of work and organising cannot be understood without considering both the technological changes and their institutional contexts. Orlikowski and Barley reviewed potential benefits of such cross-fertilisation. The danger was that humans and human behaviour are regarded as being largely determined by, rather than having influence over, technology.

BPR appeared to offer a radical solution to the competitive environment in which organisations operated. Knights and Willmott identified three key features of BPR – a shift in organisational emphasis from function to process, a belief in entrepreneurialism, and an emphasis upon the use of ICTs. However, Hammer and Champy themselves estimated a 50–70 per cent failure rate for radical-breakthrough high-risk projects.

DISCUSSION QUESTIONS

1 What potential interrelationships exist between technological change and organisational change?

2 Is technological change the responsibility of the change manager?

3 Why do competing definitions and explanations of technological change exist?

4 What are the advantages and disadvantages of using an innovation approach to explain change management?

5 Which is the preferable explanation of technological change – a technologically determinist explanation or a socially determinist explanation?

6 What possible explanations are there for the use of violent rhetoric with regard to the implementation of business process re-engineering?

Case study – Perfect Properties experiences technological change

Perfect Properties runs a chain of 300 estate agents' offices in the south of England. Up to some time ago, each office employed on average three full-time staff and two part-time staff. The day-to-day affairs of each office were overseen by the most senior estate agent, referred to as the office manager. The office managers were supported by a centralised head office function. The expectation has always been that each office would make a contribution to the overall profit of Perfect Properties. League tables have been regularly publicised within Perfect Properties, ranking the different contributions from different offices. It used to be informally understood that if an office ever failed to make a contribution to profit, the office manager would 'stand down' from his or her position. Before this year no office manager had ever been required to take this action.

The market for properties has been buoyant for many years, and profits and working life in Perfect Properties has been good. However, over the previous six months there has been a dramatic and unexpected detioration in the property market. The loss of confidence was precipitated by an international crisis and the property market is now expected to remain stagnant for the next few years. A consequence of this dramatic downturn has been that no fewer than 50 office managers have failed to make a contribution to profit. The overall financial situation is depressing in that Perfect Properties is evidently moving into a loss-making situation and there is no sign of an early recovery in the property market.

The board of Perfect Properties have reviewed four potential strategies, but in the end they have favoured an IT-based solution. The largest costs for Perfect Properties are labour costs, resulting from the large geographically-dispersed office network. Other estate agents in response to the downturn have reduced staff numbers, and Perfect Properties feels it must take a similar course of action. However, the concern is that clients who personally visit offices and talk to staff have often been a potentially lucrative source of business. The solution adopted by the board has been the introduction of a Virtual Estate Agent (VEA) in every office. The VEAs are client-friendly interactive computer terminals. Although Perfect

Properties already has a strong Internet presence with its own website, the VEAs are regarded as far more interactive. Initially, the software was designed to respond to the needs of potential purchasers, but in the longer term the VEAs are intended to deal with vendors as well. The VEAs through interactive questionnaires allow users to identify the right area and type of property for them. This is then linked to the properties that the office and other offices have available, scored against a 0–100 ranking reflecting the level of suitability.

Unfortunately, there was no opportunity to pilot the VEAs, given the unexpected nature of the downturn in the property market. The VEAs were introduced into offices over a very short time-frame. The average staff establishment for each office has meanwhile been reduced from three full-time and two part-time staff to two full-time and one part-time member of staff. Perfect Properties have always employed a proportion of the workforce on short-term contracts, which has enabled this reduction in staff numbers. However, the major staff reduction at the same time as the introduction of major technological change into the offices has not been positively received by employees. The staff disparagingly refer to the VEAs as the 'basic boxes', regarding them as giving an inferior rather than a complementary service. There have even been isolated claims that VEAs have been sabotaged by staff members ironically feeding them coffee and sandwiches. However, the VEAs have proved to be very popular with clients. The VEAs appear to appeal to clients in just the way some people prefer to use automated teller machines outside the banks instead of talking to a bank clerk inside a bank branch.

The VEAs are proving to be the salvation of Perfect Properties, attracting many new clients at a very difficult time. Although the initial implementation costs were high, the VEAs have helped to both reduce labour costs and generate more revenue. Over time even the staff in the offices have begun to appreciate how the VEAs help to deal with basic enquiries in an effective manner.

Case study questions

1 Explain the technological changes in Perfect Properties with reference to Woodward, Child and Braverman.

2 How could this case study be explained in terms of both technological determinism and social determinism?

3 Explain potential reasons why staff initially responded negatively to the introduction of the VEAs.

4 What could have been done to manage the introduction of the VEAs better?

FURTHER READING

KNIGHTS D. and WILLMOTT H. (eds) (2000) *The Re-engineering Revolution: Critical studies of corporate change*, London, Sage Publications.

This edited reader is focused upon analysing business process re-engineering, which was fashionable in the 1990s. It is recommended because it draws together a range of critical thinking about BPR. The different authors draw heavily upon social theory in developing their critiques and cite extensive empirical evidence of the failures of BPR in order to challenge the many questionable promises about radical change made for BPR. The book benefits from research-based case examples of attempts to apply BPR in a diverse range of contexts.

MCLOUGHLIN I. (1999) *Creative Technological Change: The shaping of technology and organisations*, London, Routledge.

This book addresses a central question for change management: does technology shape organisations or do organisations shape technology? This innocent question alludes to contentious yet fascinating debates about technological change. One of the strengths of the book is that it covers a wide range of theoretical debates in a digestible manner.

PREECE D. (2005) Technology and organisations, in L. J. MULLINS, *Management and Organisational Behaviour*, Harlow, FT/Prentice Hall.

Preece contributes an informative chapter to this management and organisational behaviour textbook. Although Preece is an influential writer and researcher on technological change in his own right, this chapter is recommended because it offers a broad overview of debates with extensive references for anyone interested in exploring this area in more detail.

TIDD J., BESSANT J. and PAVITT K. (2005) *Managing Innovation: Integrating technological, market and organizational change*, Chichester, John Wiley & Sons.

Innovation approaches to change have been featured in this chapter with particular reference to technological change. This textbook is one of the most respected textbooks on innovation. It will appeal to anyone who favours an economics-based approach to change and/or a strategic approach to the management of innovations. The book is a sourcebook of innovation references, as well as being very effectively presented.

Individual and organisational change

INTRODUCTION

Organisations change through individuals changing, which suggests a need for a bridge between theories of organisational change and individual change. The challenge for furthering change management understanding is concisely captured in the following quotation:

> *Organisations only change and act through their members, and even the most collective activities that take place in organisations are the result of some amalgamation of the activities of individual organisational members.*
>
> *(George and Jones, 2001: 420)*

Attempting to understand individual change raises questions about why individuals change and how individuals change. These awkward questions are often avoided in the change management literature. However, psychology of change processes may inform understanding about inertia and the inability to change in organisations (George and Jones, 2001: 437). In order to begin to understand these processes, this chapter focuses upon individual change, before making connections between individual change and organisational change. The *Critical perspective* challenges unitarist assumptions of change management, the gender blindness of change management, the ethics of changing individuals, and claims made for organisational development.

APPROACHES TO INDIVIDUAL CHANGE
The meanings and theories of individual change

The following discussion of individual change is organised in terms of three themes: individual differences, *why* individuals change, and *how* individuals change.

A precursor to understanding why and how individuals change is an acknowledgement of individual differences. Textbooks often differentiate between individuals in terms of identifying individual criteria or traits such as gender, abilities, physique, motivation and attitudes (see, for example, Buchanan and Huczynski 2004; Mullins, 2005; and Rollinson, 2005). Acknowledging individual differences highlights the uniqueness of individuals. However, in emphasising individuality there is a danger that the individual is over-emphasised at the expense of broader social factors shaping individuals. 'All that we see, learn, are and do is not just part of ourselves, but part of the social world around us' (Thompson and McHugh, 2002: 229). Individuals may put their own emphasis on being an individual or being part of groups and societies. Some individuals have a preference for their own company whereas others thrive on being part of a team. Despite such differences, all individuals are part of wider society.

The literature about individual differences is well documented in the organisational behaviour textbooks cited. One aspect of individual difference particularly pertinent to change management is perception, which is discussed here as a means of explaining the implications of individual differences for change management. Rollinson (2005: 103) defines perception as 'a mental process involving the selection, organisation, structuring and interpretation of information in order to make inferences and give meaning to the information'. Perception is often misunderstood as being merely our senses – that is, how (and what) we hear or see. However, as the definition suggests, it is concerned more with the interpretation of various inputs. The process of perception is prone to errors for everyone. Bowditch and Buono (2005: 41) note a number of distortions and illusions in our perception of other people identifiable in everyday situations, which include: stereotyping, the halo effect, expectancy, the self-fulfilling prophecy, selective perception, and projection. These distortions in perception are illustrated using hypothetical change management examples in Box 13.

'All change management consultants are only interested in making as much money as possible.' This is an example of a stereotype in terms of using a standardised impression of a group.

'The manager had a university education, so I knew he could manage the complexities of change.' This is an example of the halo effect which magnifies one characteristic (university education) thus overshadowing other characteristics.

'We repeatedly reassured employees that we anticipated Project Hercules would be successful – and it was successful.' This is an example of expectancy – in particular, the self-fulfilling prophecy. Employees help to fulfil the prophecy that Project Hercules will be successful because they believe it will be successful.

'While the new office is ergonomically designed and employs state-of-the-art technology with plenty more space for employees, I believe the magenta paint on the door of the toilets will lead to colleagues rejecting these new offices.' This is an example of selective perception by which an employee pays more attention to the colour of the toilet door than to the office as a whole.

'If only Project Daisy had commanded top management support, it would have succeeded.' This is an example of projection, which often involves blaming others rather than taking responsibility for a situation such as Project Daisy.

Box 13 – Hypothetical examples of perceptual distortions

In considering examples cited in Box 13, the issue is not about the accuracy of the statements as much as the ways in which individuals distort their perception of an individual or a situation. Individuals inevitably and regularly distort perception in different ways, and they are often unaware that they are distorting perception and that others distort perception. For example, it is impossible for 100 employees to have an identical perception of an organisational change. They may see the same PowerPoint slide show or hear the same change message, but they will perceive the stimuli in very different ways. This concern is particularly pertinent to discussions about communicating change in Chapter 13.

Triggers and drivers of organisational change were discussed in Chapter 4, but what drives an individual to change? One response to this question is to look to major life events which require individuals to change. Hayes (2002: 146–7) adapts the Holmes and Rahe (1967) Social Readjustment Rating Scale which attributes 'mean values to the degree of adjustment required after individuals experience a series of life events'. The scale ranks life events such as the death of a partner, being sacked from work, and trouble with the boss in terms of their severity.

It is important not to consider individual change as exclusively preoccupied with major and often dramatic life events. After all, for example, the ageing process involves individuals' adjusting gradually. Explaining why individuals might initiate change, Leana and Barry (2000: 753) suggest that 'individuals seek stimulation and variety in their work in order to fulfil self-development needs and maintain interest in, and satisfaction with, their jobs.' This quotation suggests that individual change may be something consciously sought, rather than something imposed upon an individual. In terms of categorising why individuals change and embracing everyday aspects of change, the work of Marris is rarely cited yet informative. Marris (1974: 20) discussed individual change with reference to balancing continuity, growth and loss, and identified three kinds of change:

- incremental/substitutional changes
- growth changes
- loss changes (either actual or prospective).

Firstly, incremental/substitutional changes are concerned with alternative means of meeting familiar needs, such as obtaining a new bicycle or buying a different coat. These changes are routine and continuity is likely to be unbroken. Secondly, growth changes may take place – for example, in terms of personal growth or security; the ageing example cited earlier fits this category. Although these changes may be profound for the individual, continuity is still unbroken. Marris refers to the third kind of change as representing loss, such as a death or discrediting of familiar assumptions: 'the thread of continuity in the interpretation of life becomes attenuated or altogether lost ... But if life is to go on, the continuity must somehow be restored' (Marris, 1974: 21).

The three kinds of change identified by Marris offer a categorisation of individual change which also explains why change is taking place and deals with the continuities and discontinuities of change. His central concern is with

how loss disrupts our ability to find meaning in experience, and how grief represents the struggle to retrieve this sense of meaning when circumstances have bewildered or betrayed it.

(Marris, 1974: 147).

105

Individual differences and reasons for individual change have been discussed, but this still leaves the question of *how* individuals change. A logical starting point is again to look to the organisational behaviour literature. But this literature is often frustratingly simplistic and anecdotal in terms of individual change. The norm is to introduce individual responses to change in terms of individual resistance contrasted with organisational resistance to change (see, for example, Mullins, 2005: 913). The real danger in these approaches is that individual change is defined in terms of *resistance*, defining the role of management as overcoming this resistance. However, individuals respond to change in many different ways.

In attempting to make sense of how individuals change, the work of Kubler-Ross (1973) has been influential. Her research was based upon individual responses to death, illuminating the stages people go through when faced with tragic news. These stages are denial, anger, bargaining, depression and acceptance. Individuals do not necessarily go through all five stages but are believed to experience at least two of them. What about changes individuals deliberately instigate as part of ongoing personal development?

Psychotherapy-based models of change are potentially useful. Matheny (1998: 396) highlighted the contribution Prochaska (1984) made to understanding planned personal change, leading to the development of an empirically-based model revealing six primary processes of change: consciousness-raising, self re-evaluation, self-liberation, reinforcement management, counter-conditioning and stimulus control. This model also suggests that there are four stages of personal change: pre-contemplation, contemplation, action, and maintenance. Whereas Kubler-Ross helped to make sense of reactions to life-changing events, Prochaska helps to explain how we can be proactive in changing our lives. In a similar manner, French and Delahaye (1996: 24) have proposed a four-phase individual change transition model involving the phases of security, anxiety, discovery, and integration.

In considering commonalities and differences between these models, there are parallels between models of individual change and the learning cycle proposed by Kolb (1984). Kolb suggested a learning cycle incorporating a concrete experiences stage, an observational and reflective stage, an abstract conceptualisation stage, and an active experimentation stage. Overall, the Kolb learning cycle encourages reflection, which according to Ash *et al* (2001: 5) 'appeared to be of a paramount importance for learning and growth. As change is about learning and growth, the two seemed to go hand in hand.' Similarly, Randall (2004: 87) believes that 'learning is a prerequisite for successful human survival and development,' which implies that individuals change in order to survive, and that this process is informed by learning.

Individuals experiencing organisational change

A good starting point for explaining how individuals experience major organisational change is again in terms of Kubler-Ross (1969) – denial, anger, bargaining, depression and acceptance – cited earlier. Burke (2002: 92) has effectively drawn comparisons (see also Conner, 1998, and Stuart, 1995). However, Burke furthers understanding by suggesting that:

> *Some organisational members fight the change 'to the death', constantly denying that the change is necessary. Others embrace the change readily and move with it. Most people are somewhere in between and move through all stages.*

The quotation with its strange mix of metaphors, is not supported by empirical material, but it does suggest that individuals approach organisational change in very different ways.

Woodward and Hendry (2004: 162) undertook empirical work involving surveying individuals experiencing organisational change in the City of London's financial services sector. Examples of the problems individuals encountered in a changing environment included:

■ increased accountability but reduced resources

■ a focus on tasks with a corresponding neglect of employees, and

■ feelings of insecurity and uncertainty in roles and direction.

In drawing this discussion to a conclusion it is important to acknowledge that individual experiences of change may be either negative or positive. In keeping with the theme of this chapter, 'the experience of change will vary over time and across individuals and groups'(Dawson, 2003: 179). The quotation reminds us that just as organisational change is a dynamic process, so is individual change.

Managing individual change as part of organisational change

Kotter (1996: 4) acknowledges that the pain of change is ever-present; however, he believes that 'a significant amount of the waste and anguish we've witnessed in the past decade is avoidable.' These concerns are echoed by Woodward and Hendry (2004: 164) and supported through their empirical work:

> *Much of the pressure created by organisational change may be alleviated if those leading change focus on people aspects in addition to strategy and other organisational elements. However, this crucial element is still ignored by a sizeable minority, with a third of senior managers acknowledging that people aspects were ignored in their change programmes.*

Leading change is the focus of Chapter 12 – however, what stands out in this quotation is that one third of senior managers surveyed ignored people aspects in their change programmes. The quotation raises the question that if managers were not managing the people aspects, what *were* they managing? Part of the explanation for this ignorance may be historical. French and Delahaye (1996: 22) explain that 'there is little information on individual change in organisations because approaches to managing change have been developed at a group or systems level.' More problematic has been the tendency to deal with organisational change and individual change as if they were synonymous. Randall (2004: 79) highlights the problem as follows: 'Writers may conflate the process of change at the different levels of individual, group and organisation learning into one seamless series of events.'

Earlier, Prochaska (1984) was cited suggesting four stages of personal change – pre-contemplation, contemplation, action, and maintenance. What all the models of individual change appeared to suggest was that individuals go through a process of change rather than change as a single event. Individual change often involves some form of contemplation as a precursor to changing. The concern here relates to the readiness of individuals for organisational change. 'Organisations often move directly into change implementation before the individual or the group to be changed is psychologically ready' (Jones *et al*, 2005: 362). Similarly, Bridges (1995: 32) perceptively warns that 'planners and implementers usually forget that people have to let go of the present first.'

One approach to managing individual change as part of an organisational change process is through change agency – introduced in Chapter 5 – for which different skill requirements have been identified. For Carnall (2003: 226) there is a need to manage transitions, deal with organisational cultures and the politics of organisational change. For Balogun and Hope Hailey (2004: 8) 'change agents need to develop their analytical, judgemental and implementation skills'. Although such skills are relevant to the change process, earlier discussions suggest that individuals may also have deeper issues arising out of the processes of change. Burke (2002: 95) identified three means of helping organisational members deal with change: conceptually, achieving closure, and participation. In a similar way, Carnall (2003: 238) suggests that

> *coping with the process of change places demands on the individuals involved. Various issues need to be faced either by the individuals or by managers.*

Organisational changes present opportunities for learning. The answer to the question of what managers can do to help individuals change may be to enable change through facilitating learning for individuals both about themselves and the processes of change:

> *Change doesn't happen because a chief executive or other top management figure says it should; change happens because the majority of people involved willingly or unwillingly agree to change their behaviour.*
>
> *(Conner, 1998: viii)*

This quotation equates with many of the arguments in this textbook – but the realisation of what Conner is proposing may be more difficult to achieve. Certainly, the high incidence of change management failure (discussed in Chapter 15) may to some extent be explained in terms of a failure to engage with individuals as part of organisational change processes as evidenced at the beginning of this discussion.

CRITICAL PERSPECTIVE

The following critical perspective on individual change as part of organisational change is organised around four challenges:

- the prevalence of unitarist assumptions in change management literature
- the gender blindness of change management literature
- the ethics of senior managers who change individuals, and
- the shortcomings of organisational development.

The following discussion elaborates upon each of these challenges.

The unitarist assumptions of organisational change

Goals represent results or end-points toward which organisational efforts are directed (Daft, 1995: 42). When Mullins (2005: 145) writes about the goals of an organisation being the reason for its existence, he is reflecting the orthodoxy of management thinking about goals. However, the notion of organisational goals existing independently of senior management goals has been repeatedly challenged (see, for example, Silverman, 1970). Annoyance relates to the misrepresentation of organisational goals masking the existence of privileged individual goals of managers.

> *We are informed that the organisation has needs, or has goals. We are left with the implication, therefore, that it is 'the organisation' and not managers which changes workers' feelings and attitudes.*
>
> *(Collins, 1998: 92)*

Unitarist assumptions about a commonality of interests is very evident in the more applied change management literature, which prescribes that individuals ignore their individual differences and pull together to serve the best interests of the organisation. However, as the quotation of Collins suggests, the needs or goals are those of senior managers. Individuals may choose an organisation based upon its goals, and they may have goals which are contradictory to senior management, creating gaps between formal and informal, official and operative, goals and actual policies. Organisational and individual goals are not always compatible. Despite this incompatibility, however, organisations may still function.

The problem for change management is that an organisational change may cause incompatibility between previously compatible individual and organisational goals. This situation is likely to be exacerbated when organisational goals explicitly change. The goals that are pursued within organisations change over time, as political alliances between dominant interest groups shift and external pressures and events change (Dawson 1996: 45). Earlier, Randall (2004: 79) highlighted the problem of writers conflating the process of change at the different levels of individual, group and organisation. The dominance of unitarist assumptions about individuals, groups and organisations' sharing common goals may be another explanation for the neglect of individual-level analysis in accounts of organisational change.

Gender and change management

Orthodox approaches to individual change neglect important differences such as class, race and gender (see Grint, 1998, for an informative introduction to class, race and gender with regard to the workplace). The rationale for seriously considering gender is captured by Calas and Smircich (1996: 222–3) when they suggest: 'organisational scholarship has been, primarily, a literature written by men for men and about men.' This caustic quotation succinctly captures a criticism that can be levelled at this textbook as well as at the wider change management literature. More specifically, Foreman (2001: 215) warns that 'contemporary literature on the management of organisational change rarely discusses the issue of gender.'

A critical gendered perspective is more than an acknowledgement of the under-representation of women change management theorists. Alvesson and Billing (1997: 191) note that empirical evidence does exist to view gender as a central organising principle in organisations. The following discussion considers empirical work undertaken by Leonard (1998) and Paton and Dempster (2002) focusing upon gender and organisational change.

Leonard (1998: 82) undertook research into the incorporation of further education (FE) institutions in the 1990s. Her research revealed that 'the changes in the management and organisation of FE brought about by incorporation have had a gendered impact on FE institutions.' She argues that the culture has shifted from educational philosophy and professional concerns to the economic principles of marketisation, unit autonomy and performance targets. She found that a consequence of this shift has been that men have reclaimed 'these organisations as both male-dominated and masculine'.

Paton and Dempster (2002) in their exploratory work reviewed contentious research specifically considering differences between women and men in areas such as spatial awareness and information-processing. As well as reviewing relevant literature, empirical work was undertaken in the Department of Social Security. Their study raised policy implications for organisations including the existence of a female preference for a more open and collegiate approach to change management, and the fact that ignoring gender differences disadvantages a significant proportion of the workforce (Paton and Dempster, 2002: 546).

Their study also has implications for change management academics, warning against the tools for change which 'tend to offer mechanistic, systems-oriented and results-driven solution methodologies and techniques' (2002: 546). These research studies encourage thinking about organisational change in radically different ways, and the potential this has for both understanding and managing change. 'Our understanding of organisational change and the ways change is managed is enriched by an analysis of gender' (Foreman, 2001: 233).

Because this textbook does not feature gender differences in other chapters, there was an argument for omitting this short discussion. However, a short discussion is on balance believed to be marginally preferable to no discussion.

The ethics of changing individuals

Stuart (1995: 4) posed the question 'Just how are individuals experiencing their current world of organisational change?' However, his research interests were focused upon the experiences of managers, rather than those of employees in general.

RESEARCH CASES IN JOURNALS NO.6 – INDUSTRIAL ORGANISATION X 2

In this particular paper, the managers experiencing organisational change are the cases studied, rather than the organisation to which they belong. The managers who were interviewed for the research are drawn from two large industrial organisations that were attempting radical organisational change. The research was sponsored by the senior management of one organisation in the belief that the findings would inform the achievement of strategic management development objectives. The author respects the sensitivity of the information gathered and does not share any information that would reveal the identity of the managers. However, the managerial quotations offer insights into managers' experiences of organisational change. A strength of the paper is the extensive discussion of the experiences of managers in terms of 'change journeys'.

Sector: Manufacturing
Research methods: Research interviews and documentation.
Authors: Stuart, R.
Paper title: Experiencing organizational change: triggers, processes and outcomes of change journeys
Journal details: *Personnel Review*, Vol.24, No.2, 1995, pp.3–88

Any understanding of individual change as part of organisational change requires an appreciation of the different ways in which individuals, not just managers, experience change. Both Huczynski (1996) and Collins (1998) highlighted the prevalence of hero-manager accounts of the experience of change in which successful senior managers commit their thoughts to print.

The existence of this literature raises questions about how individuals working in these 'successfully' managed organisations experience change. Collins (1998: 64) warns that 'student-oriented texts on change and its management tend to work towards meeting the needs of one particular constituency over the needs of other groups at work and in the wider society.'

This textbook has argued for greater acknowledgement of individual change as part of organisational change processes. Organisations do not change regardless of individuals, they change through individuals' changing. This line of reasoning raises ethical dilemmas about the legitimacy of senior managers attempting to change individuals as part of the employment contract. Individuals are not impersonal resources in a change management equation:

> *The individual also takes with them an identity and a biography as well as various values and feelings or emotions about the world. The human being approaching employment is a whole human being, not just a human resource.*
>
> *(Watson, 2002: 128)*

This quotation should raise questions about what aspects of yourself you would allow to be changed ... and what aspects you would not allow to be changed.

- Would you allow your employer to influence your attitudes towards your family or partner?
- Would you allow your employer to challenge your religious beliefs?
- Would you adopt the political beliefs of your employer?

Even such questions, however, assume that consent would be requested and that attempts to change individuals would be overt rather than covert. The concept of psychological contracts offers a means of considering the ambiguities of employment relations. As well as the more tangible employment contract, workplace relationships are believed to be governed by less tangible psychological contracts. Psychological contracts are not written documents, but they do imply 'a series of mutual expectations and satisfaction of needs arising from the people-organisation relationship' (Mullins, 2005: 37). Morrison (1994: 365) believes that the psychological contract relates to change in three ways: the contract is dynamic, change alters the contract, and there are unspoken expectations about the contract. Individual changes required as part of organisational change have implications for psychological contracts. Organisational change may benefit individuals, but equally, change may be to the detriment of individuals. As Bowditch and Buono (2005: 5) warn, 'A fine line exists between motivation and manipulation, participation and deception, goal-setting and coercion, and other central facets of organisational life.'

Explicit and implicit coercion have been identified as potential styles of managing resistance to change (Kotter and Schlesinger, 1979). Coercion may be defined as 'an extension of direction. Here, change is imposed on staff, rather than staff having the idea of change sold to them' (Balogun and Hope Hailey, 2004: 36). Coercion is an illustration of a style of change management potentially impacting upon individuals. In Chapter 1, the identification by Weiss (2001: 421) of ethics-related issues relevant to change management highlighted the need to respect the rights of individuals, for justice towards individuals and for the fairness of plans. However, it is difficult to reconcile coercion as an approach to change management against such ethical criteria. Cummings and Worley (2005: 60) have written about ethics and coercion with reference to organisational development interventions, believing that 'people should have the freedom to choose whether to participate in a change programme if they are to gain self-reliance to solve their own problems.'

In terms of ways forward, Woodd (1997: 115) has made the case for human resource specialists acting 'as the guardians of ethical conduct in the employment of people'. One of the dilemmas of this discussion is its inevitably generalised nature. Ethical dilemmas raised by changing individuals as part of organisational change are likely to be at their most explicit and tangible in very specific instances.

Critically reviewing organisational development

Organisational development (OD) was introduced in Chapter 2 in terms of the origins of change management. OD and OD theorists have also been referred to at other points in this textbook. In this discussion, arguments for and against OD are reviewed. Dawson (2003: 32) acknowledged that the OD model of planned change remains part of the orthodoxy in terms of what is taught in universities, although himself favouring alternative strategies. He challenges the normative framework assumptions that there is one best way to manage change. He also challenges consultants who deliver OD for not being concerned with the development of theory or developing systematic programmes of research.

In exploring Dawson's challenges, there are signs that OD practioners have sought to develop their 'toolkits' and to undertake research. King and Anderson (2002: 192) in answering the question 'Does OD work?', write as follows:

> *Those who have experienced poorly designed and validated OD interventions have become increasingly cynical. Particularly where an organisation has imposed a rapid series of ill-conceived change initiatives upon staff it can begin to feel as if each successive programme is just the latest in a long line of faddish interventions.*

In terms of empirical evidence to support or refute such a view, they cite the review undertaken by Sinangil and Avallone (2001) offering qualified support for OD interventions which were theory-driven, competently implemented, and validated post-hoc. Wirtenberg *et al* (2004: 465) report on a survey questionnaire sent out to more than 6,000 members (response rate approximately 15 per cent) of the Organisation Development Network, Organisation Development Institute, and International Organisation Development Association assessing strengths and weaknesses of the field of OD.

Strengths included systemic orientation, change management, teamwork leadership development and values. Weaknesses included lack of definition and distinctiveness of OD, lack of quality control of practioners, insufficient business acumen of practioners/insufficient emphasis on customer needs, and insufficiently clear return on investment/value of the work.

These survey findings offer interesting insights into OD from the perspective of practioners, mirroring academic concerns about the ambiguity of OD but also highlighting the potential practical applicability of OD to change management challenges. In a similar vein, interviews with 21 thought leaders and pioneers in the field of OD revealed answers that confirmed 'some doubts about the field's current state, but also provided hope by charting some paths to renewed rigour and relevance' (Worley and Feyerherm, 2003: 114). It is difficult to offer a universal conclusion to this review of OD, given the wide range of practices and practioners in the field. Although it would be easy to condemn OD as a poorly regulated and outdated approach to contemporary challenges of change management, the soul-searching in OD practioners' attempts to critically review the field of OD is encouraging.

SYNOPSIS

Individual differences were identified, and these differences were influenced by society. One example of differences particularly relevant to change was that of perception. Major life events require individuals to change, but individual change was not exclusively preoccupied with major life events. Marris discussed individual change with reference to balancing continuity, growth and loss.

Understanding individual change as part of organisational change required an appreciation of the different ways in which individuals experience change, and the Kubler-Ross model (denial, anger, bargaining, depression and acceptance) was identified as applicable to major changes.

The pain/pressure of organisational change may be alleviated if those leading change focus on aspects of individual change. However, approaches to managing change had been developed at a group or organisational level, rather than at an individual level. Models of individual change suggested that individuals go through a process of change rather than change as a single event. One approach to managing individual change as part of an organisational change process was through change agency with different skill requirements identified.

The goals of an organisation have been regarded as the reason for its existence. However, such orthodoxy has been challenged. Members of organisations may have goals which are contradictory to those of senior management, creating gaps between formal and informal, official and operative, goals and actual policies.

Orthodox approaches to individual change neglect important differences such as class, race and gender. Foreman warned that literature on the management of organisational change rarely discusses the issue of gender. Empirical work undertaken by Leonard and Paton and Dempster focusing upon gender and organisational change was considered.

As well as by the more tangible employment contract, workplace relationships are believed to be governed by less tangible psychological contracts, implying a series of mutual expectations and satisfaction of needs arising from the people-organisation relationship. Organisational changes may benefit individuals, but equally, changes may be to the detriment of individuals. The identification by Weiss of ethics-related issues relevant to change management highlighted the need to respect the rights of individuals, for justice towards individuals and for the fairness of plans.

The organisation development (OD) model of planned change was seen as part of the orthodoxy. However, OD may be questioned in terms of the normative framework assumptions that there is one best way to manage change and that consultants who deliver OD are not concerned with the development of theory or with developing systematic programmes of research. In terms of empirical evidence, Sinangil and Avallone offered qualified support for OD interventions which were theory-driven, competently implemented, and validated post-hoc.

DISCUSSION QUESTIONS

1 What happens to an organisation if individuals do not change as part of an organisational change? (Think in terms of specific changes)

2 What encourages and discourages us to change as individuals?

3 Why in the management literature is there more emphasis upon senior managers' experiences of change than employees' experiences?

4 Should individuals embrace the goals of organisations in which they work?

5 How can women in changing organisations be more fully acknowledged without stereotyping women?

6 What is the case for and against organisational development existing in ten years' time?

Case study – Experiencing change in Greenshires County Council

Among other things, the social services department of Greenshires County Council processes documentation relating to elderly people going into care – in particular, the department is responsible for the generation of a contract between the individual, the residential home and the Council. The process inevitably generates large amounts of paperwork from a wide range of interested parties. Traditionally, one administrator has been tasked with processing all this paperwork from the initial enquiry through to the time the person takes up residence in his or her new home, and to processing the payments. The process has included gathering reports from social workers, estimates from residential homes and invoices from the Council's finance department. The process is invariably time-consuming and has to be dealt with professionally and sensitively. After many years of working in this way the manager of the department has decided to change the way contracts are processed. His story is told in his own words, together with the stories of two administrators who worked in the department.

Departmental manager's story

I have enjoyed running this department, but it is not the job it used to be. I pride myself that all contracts are processed as quickly and efficiently as possible, and I believe that the low labour turnover reflects a relatively content workforce. My problem in recent months has been that the Head of Finance required me to achieve major cost savings in order to address a significant Council budget deficit. I explained that due to demographic changes the contract work was expanding and that administrators were working to full capacity. He was not satisfied with my answer and demanded a 20 per cent cut in labour costs while simultaneously acknowledging that the work of the department will continue to increase. If that was not enough, the Council's quality guru has insisted that the department must dramatically improve customer service ratings or face processing work being outsourced to a private contractor who is keen to take over from us. I seriously considered resigning when faced with these challenges, but because of my loyalty to my team, I have decided to go for one last roll of the dice. I decided not to tell my team anything about the organisational politics or potential job losses, but to present the changes as positive improvements to service delivery.

The changes which came into force three months ago are quite radical by our standards. My thinking has been influenced by writings about scientific management I read years ago and more recently in an article by Hamper and somebody who advocated radical change around processes. The contract generation process has been divided into five stages and a separate team now works on each stage, rather than individuals' working on individual cases as they used to in the past. It has been a revelation to me in that I have been able to identify bottlenecks in the process which I never knew existed. Also, there is a progress wall-chart in the open-plan office which allows us all to gauge the progress that we are making. I am currently working on some interesting enhancements to the processes. However, I hear mixed reports from staff, so I have decided to talk to two of the longer-serving administrators.

Administrator's story (Justin Hinds)
Yes, it's OK. It took a while for me to get used to it, but I like it. As I think you know, I enjoy my work, but generally I am quite laid-back about life. I used to find working on individual cases interesting but it could be very intense. I didn't like the phonecalls from the relatives enquiring about the contracts. I'd tell them to chill out, but they just got more uptight. I now work in a small team with Tina, Eric and Paula. We call ourselves the A Team, although officially I think we are the Finance Communications Team. It took a few weeks for us to 'sus' each other out and at first I thought Eric was odd, but it is just his way of working with people. We go for a beer every Friday after work and whinge a bit, but generally the team is upbeat. I don't mind the new open-plan office – although now that I am away from the window, my special plant does not seem to grow so vigorously, and that annoys me. If you'd told me six months ago we would be working in this new way, I would have laughed. That said, I take each day as it comes and life is too short to worry. Somebody told me that the new business processes had been designed by those re-engineering blokes, which I thought was probably a good thing. You get an impression of everyone pulling together in the Council these days, which must be good. I do think things will get better if we all work together and chill a little.

Administrator's story (Virginia Astley)
When you asked to see me, I was going to decline the invitation because I am still very annoyed. I prided myself on my attention to detail and the attentive customer service that I always provided. It was a bombshell when you announced that we had to change because we had failed to deliver effective customer service. On the Friday you made your damning announcement, and on the Monday I came in to work to find all the offices had been refurbished as one open-plan office. My desk used to overlook a lovely little garden. Now I find myself sitting opposite a fire exit. At first I could not comprehend what was happening, and then an intense anger erupted inside me. I apologise most sincerely for kicking the cabinet door – that was probably the lowest point in my 20 years of working here. After my sick leave I have felt a bit more positive, and Justin has helped. All the same, my impression of the new arrangements is that it is a weary rehash of scientific management that my university lecturers were so critical about. I'm in a pleasant enough workgroup with

Tracy, Sally and Jane, but they talk a lot about shoes and make-up and to me they are 'bimbos'. When I try and jolly them along, they say that as long as we deal with our bits of 20 contracts a week we are sorted. I have started to go with the flow, or lack of flow [nervous laughter]. What keeps me sane is the knowledge that in six months' time I will be out of here and studying for my PhD. If I had wanted to work in a factory I would have worked at Higson's Plastic Parts (who, incidentally, pay more money).

Case study questions

1 What is happening in the three accounts of change with specific reference to perception and, in particular, perception distortions?

2 Explain with reference to discussions in the chapter what was hindering Virginia in changing.

3 If you had been the departmental manager, what might you have done differently to have managed this process of change?

FURTHER READING

CONNER D. R. (1998) *Managing at the Speed of Change*, Chichester, John Wiley & Sons.

This book is a bit different from the norm in that Conner – now working successfully as a consultant on large change management projects – originally worked as a psychologist. He is able to effectively apply his interest and knowledge about individual transitions to organisational changes. The book at times has a strange feel as Conner writes, for example, about the hard-nosed metaphor of the burning platform as part of change management, whereas at other times he displays a humanist perspective on the difficulties individuals encounter during transitions.

HAYES J. (2002) *The Theory and Practice of Change Management*, Houndmills, Palgrave.

In the context of a textbook on change management Hayes offers a very readable account of 'Managing personal transitions'. Although the book as a whole has a managerial/consultancy feel, this chapter is particularly recommended for its emphasis upon the needs of the individual over the organisation. There is enough food for thought in this chapter for anyone who wants to further understand the transitions that we constantly experience.

STUART R. Experiencing organisational change: triggers, processes and outcomes of change journeys, *Personnel Review*, Vol.24, No.2, 1995, pp.3–87.

A whole issue of *Personnel Review* was devoted to this monograph by Roger Stuart concerned with identifying individuals' experiences of organisational change. The strengths of the monograph are twofold in that it pulls together a disparate literature and it draws upon original empirical research undertaken by the author. Stuart deliberately went beyond familiar frames of reference in terms of the literature to offer insights into the experience of change from many different perspectives. For anyone interested in delving more deeply into this fascinating area, the 67 references at the end of the monograph offer a good reading list. The monograph also benefits from empirical insights, although at times it would have been good to have been able to read case studies of the experiences of change rather than 'soundbites' from the research interviews.

WILSON E. (ed.) (2001) *Organizational Behaviour Reassessed: The impact of gender*, London, Sage Publications.

The chapter by Foreman on 'Organisational change' is particularly recommended for anyone interested in change from a gendered perspective. Also, the book as a whole is recommended in that it considers other areas featured in this chapter from the perspective of gender.

Resistance to change

LEARNING OBJECTIVES

To:

- review the meanings and theories of resistance to organisational change

- consider options for managing resistance to organisational change

- explore the concept of resistance as an organisational stabiliser

- introduce the politics of change as a perspective on resistance

- re-evaluate resistance to organisational change.

INTRODUCTION

We may like change and regard it as an essential feature of living: it does not mean that we always welcome it.

(Fransella, 1975: 135)

This chapter in focusing upon resistance to change addresses a significant aspect of change management. Stickland (1998: 136) has described resistance as an ongoing problem for change managers, and Randall (2004: 37) believes that the problem of resistance 'lies at the heart of most change programmes...' In organisational settings resistance is frequently presented and perceived as irrational and problematical – something that requires to be dealt with as an integral element of any change management initiative.

As well as potential resistance to change by employees, it is worthwhile acknowledging that organisations may face resistance to change from other groups such as suppliers, distributors, stakeholders and consumers (Paton and McCalman, 2000: 47). Also, resistance to change may be evident in group behaviours (see Chapter 11 for a discussion of group-/team-based change).

The *Approaches* section of this chapter begins with a discussion of the meanings and theories of resistance to change. The problematic nature of resistance to change depicts resistance as something that has to be managed. In reviewing classic texts on resistance, King and Anderson (2002: 10) conclude:

The common theme binding all of them being, we argue, a naïve and managerialist assumption that resistance is counterproductive – even irrational – behaviour which needs to be overcome.

In the *Critical perspective* section functionalist assumptions about resistance will be challenged in terms of the notion of resistance as a stabiliser, political aspects of change, and the need to re-evaluate resistance to change.

APPROACHES TO RESISTANCE TO CHANGE
The meanings and theories of resistance to change

In the *Critical perspective* section, resistance terminology will be challenged. However, the following definition of resistance to change offered by Lines (2004: 198) provides a useful starting point:

> *Resistance towards change encompasses behaviours that are acted out by change recipients in order to slow down or terminate an intended organisational change.*

The quotation raises the question of why groups and individuals should behave in this way – and many explanations have been offered, although often with little research evidence to support the theorising. Dawson (2003: 19) identifies the following examples of organisational factors from which resistance can result:

- substantive change in job
- reduction in economic security or job displacement
- psychological threat
- disruption of social arrangements, and lowering of status.

Similarly, Paton and McCalman (2000: 47) have identified reasons why organisations, individuals and groups fear change which include the resulting organisational redesign, new technological challenges, and challenges to old ideas. One explanation for why we are selective in the changes we resist has been offered by Burke (2002: 93), who cites the research of Brehm (1966): 'What comes closer to a universal truth about human behaviour is that people resist the imposition of change.'

Four predominant perspectives on resistance to change have been identified (Graetz *et al*, 2002: 260):

- the psychological model
- the systems model
- the institutional approach, and
- the organisational cultures approach.

The psychological model specifies causes of resistance to change in terms of individual behaviours. The systems model suggests that it is not change as such that people resist, but that instead people resist losing something. According to the institutionalised approach resistance becomes embedded in organisational structures, decision-making processes and resource allocation. Resistance may also be explained in terms of the existence of organisational cultures (see Chapter 7 for a discussion of cultural change). Another classification of perspectives on resistance has been identified by King and Anderson (2002: 215) who described resistance as:

- an unavoidable behavioural response
- a politically motivated insurrection and class struggle
- a constructive counterbalance, and
- cognitive and cultural restructuring.

Similarly, Piderit (2000: 785) in her review of previous empirical research identifies three different conceptualisations of resistance 'as a cognitive state, as an emotional state, and as a behaviour'.

In the above overviews of explanations of resistance to change there are similarities and differences. The main conclusion to be drawn from these different classifications is that no consensus explanation of resistance to organisational change currently exists. In the light of the wide range of organisational changes and organisational contexts that occur, it is unlikely that a single universal explanation of resistance to change will ever be sufficient. Burke (2002: 93–4) cites the work of Hambrick and Cannella (1989) distinguishing between blind, political and ideological resistance. Individuals in the 'blind resistance' category are believed to be afraid or intolerant of any change. Individuals in the 'political resistance' category believe they may lose something of value if change is implemented. And individuals in the 'ideological resistance' category believe that change is ill-fated or against their deeply-held values. The political/ideological roots of resistance to change tap into industrial sociology literature.

> *The overt resistance of the recalcitrant worker and the associated tendency to work limitation has been discovered again and again in the annals we have reviewed. The related phenomenon of absenteeism, sabotage and pilferage have also been repeatedly noted by researchers.*
>
> *(Ackroyd and Thompson, 1999: 53)*

Again, notions of recalcitrant workers emphasise that resistance is not always overt. Also, the quotation reminds us that resistance is not a new phenomenon but one that may be traced back through the history of industrial relations.

As well as broad classifications of explanations of resistance to change, there have been more specific classifications of resistance to change. Resistance to change may be covert or overt, or a combination. Examples of covert resistance at an individual level include demotivation, intentional underperformance and purposeful lack of realisation of potential (King and Anderson, 2002: 210). Graetz et al (2002: 255) differentiate between active and passive resistance 'noting that resistance may manifest in a variety of forms, ranging from active resistance (where change is aggressively challenged) to passive resistance (where change is indirectly undermined)'.

Although the change literature often speaks of the problem of active resistance to a particular change, passive resistance can be more of a problem yet less tangible and less explicit. In considering the potentially problematical nature of resistance to change it is useful to consider the opposite of resistance. Graetz et al (2002: 254) conceptualise a continuum stretching from commitment to resistance, with acceptance and rejection as positions along this continuum. The notion of a continuum acknowledges the different degrees of resistance that may exist and again is more sophisticated than a universal concept of resistance.

Managing the problem of resistance to organisational change

Because people respond to change through diverse defence mechanisms, implementation of change may be regarded as more crucial than conceptualisation (Sorge and Van Witteloostuijn, 2004: 1207). Any attempt to manage resistance to change is likely to be informed by the analyses offered in the previous discussion. Although a manager may not make explicit reference to particular theories, whether he or she regards resistance as an individual psychological problem, for example, or as an institutional problem will influence how he or she manages resistance.

If resistance relates to uncertainty rather than change, then resistance is a consequence of how a change is managed rather than the change itself (Carnall 2003: 1–2). Burke (2002: 93), drawing upon the work of Brehm (1966), writes:

> *The degree of ease and success with which an organisation change is introduced is therefore directly proportional to the amount of choice that people feel they have in determining and implementing the change.*

The dilemma with such an approach is that there are a range of related issues such as management and leadership styles and power. Similarly, Dawson (2003: 19) regards one of the main reasons for resisting change as that 'the proposed change may break the continuity of a working environment and create a climate of uncertainty and ambiguity.' Again, managerial analysis of the change may be a prerequisite for managerial intervention.

King and Anderson (2002: 196) note a steady flow of published literature advising managers on how to overcome resistance to change in organisations. They identify the following writers as influential examples of classical writing on resistance to change: Coch and French (1948), Lewin (1951), Lawrence (1969), Shepard (1967), Dubrin (1974), and Kotter and Schlesinger (1979).

While acknowledging the subtleties and complexities of resistance, Dawson (2003: 20) identifies strategies that change agents have utilised to overcome resistance. 'Typically, these centre on participation, communication and support at one end of a continuum through to negotiation, manipulation and coercion at the other.' Organisational development approaches tend to opt for participative approaches, whereas contingency approaches tend to opt for more coercive strategies (Dawson, 2003: 20). In Chapter 12, power is discussed in terms of leading change. One perspective is in terms of the power bases; reward, coercive, referent, legitimate and expert popularised by French and Raven (1959). According to Graetz *et al* (2002: 242–3) the use of these power bases may be a means of managing resistance to change.

Although research evidence will be cited in the penultimate chapter suggesting that change management initiatives often fail, resistance may paradoxically have a constructive role to play in change management.

> *It is perhaps ironic that, given the number of failed change initiatives, those who question the need for change are often cast as the villains of the piece, as unable to adapt to the dynamic changing conditions of the modern world.*
>
> *(Dawson, 2003: 20)*

This quotation encourages a more participative approach to change management compatible with earlier discussions. Instead of the caricature of senior management imposing change which employees then resist, employees become involved in the change process in a more real sense. At the very least, senior management could encourage the active expression of resistance. 'Where there is major change, there is resistance; but you can minimise negative effects by encouraging resistance to be expressed openly instead of secretly' (Conner, 1998: 128). Otherwise, the danger is that although overt resistance may be suppressed, it may be replaced by more covert resistance to change. Conner is suggesting from a managerialist perspective that overtly expressed resistance will be more manageable than covert resistance. King and Anderson (2002: 220) offer the colourful metaphor of the management of resistance as medicine for the bad patient, so that resistance is regarded as 'a defence mechanism against the pathogens of change'.

There is a need to be resourceful when dealing with resistance, rather than relying upon generalised remedies to overcome resistance to change. King and Anderson (2002: 208), in reviewing literature relating to resistance to change, draw the conclusion that 'proffering highly general models and advice on how to overcome resistance is clearly fraught with danger.' This quotation suggests that even for the manager who still regards resistance as a problem to be managed there would be benefit in a more sophisticated analysis of the nature of the resistance in different contexts.

CRITICAL PERSPECTIVE

This critical perspective challenges assumptions that resistance to organisational change is a problem that always requires management. The following quotation is particularly pertinent because it is taken from a guide to effective implementation of change management:

> *Change for change's sake, change for short-term commercial advantage or indeed change which may adversely affect the 'common good' should be resisted, not only on moral grounds, but also on the basis that the adverse long-term financial consequences are likely to outweigh any short-term gain.*
>
> *(Paton and McCalman, 2000: 49)*

The following critical perspective on resistance to organisational change is organised around three challenges:

- resistance may help to stabilise an organisation
- resistance is an important and integral element of the organisational politics of change
- there may be benefit in terms of thinking about responses to change rather than about resistance.

The following discussion elaborates upon each of these challenges.

Change and stability

RESEARCH CASES IN JOURNALS NO.7 – MIDDLE MANAGERS

Middle managers are a potentially powerful group in terms of resisting change. However, given the contentious nature of resistance, it can be difficult to research resistance inside organisations. The authors gathered case illustrations of resistance to change at an open-space conference themed around management development and from participants on an MSc/MBA course in technology management. The ten short real-life cases presented in the paper illustrate how change was perceived to have been successfully resisted by middle managers. Based upon the case studies of resistance by middle managers, the authors illustrate tactics used for resistance including: feigning agreement to change and obtaining control of the change process; saying No, and linking reasons to the core values of the organisation; delaying by continuously requesting further information; and setting managers involved with change against each other. They identify a potential organisational benefit of resistance as preventing folly.

Sector: Various
Research methods: Narratives told at an open space conference and on an MSc/MBA course.
Authors: Perren, L. and Megginson D.
Paper title: Resistance to change as a positive force: its dynamics and issues for management development
Journal details: *Career Development International*, Vol.1, No.4, 1996, pp.24–8

Individuals have a strong preference for stability (De Wit and Meyer, 2004: 177), yet the management of stability may be regarded as the antithesis of much of the popular rhetoric of change, particularly the espousal of constant change. But what if commentators such as Abrahamson (2000: 75) were correct in suggesting that in changing successfully, companies should stop changing all the time? This type of view is certainly not the orthodoxy. For example, Matheny (1998: 394) suggests that 'in today's volatile marketplace, maintaining an organisation's status quo can be equivalent to self-destruction', and Eccles and Nohria (1992: 192) claimed that arguments for maintaining the status quo were hard to find and even harder to defend. Both change management success and change management failure breed new demands for change, and only the absence of change is regarded as deficiency (Sorge and Van Witteloostuijn, 2004: 1207). Managers and employees are judged on their ability to cope with and manage change (Paton and McCalman, 2000: 96, and Sorge and Van Witteloostuijn, 2004: 1213).

The emerging concern relates to whether constant change benefits either institutions or individuals. The critical change literature is more circumspect about the espoused case for constant change. 'With all the hype these days about change, we desperately need more messages about some good old-fashioned stability' (Mintzberg *et al*, 1998: 281). The idea of such messages may initially appear nostalgic, but the implication is that we can learn from past change in terms of learning what was bad but equally what was good. Reed (2001: 24) argues that the belief in constantly re-engineering existing processes gives rise to anxiety and ignores much of the good in what has gone before. Abrahamson (2000: 76) has gone as far as to offer a new phrase 'dynamic stability', defined as 'a process of continual but relatively small change efforts that involve the reconfiguration of existing practices and business models rather than the creation of new ones'.

Cummings (2002: 279) has highlighted the paradox that 'managing change requires continuity.' Cummings is sceptical about greenfield site notions of change which advocate fresh starts, believing that it is difficult for people to forget histories and traditions. Similarly, Sturdy and Grey (2003: 652) caution against change and continuity as alternative states: 'They are typically coexistent and coterminous; and they are not objective because what constitutes change or continuity is perspective dependent.' Resistance to change may enable an organisation to maintain stability in times of change in a manner similar to how the stabilisers on a child's bicycle enable a child to achieve simultaneous stability and progress. Gravenhorst and In't Veld (2004: 320), whilst subsequently offering alternative explanations of resistance to change, cite Watson's (1969) definition of resistance to change:

As all the forces that contribute to stability in personality or social systems ... He sees resistance to change as a natural reaction of individuals and social systems, originating from the need for a relatively stable situation.

Although stability may appear to be the antithesis of change, according to such a perspective stability may be a natural state. Managers in seeking to overcome resistance to change may be misunderstanding the processes of organisational change. The following quotation is particularly notable both because Schon (1963: 82) was writing in the early 1960s and because as a mainstream writer he may be differentiated from the more radical writers cited in this chapter.

Resistance to change is not only normal but in some ways even desirable. An organisation totally devoid of resistance to change would fly apart at the seams.

King and Anderson (2002: 217), in reviewing perspectives on resistance to change, point out that resistance 'can thus act as a counterbalance to change which is ill-conceived, poorly enacted, or simply detrimental to the productive efficiency of the organisation'. One characteristic which may influence choices to resist certain changes and embrace other changes is the conservative impulse:

Thus the impulses of conservatism – to ignore or avoid events which do not match our understanding, to control deviation from expected behaviour, to isolate innovation and sustain the segregation of different aspects of life – are all means to defend our ability to make sense of life.

(Marris, 1974: 11)

This is an eloquent explanation of why certain individuals may resist certain changes. Whereas resistance to change in organisations is often presented as irrational, the impulse of conservatism suggests that resistance may be a rational attempt to maintain stability.

The politics of change

In addressing the politics of change, it is necessary to consider the broader topic of organisational politics. Organisational politics/micro-politics has been defined as:

Processes occurring within work organisations as individuals, groups and organisational 'sub-units' compete for access to scarce and valued material and symbolic resources.

(Watson, 2002: 326)

Watson (2002: 327–8) writes about micro-politics as being 'an inevitable and intrinsic part of organisational life and activity'. He offers three reasons for such inevitability. Firstly, because individuals are 'strategic animals' they continually have to compete and/or co-operate with others. Secondly, through the process of being allocated to 'sub-units' of an organisation, individuals identify with that grouping rather than with the organisation as a whole. Thirdly, due to the ambiguity and uncertainty of organisational situations, no one individual will possess all the facts. Mintzberg *et al* (1998: 242–4) identify dysfunctional effects of politics which include that it can be divisive and costly, uses up energies which could be better utilised, and can lead to aberrations. However, they (1998: 243–4) do identify four benefits that may arise out of the exercise of politics. Firstly, politics in a Darwinian sense encourages the strongest organisational members into leadership positions. Secondly, politics ensures a full debate of issues from all sides. Thirdly, politics may encourage change which has been blocked by more legitimate systems. And fourthly, the path of executing a change may be eased through politics.

In reviewing the discussion so far it is apparent why commentators have become interested in the politics of change and how such a perspective can inform our understanding of resistance to change. Buchanan and Badham (1999: 5), in one of the most influential texts on power, politics and organisational change, warn that change agents striving for political neutrality face double jeopardy. Firstly, a politically neutral approach is likely to be ineffective in the face of self-interested resistance, and secondly, ignoring political realities could be viewed as 'unskilled, incompetent, unprofessional and unethical'. Four arguments for understanding politics in the context of change have been offered (Buchanan and Badham, 1999: 1–3):

- political behaviour is more significant in organisations than is realised
- the role of political behaviour in organisational change is not sufficiently addressed in the academic management literature
- political behaviour can be both positive and negative, and
- management development should help change agents to deal with political behaviour in organisations.

In terms of the politics of change, resistance may be regarded as an inevitable consequence of the organisational politics that exist inside any organisation. There are likely to be organisational advantages and disadvantages arising out of these political processes relating to resistance.

Re-evaluating resistance to organisational change

This chapter has been sceptical of claims that resistance should be regarded as an unfortunate aberration which change managers need to overcome. Instead, there is a need for a re-evaluation of resistance to change, particularly in terms of the lack of sophistication of the analyses and the semantics of resistance to change.

The first concern is with the lack of sophistication of analyses. Resistance is a rich and complex concept, and deserves much greater attention than it often gets during change management exercises (Stickland, 1998: 138). This textbook has emphasised the role of individuals in the processes of organisational change. However, Ford et al (2002: 106) would challenge individual-based explanations of resistance to organisational change. 'Resistance, therefore, is not to be found "in the individual" but in the constructed reality in which individuals operate.' Their complex although potentially enlightening argument is that resistance results out of 'background conversations' that create a reality for individuals, which is very different from resistance existing within individuals. They identify three background realities: complacency, resignation, and cynicism. Anyone who has experienced organisational change should be able to identify with these often negative background conversations. This form of analysis may be regarded as bringing sophistication to the functionalism of earlier analyses. It seems obvious, but in terms of more sophisticated analyses there is a need to take into account the inevitably varied responses individuals will make to change:

> *Conceptualising employees' responses to proposed organisational changes as multidimensional attitudes permits a richer view of the ways in which employees may respond to change.*
>
> *(Piderit, 2000: 789)*

In drawing conclusions, Piderit (2000: 789) notes that this conceptualisation is 'intended to encourage an appreciation for the prevalence of ambivalence in individuals' responses to change'.

The second concern relates to the semantics of explanations of resistance to change. Resistance to change is commonplace in our everyday lives, yet we are far less likely to hear such terminology outside the workplace. When your partner 'contests "another" late night at the office, or when your child balks at a new baby-sitter, they are resisting change' (Conner, 1998: 125). Whereas as individuals we may have a very positive attitude to change, this does not mean that we will not resist certain changes. 'Resistance is a natural human response and, like one's defence mechanisms, should be respected' (Burke, 2002: 94). For example, elections are an integral part of democracies and offer us a chance to resist particular changes proposed by politicians through the ballot-box. However, as Collins (1998: 92) explains, the semantics of government and *opposition* is employed, rather than government and resistance.

The terminology of resistance intentionally suggests something dysfunctional, whereas *opposition* to change (rarely-used terminology) would be a more honest and constructive approach to explaining change. Opposition becomes resistance, with resistance being futile. 'The term seems to imply that those who resist are setting themselves to struggle against the inevitable...' (Collins, 1998: 91). Kirton (2003: 293) takes arguments about terminology further, noting that:

> *The term is resistance to change – not to this change or my change. This is not to be dismissed as a subtle difference. There are no organisms that are resistant to all change – all are selective as to what change to accept and what not.*

So why is the term 'resistance to change' so frequently used in the context of change management? Possibly because it throws the entire blame for rejection (or even delay in acceptance) of a proposal for change onto those to whom it is proposed (Kirton, 2003: 293). This chapter has argued that individuals do not so much resist change as resist the uncertainty arising out of change; 'people do not resist change as much as the ambiguity that results when the familiar ceases' (Conner, 1998: 126). The favoured change management terminology of 'resistance to change' may be misleading for those seeking to understand this concept, and may paradoxically be unhelpful in terms of change management.

> *The complementary term to 'resistor to change', in popular currency, is 'change agent'. The dangerous element here is that it seems to imply that most of us are not change agents.*
>
> *(Kirton, 2003: 293)*

As Piderit (2000: 792) concludes, the metaphor of resistance to change may have taken us as far as we can go. Instead, she favours retiring the phrase (see also Dent and Goldberg, 1999, and Merron, 1993) in favour of research into employees' responses to change – in particular, their multidimensional attitudes.

One of the concerns with the label 'resistance' is that it 'can be used to dismiss potentially valid employee concerns about proposed changes' (Piderit, 2000: 784). It is time to retire 'resistance to change' terminology ... although there would probably be considerable resistance from managers and management writers.

SYNOPSIS

Resistance towards change was defined as encompassing behaviours acted out by change recipients in order to slow down or terminate an intended organisational change. Examples of organisational factors from which resistance could result included substantive change in a job and reduction in economic security or job displacement. Four perspectives on resistance were identified: the psychological model, the systems model, the institutional approach, and the organisational cultures approach.

King and Anderson identified classic writers on resistance to change: Coch and French, Lewin, Lawrence, Shepard, Dubrin, and Kotter and Schlesinger. Strategies that change agents had utilised to overcome resistance were identified, with participation, communication and support at one end of a continuum through to negotiation, manipulation and coercion at the other.

Individual preferences for stability were acknowledged. Mintzberg *et al* argued that with all the hyperbole these days about change, we desperately need more messages about some good old-fashioned stability. Sturdy and Grey were cited cautioning against popular differentiations between change and continuity, because they are typically coexistent. Resistance to change may enable an organisation to maintain stability in times of change. King and Anderson reviewing perspectives on resistance to change, highlighted that resistance can act as a counterbalance to change which is ill-conceived, poorly enacted, or simply detrimental to the productive efficiency of the organisation.

Organisational politics was defined as processes occurring within work organisations as individuals, groups and organisational 'sub-units' compete for access to scarce and valued material and symbolic resources. In terms of the politics of change, resistance may be regarded as an inevitable consequence of the organisational politics that exist inside any organisation regardless of change.

The chapter suggested a need to re-evaluate resistance to change, particularly in terms of the lack of sophistication of the analyses and the semantics of 'resistance to change'. Resistance to change is commonplace in our everyday lives, yet we are far less likely to hear such terminology outside the workplace.

DISCUSSION QUESTIONS

1 Is it possible to live a fulfilling life without resisting certain changes in everyday life?

2 What are the tangible and intangible manifestations of resistance to change in organisations?

3 Why is resistance to change problematic for those managing change?

4 What are the potential benefits of management's perceiving resistance as a stabiliser?

5 Why is resistance to change invariably thought about in organisations as something that has to be overcome?

6 In updating the language of change, what alternative terminology to 'resistance' could be used?

Case study – Resistance to change in Happy Homes call centre

Happy Homes call centre customer advisers design high-quality customer-focused solutions to meet all their customer's home insurance needs. This is marketing terminology for the call centre operation. The reality has been slightly different. The call centre function of Happy Homes is subcontracted to Express Efficient Calls Ltd (EEC) based in Unit B on an industrial estate. The terms of the contract between Happy Homes and EEC are very specific, involving measurable standards of service delivery and the conversion of calls into sales. The contract is regularly reviewed by Happy Homes. The manager of the call centre is Sarah Cracknell. She knows she is in fierce competition not just with call centres in this country but also call centres globally.

Ms Cracknell is proud of EEC which she has built up from nothing after spotting a niche for call centres 15 years ago. At any one time there might be up to 100 staff working in the call centre, working on the dawn, daylight or twilight shifts. The majority of employees work part-time. The call centre has the look of a hybrid between an open-plan office and a factory. There are rows and rows of desks, with computer monitors on each desk. Ms Cracknell has a raised glass office in one corner of the building. The walls of the building are very bare, only interrupted by neon signs flashing up details of targets and calls answered on time. Employees are divided into four colour-coded teams of approximately 25 employees. A supervisor is allocated to each team and can be seen moving from desk to desk because they wear suits reflecting the colour of their particular team.

Ms Cracknell runs a very efficient operation and everything has been going smoothly. Happy Homes have been pleased with the service delivery and sales, although enough has never quite been enough for Happy Homes. Through focus group work they have identified an innocent question for customer advisers to ask mid-way through each call: 'Do you enjoy living in your current home?' Their research has revealed that this question encourages customers to access good feelings about their home, and also introduces an element of informality into the conversation, yet because it is a closed question it will not lead to a discussion. Ms Cracknell has been instructed to ensure that all customer advisers ask this question during every call. She has also been warned that Happy Homes will be sampling monitored calls to ensure that this requirement is being met. Being proactive, she has decided to undertake her own monitoring in anticipation of future Happy Homes monitoring of calls.

She monitors the calls of customer advisers for one week on the busy daylight shift. Out of 100 of her employees, 80 are asking the question, and 20 employees are not asking the question. She interviews all those 20 employees to establish why they are failing to ask the question as instructed. At this stage three employees resign, stating that the job is not worth the hassle. The other interviewees are more forthcoming and explain their reasoning as best they can. Her initial hunch was that the 20 might have all come from one team, but they are from across all four teams. When she analyses the interviews, it is possible to group individuals in terms of three main reasons for resistance.

The first grouping of reasons is couched in terms of an expressed preference to stick with the status quo. Customer advisers claim that they do not want to change the way that they have always worked.

- 'It worked well before, so why change it?'
- 'Why do we have to ask this silly question?'
- 'I am happy continuing as I always have done.'

The second grouping of reasons relate to terms and conditions of employment and industrial relations. Only 10 per cent of employees are in a trade union and EEC does not recognise this union as negotiating on behalf of employees. Individuals claim (erroneously, as it emerges) that any changes to their work have to go through a process of negotiation.

- 'I don't mind asking any question, but I must be properly reimbursed for asking the question.'
- 'The regional union official is due to call me back on this one.'
- 'Most employees feel the same as me – they are just reluctant to take industrial action.'

The third grouping of reasons is the most illuminating. Individuals acknowledge that they should be asking the question – and that initially they were asking the question – but they are gaining negative customer responses to the question, and believe this will be bad for their individual customer service ratings and the overall customer service ratings for EEC.

- 'Their [the customer's] tone changes negatively after you have asked the question.'
- 'One customer asked if I was having a laugh.'
- 'A customer asked if I was a robot programmed to ask the same question that I had asked them yesterday.'

Ms Cracknell now realises that an innocent question that is so important to Happy Homes has the potential to derail a lucrative contract upon which EEC is utterly dependent.

Case study questions

1 Explain the three groupings of responses with specific reference to theories of resistance introduced in this chapter.

2 If you were Sarah Cracknell, how would you deal with each of these three forms of resistance?

3 How would thinking in terms of responses to change rather than resistance to change alter your understanding of this case study?

FURTHER READING

BURKE W. (2002) *Organization Change: Theory and practice*, Thousand Oaks, Sage Publications.

Although the coverage of resistance is rather short in quantity, in terms of quality Burke shares some illuminating references which form the basis for a more sophisticated understanding of resistance. A strength of the writings of Burke is that he is interested in both the practical challenges of change management and academic understanding of change management.

KING N. and ANDERSON N. (2002) *Managing Innovation and Change: A critical guide for organizations*, London, Thomson Learning.

A chapter is devoted to 'Resistance to change' in this accessible business psychology textbook. In particular, the chapter reviews six pieces of literature which have been influential in advising managers on how to overcome resistance to change in their organisations. As the authors acknowledge, it would be a 'gargantuan task' to review all the resistance to change literature, and they have identified some of the more influential literature.

KOTTER J. P. and SCHLESINGER L. A. (1979) Choosing strategies for change, *Harvard Business Review*, March/April, Vol.57/Issue 2; pp.106–14.

This paper is frequently cited in the change management literature and, time permitting, it is worthwhile checking out the original reference. The main focus of their paper is resistance to change. They offer four reasons for resistance, as well as discussing their famous strategies for change. They suggest that the methods described are based upon an analysis of dozens of successful and unsuccessful organisational changes.

PIDERIT S. K. (2000) Rethinking resistance and recognizing ambivalence: a multidimensional view of attitudes toward an organizational change, *Academy of Management Review*, Vol.25, No.4; pp.783–94.

This journal paper offers a comprehensive critical review of studies in resistance to change. The paper highlights competing explanations of resistance to change, as well as offering new explanations in terms of acknowledging the existence of ambivalence to change and the multidimensional nature of our responses to change. Although the paper has a very scholarly feel, working with ambivalence and multidimensional responses to change appears to be pertinent to the practice of change management.

Group- and team-based change

11

LEARNING OBJECTIVES

To:

■ understand the meaning and theories of groups and teams in organisations

■ explore group- and team-based responses to change

■ find out how change can be managed through groups and teams

■ question group- as opposed to individual-level analysis

■ consider the downside of groups and teams

■ critically review the concept of self-managed teams.

INTRODUCTION

Teams are replacing individuals as the basic units of work organisation (Thompson and McHugh, 2002: 324). Although cynicism about excessive meetings and committees in organisations is common, organisational decisions do tend to be made by groups rather than by individuals (Arnold, 2005: 435). Against such a backdrop this textbook has to acknowledge the increasing emphasis upon group- and team-based working with particular reference to change. In organisations undergoing change it is unrealistic to work with every single one of the individuals who comprise the organisation – consequently, 'organisation change efforts typically rely heavily on the use of work groups' (Burke, 2002: 98). Lewin was influential in encouraging such an emphasis. He maintained 'that it is fruitless to concentrate on changing the behaviour of individuals because the individual in isolation is constrained by group pressures to conform' (Burnes 2004b: 983). This belief in change through groups, rather than through individuals, is explored throughout this chapter.

The chapter's *Approaches* section first introduces meanings and theories about groups and teams, and then describes the responses of groups and teams to change and how change is facilitated through groups and teams. The *Critical perspective* explores the case for group-level change versus individual-level change, and challenges the hyperbole around groups and teams. Finally, team-based change is critically reviewed in terms of the concept of self-managed teams.

APPROACHES TO GROUP- AND TEAM-BASED CHANGE

In seeking to understand change, a distinction made commonly (as discussed in Chapter 1) was between the individual, group and organisational levels of analysis. It is possible to initiate change at each and/or all of these levels. Another distinction has been made between macro-level and micro-level organisational variables. Macro-level variables affect the entire institution whereas micro-level variables affect individuals (Haddad, 2002: 69). These distinctions help to locate groups and teams between the macro organisational level and the micro individual level. Groups and teams are likely to influence and be influenced by both individuals and organisations.

The meanings and theories of groups and teams in organisations

The literature often treats groups and teams as indistinguishable, despite the existence of crucial differences (Cameron and Green, 2004: 55). Bowditch and Buono (2005: 137), in differentiating between groups and teams, define a group as consisting of '(1) two or more people who are (2) psychologically aware of each other, and who (3) interact to fulfil a (4) common goal'. Conversely, they (2005: 167) define a team as:

> *A distinguishable set of people (1) who interacts with each other dynamically, interdependently, and adaptively, (2) who work toward a common and valued goal, and (3) who each have specific roles or functions to perform.*

These definitions of groups and teams highlight similarities and differences between groups and teams. Although all teams are by definition groups, not all groups are teams. Often emphasis is placed upon the applied work-based nature of teams. 'A major characteristic that distinguishes groups from teams is that the latter focus on a specific output, and teams are generally held accountable for the completion of their output'(Weiss, 2001: 135). Brooks (1999: 75) neatly captures the difference when he writes: 'Social psychology may still talk about groups and group work, but organisations are primarily interested in teams and effective teamworking.' Because the early pioneering work of Lewin made reference to 'groups' and more recent change management literature refers to 'teams', the label 'group and team' will be used in the chapter except for those instances where a commentator is referring specifically to a group or a team. As well as differentiating between groups and teams, it is common to classify different types of group. Classifications include:

- primary groups versus secondary groups
- formal groups versus informal groups
- permanent groups versus temporary groups.

Individuals belong to many different groups inside organisations and in the wider society. For example, an individual may be a member of a large factory trade union. This group may be classified as secondary in terms of limited social interaction amongst members, formal in terms of being a formalised group, and permanent in the sense that it seeks to tackle ongoing issues. By contrast, the same individual may be a member of the group campaigning for a vending machine in the staff room. This group is a primary group in that the six employees lobbying for the vending machine regularly interact with each other. It is informal in that the group simply came together out of their collective annoyance at the lack of a vending machine. And it is temporary because the group will cease to exist once the vending machine has been installed or if it has no success in the campaign.

Teams may also be classified. For example, the following differentiation between project development teams has been suggested: functional team structure, lightweight team structure, heavyweight team structure, and autonomous team structure (Clark and Wheelwright, 1992: 420). Mckenna (2000: 329) identifies examples of different types of teams, including work teams, management teams, cross-functional teams and quality circles.

The important point here is not so much to note the variety of classifications as to acknowledge that groups and teams differ considerably contingent upon a range of variables such as type of task, type of organisation, level in the hierarchy, and sectoral background. Every group and team is unique in a manner similar to the unique nature of organisations and individuals.

The primary work group has been described as the most important subsystem within an organisation, always crucial for organisational effectiveness (Burke, 2002: 97). This may explain why, historically, there has been considerable interest in groups among management and organisational behaviour writers. Major contributions to our understanding about groups and teams include:

- Asch (1952): group norms
- Tuckman (1965): stages of group development
- Janis (1972): groupthink
- Belbin (1981): team roles.

Norms are the 'unwritten rules' of a group, constituting the 'atmosphere' of a group (Coghlan, 1994: 19). However, norms are only guides or expectations about behaviour, offering potential indications as to how others will behave. Researchers have found that group norms can exert a considerable influence over individuals. Asch (1952) conducted one of the most frequently-cited studies in this field, asking individuals in a group to judge the lengths of different lines. Seven of the eight individuals gave the wrong answer in collusion with the researcher; their answers tended to influence the answer of the eighth individual (unaware of the research) who often gave a wrong answer in order to conform to the group norm.

Another important contribution to our understanding of groups was the identification of the concept of groupthink by Janis (1972). Groupthink is believed to occur when group members' motivation for unanimity and agreement overrides their evaluation of the risks and benefits of alternative choices. Janis was able to demonstrate real-life policy-making groups making poor choices. He cited the highly visible example of US foreign policy fiascos such as that of the Bay of Pigs in the 1960s. The symptoms of groupthink identified by Janis were: the illusion of invulnerability, assumptions of morality, rationalisations, stereotyping, self-censorship, illusions of unanimity, mind-guarding and direct pressure. The concept still appears relevant today when analysing irrational senior management team decisions in teams composed of apparently able and rational individual senior managers.

Groups in going through a continual state of activity and change are dynamic (Bowditch and Buono, 2005: 150). An influential contribution to our understanding of group development was Tuckman (1965). Tuckman proposed that permanent groups go through four stages of development, which he described as forming, storming, norming and performing. In the case of temporary groups there was believed to be a fifth stage: adjournment.

Finally, Brooks (1999: 89) describes Belbin's team role categorisation as probably the most popular team categorisation. Belbin (1981) was interested in team roles in terms of making an effective team. He identified nine roles that required to be fulfilled in an effective team: co-ordinator, shaper, 'plant', monitor/evaluator, implementer, teamworker, resource investigator, completer/finisher and technical specialist.

Group- and team-based responses to change

The responses of groups and teams to change will vary depending upon many factors such as the classification of the change, the type of organisation and the members of the group or team. Group and team responses to change are discussed here in terms of how groups and teams may resist change, how groups and teams shape norms about change, and how groups and teams may encourage involvement and participation.

The previous chapter highlighted debates about resistance to change. Coghlan (1994: 18), however, warns that focusing upon individual resistance to change may be deficient in that individuals are dealt with in isolation from the groups with which they identify. This warning is taken further by Thompson and McHugh (2002: 330), who acknowledge that groups are sites of resistance and bearers of sectional and cultural interests. This observation has reinforced the conception of groups as conveyors and communicators of oppositional values.

The following forms of group-based resistance illustrate such views (Burke, 2002: 103):

- turf protection and competition: this is the group fighting for survival
- closing ranks: this may be paraphrased as 'one for all and all for one'
- changing allegiances and/or ownership: the wish to depart from the parent organisation in some way
- the demand for new leadership: seeking to replace the leader.

Norms arising in groups exert a considerable unacknowledged influence upon individuals, particularly in terms of how groups and teams respond to change. Norms can be prescriptive, suggesting what behaviours should occur, or proscriptive, suggesting behaviours that should not occur (Furnham, 1997: 441). One of the many contributions Lewin (1951) made to understanding organisational change was to link the concepts of norms and change as part of his field theory. Burnes (2004a: 480) in an important reappraisal of Lewin's work highlights the centrality of groups in change processes:

> *[Lewin] demonstrated that the most effective method of convincing people to change their behaviour was by providing groups with information for them to evaluate and discuss, and letting the group come to its own decision. Once the decision had been made by the group, it exerted a strong pressure on all the individuals concerned to adhere to the group's decision.*

The pioneering work of Lewin was to become the catalyst for the group dynamics school, which emphasised the influence of the role of groups in change. As Cummings (2004: 34) notes, groups exert pressure on members to conform to group norms. Changing individual behaviour can be extremely difficult, because group members may resist organisational changes that run counter to group norms and expectations. In this discussion the idea of change management as managing group norms becomes evident. Burnes (2004b: 986) effectively clarifies why Lewin advocated the often derided 'refreezing' element of his three step model. 'Lewin saw successful change as a group activity, because unless group norms and routines are also transformed, changes to individual behaviour will not be sustained.' This appears to be an important clarification of a frequently misunderstood concept. It is unfortunate that general interest in field theory waned with Lewin's death (Burnes, 2004b: 982) – an appreciation of field theory contributes considerably to the integrated system that Lewin was proposing.

Therefore, individual behaviour is a function of the group environment or 'field', as he termed it. Consequently, any changes in behaviour stem from changes, be they small or large, in the forces within the field.

(Lewin, 1947)

Burke (2002) highlights the work of Argyris (1971) on changing values through groups, and the work of Bion (1961) who focused upon the 'collective unconscious' of the group, as further potential avenues.

Another way groups and teams may respond to change is through becoming involved in and participating in larger change initiatives. The belief here is that work units through being involved in helping to plan and implement change are more likely to embrace than to resist an organisational change (Burke, 2002: 103). Change management may be aided through the involvement of groups and teams in change processes at various stages of a change initiative:

Greater involvement in change might be achieved by encouraging work group leaders to take greater ownership of the change, and allowing work groups to have more control over the means through which a change is implemented.

(Griffin et al, 2004: 568).

Cummings (2004: 34) believes that 'when group members are involved in making decisions about what changes are most appropriate to their situation, their interests are likely to be taken into account in those changes.' However, in terms of power (discussed in Chapter 12), involvement may range from shaping changes to merely attending a meeting at which changes are explained and questions fielded. The problem is that senior management may seriously involve groups in change management processes or employ the rhetoric (discussed in Chapter 14) of involving groups in change processes. King and Anderson (2002: 196) cite the research of Coch and French (1948) in a pyjama factory involving one group of workers who attended a series of planned group meetings around a change and another group who were purposely excluded. Understandably, they found that the group involved in group meetings exhibited less resistance than the excluded group.

In summary, this discussion has suggested that groups may respond to change in terms of resistance, and that such responses may be influenced through the existence of powerful unwritten group norms. However, it is believed that such norms may be more positively influenced through the active involvement and participation of groups in changes.

RESEARCH CASES IN JOURNALS NO.8 – BETA CO.

The case study of Beta Co. is referred to here because the authors gained access to the workings of a senior management team. Many of the issues raised in this case study are, however, equally relevant to the discussion about organisational learning in Chapter 15. Beta Co. represents a pseudonym for a global publishing business which was described as having a reasonably secure short-term future but a highly uncertain longer-term future. The authors focused their qualitative research upon the senior management team including the chief executive officer. They were working with the senior management team and facilitating the use of scenario-planning techniques and related procedures. The authors admit that their attempts were largely unsuccessful. But they offer extensive discussions of their interactions with the senior management team and use theories to explain the defensive avoidance strategies at work. They argue that the reality of a team faced with an uncertain future proved too stressful for the team members, giving rise to a variety of coping strategies.

Sector: Publishing
Research methods: Multiple methods including interviews and workshop activities.
Authors: Hodgkinson, G. P. and Wright, G.
Paper title: Confronting strategic inertia in a top management team: learning from failure
Journal details: *Organization Studies*, Vol.23, No.6, 2002; pp.949–77

Changing organisations through groups and teams

Despite the existence of a large body of change management literature, this literature has not provided any lasting answers (Dawson, 2003: 11). However, literature relating to groups and teams in general is far more established. Literature cited earlier may be drawn upon to further understand change in terms of norms, stages of group development, groupthink and effective teams. The work of Lewin and the wider group dynamics school offered an approach to change management which acknowledges the importance of group norms in change processes. As for the practical application of Lewin's work, Burke (2002: 159) describes the process focus of a Lewinian intervention as follows:

> *(a) changing group norms, (b) reducing restraining forces instead of increasing driving forces (the latter increases resistance, after all), and (c) increasing owned forces and decreasing imposed forces.*

The Tuckman (1965) model may inform change management. When using groups as a medium and target of change, there is a need for attention to forming and maintaining groups in order to enable them to function effectively (Coghlan, 1994: 21). The formation of a group is a dynamic process which has similarities to the dynamic processes of organisational change.

Groupthink (Janis, 1972) offers an explanation for apparently irrational senior management change decisions. In essence, employee resistance may be a rational response to poor decision-making by senior managers, although ironically, the resistance of employees is often depicted as irrational.

The work of Belbin (1981) offers prescriptions on how to create the most effective change management teams for particular change initiatives. West *et al* (2004: 269) have advocated change through the development of innovative teams: 'In order to manage and implement change we therefore need to understand how to develop innovative teams.' They draw upon research and theory in order to prescribe 12 steps to successfully managing change through teams. These steps include ensuring that the team task is intrinsically motivating, selecting a team of innovative people, providing organisational rewards for innovation, and creating a learning and development climate in the organisation.

A change team may be formed specifically to facilitate a change process. However, major generic change initiatives such as the learning organisation, TQM and BPR place emphasis upon teamwork. Cameron and Green (2004: 55) have defined a change team as 'often formed within organisations when a planned or unplanned change of significant proportions is necessary'. As well as the benefits of groups' potentially shaping norms, there is a pragmatism to the promotion of groups and change. Galpin (1996: 17) offers very practical guidance on establishing teams as part of a change effort, in particular emphasising the need to get the team infrastructure right.

Finally, rather than forming a change team, changing an existing team as a means of facilitating change may be an option. Burke (2002: 104) in his discussion of group responses to change suggests that 'there is always the option to change the group itself as a means of facilitating change...'

CRITICAL PERSPECTIVE

The following critical perspective on groups and teams and change management is organised around three challenges:

- group-level analysis may be emphasised at the expense of individual-level analysis
- there is hyperbole about the benefits of groups and teams in organisations
- the concept of self-managed teams may be critically questioned.

The following discussion elaborates upon each of these challenges.

Group-level analysis versus individual-level analysis

This textbook has emphasised the need for individuals to change as part of organisational change. However, the dilemma highlighted in this chapter is that groups both formal and informal are an integral part of organisations, raising questions about the most appropriate level of analysis and intervention – group or individual or both? Lewin made a convincing case, cited earlier in this chapter, for changing individuals through groups, acknowledging the ways in which groups shape norms of individuals about change.

In assessing the significance of group-level analysis it is informative to look at the historical origins of group-level analysis in psychology. Rose (1989: 40) documents how experiences of the World Wars shaped psychological research and theorising about groups. 'Crucially, the role of the individual was increasingly viewed from the perspective of a larger entity – the group.' War provided both the impetus to research group processes and the means by which real groups could be researched. Rose (1989: 44) notes that behaviour during combat appeared to relate to bonds between the soldier and his buddies, rather than to the unreal and distant principles and causes of war. These insights are useful in contextualising the body of management and organisational behavioural work that has developed in relation to groups.

> *The concept of the group was to become the organising principle of psychological and psychiatric thought concerning the conduct of the individual... The invention of the 'group', the conception of 'social' or 'human' relations as key determinants of individual conduct, were the most consistent lessons of the psychological and psychiatric experience of war.*
>
> *(Rose, 1989: 48)*

The writings of Rose help to explain the fetish of strategists for employing war metaphors to understand management and organisational behaviour. Also, debates about the semantics of resistance to change appear more understandable when explained in terms of groups at war. 'The problems of economic reconstruction would insert these issues of the group into the heart of economic debate, managerial practice and psychological innovation' (Rose, 1989: 52). Since World War II, individuals have increasingly been understood in relation to the groups to which they belong.

This may be regarded as a more sophisticated/contextualised approach to understanding individuals. However, the concern is that we begin to lose sight of individuals when the unit of analysis becomes the group. Also, the reification of the group as a manageable thing suffers from deficiencies similar to the reification of organisations as manageable things.

Burnes (2004a: 261) has identified three schools of thought which form central planks on which change management theory stands: the individual perspective school, the group dynamics school and the open systems school. Each of these schools of thought may be regarded as in competition yet simultaneously complementary. In terms of the theme of this discussion, the emphasis placed upon group-level change will be very much dependent upon which school of thought is favoured. Group dynamics offer important explanations of change processes, but not the only explanations.

> *Understanding change – how it works and how it does not – involves an understanding of how individuals react to change and how groups and teams function and deal with change.*
>
> *(Coghlan, 1994: 22)*

This discussion suggests that change can be explained exclusively in terms of neither individuals nor groups – both elements are important ingredients in developing a more comprehensive understanding of change management.

The downside of groups and teams

There is an almost evangelical feel to the groups and teams literature, implying that anyone who is not part of a group is in some way deviant. This chapter has highlighted the advantages arising out of group- and team-based change. However, inevitably, there are disadvantages to working in groups and teams. Potential disadvantages are the problematic nature of teamworking, social loafing, de-individuation and inter-group conflict.

In a polemical yet practical critique of teamwork, Robbins and Finley (1998: 21) shared their concerns. 'Despite human beings' attraction to belonging to a team, we are not willing to uproot our individual lives and priorities for the sake of some lousy workgroup.' Robbins and Finley (1998) explain why they believe teams do not work. Among the problems identified are mismatched needs, unresolved roles, personality conflicts and bad leadership. They believe there is no one single reason why teams do not work.

There is considerable research evidence to suggest that groups and teams may make a positive contribution to organisations. However, the concept of social loafing is often cited as an example of the potentially negative side of group work which appears particularly pertinent to the practical challenges of change management. Bowditch and Buono (2005: 149) describe social loafing in the following terms:

> *The tendency toward diminished performance in groups appears to be a universal phenomenon. It has been observed in a variety of groups working on an array of*

*different tasks, among both males and females, across people of all ages and in
many different cultures.*

The phenomenon is different from a reluctance to participate due to shyness or discomfort.
Ringelmann, a German psychologist, identified social loafing 80 years ago at a time when
organisational change was less prevalent.

As well as social loafing, groups may encourage de-individuation. Buchanan and Huczynski
(2004: 377) have defined this concept as follows.

> *De-individuation refers to a person's loss of self-awareness and self-monitoring. It
> involves some loss of personal identity and greater identification with the group.*

In terms of change management, social loafing and de-individuation – as potentially negative
responses to the change management concerns of this textbook – appear pertinent.

Much of the previous discussion has chosen to consider groups and teams in isolation from
the larger organisation. However, it is likely that groups will interact with each other, which
may potentially be a source of inter-group conflict. Such conflict may take the form of
disagreements or differences between groups rather than within groups. Daft (1995: 446)
identifies three ingredients required for inter-group conflict as: group identification, observable
group differences, and frustration. Daft notes that such conflict can occur vertically and
horizontally in terms of the organisational hierarchy. The negative consequences of conflict
include: diversion of energy, altered judgement, loser effects and poor co-ordination (Daft,
1995: 460). Coghlan (1994: 20) relates what he refers to as inter-team conflict to change
processes:

> *A change process frequently involves inter-team conflict in organisational settings
> where change is promoted by a management/administration group and those
> affected by the change feel apart from that group and oppose the change.*

In the concept of inter-group conflict it is possible to see how a group intended to facilitate the
process of change becomes a source of resistance to change. In terms of this discussion of
the downside of groups and teams it is worthwhile acknowledging that 'whether teams help or
hinder change at the organisational and personal level depends on a number of factors'
(Graetz *et al*, 2002: 309).

Critically reviewing the concept of self-managed teams

West *et al* (2004: 270) believe that 'teamworking offers a powerful strategy for managing
organisational change.' Team-based change initiatives in organisations are many and varied
and may be a component of larger change management initiatives such as total quality
management, business process re-engineering and the learning organisation. This review will
focus upon self-managed teams (sometimes referred to as self-managed work teams). Iles
and Sutherland (2001: 55) define self-managed teams as follows:

> *In this approach, teams are responsible, and collectively accountable, for
> performance and monitoring of one or more tasks (often an entire product or
> service) and managing interpersonal processes within the team.*

Burke (2002: 100) believes that there will have to be more reliance on self-directed groups
now and in the future. These groups encourage individuals to manage themselves both

individually and as part of the group. As part of their review of organisational change for health care managers, professionals and researchers, Iles and Sutherland (2001: 55) evaluated the evidence relating to self-managed teams. They cite the research of Cummings and Molloy (1977) and Pearce and Ravlin (1987), highlighting improvements arising out of the introduction of self-managed teams. Beekun (1989) and Macy, Bliese and Norton (1994) were conversely more circumspect in their evaluations of self-managed teams. Salem, Lazarus and Cullen (1994) identify both advantages and disadvantages of self-managed teams. Potential advantages include reduced absenteeism, increased productivity and a decreased need for managers, whereas potential disadvantages were difficulties in rescinding the system once established and varying levels and degrees of resistance. Elmuti (1997), in his paper reviewing the case for and against self-managed teams, is able to draw some relevant conclusions. In particular, he draws comparisons with empowerment in that self-managed teams require senior management to fully and tangibly support the teams. Overall, Elmuti believes that they can make a positive contribution to organisations.

SYNOPSIS

The literature often treats groups and teams as indistinguishable, despite the existence of crucial differences. Bowditch and Buono defined a group as consisting of two or more people who are psychologically aware of each other and who interact to fulfil a common goal. Classifications of groups included primary versus secondary, formal versus informal, and permanent versus temporary groups. Major contributions to understanding groups and teams included the writings of Asch on group norms, Tuckman on stages of group development, Janis on groupthink, and Belbin on team roles.

Responses of groups and teams to change varied depending upon factors such as the classification of the change, the type of organisation and the norms. Groups exerted a considerable unacknowledged influence upon individuals: Lewin linked the concept of norms with change as part of his field theory.

The work of Lewin and the wider group dynamics school offered an approach to change management which acknowledged the importance of group norms in change processes. Subsequently, organisation development has placed emphasis upon groups.

The experiences of the World Wars shaped psychological research and theorising about groups. The invention of the 'group' was the most consistent lesson of the psychological and psychiatric experience of war. The concern was that we begin to lose sight of individuals when the unit of analysis becomes the group. Also, the reification of the group as a manageable thing suffers from deficiencies similar to the reification of organisations as manageable things.

There was an almost evangelical feel to the groups and teams literature. Potential disadvantages of groups and teams were the problematic nature of teamworking, social loafing, de-individuation and inter-group conflict.

Evaluation focused upon self-managed teams. Salem, Lazarus and Cullen described both advantages and disadvantages of self-managed teams. Potential advantages included reduced absenteeism, increased productivity and a decreased need for managers, whereas potential disadvantages were difficulties in rescinding the system once established and varying levels and degrees of resistance.

DISCUSSION QUESTIONS

1 Why do writers attempt to differentiate between groups and teams, and does such differentiation help or hinder the study of change management?

2 What influences individuals to behave differently in groups from when they are on their own?

3 What is the main pragmatic advantage of managing change though groups rather than through individuals?

4 If the experiences of the World Wars had not shaped the study of groups, how might understanding of groups have been different?

5 Why are groups and teams popular with individuals working in organisations?

6 Do you believe groups and teams will play a greater or a lesser role in change management in the future?

Case study – All change in the technical support team

A total of 250 people work at the head office of the Mighty Lemon Drop Company (MLDC). The head office covers all the functional areas of the business such as personnel, marketing and finance, and has been located on the same site for the last 30 years. It has something of a hierarchical feel to it, with the more senior staff located at higher levels in the multistorey building. The technical support team are located in the basement of the building. In their large artificially lit rooms there are many metal shelves on which computers and parts are stacked neatly. The rooms have also been personalised with old chairs and equipment salvaged from the building over the years, and unlike the rest of the building there are many inappropriate posters.

The technical support team provide day-to-day technical support for the whole head office. The workload of the team has increased over the years reflecting the increasing workplace emphasis upon IT, although more strategic large-scale IT projects have been subcontracted to external providers. The members of the team used to be Alf, Bill, Jane and Ted. Bill was the team leader and was referred to as Head Technician. Jane's specialism was software problems, whereas Ted's specialism was hardware problems. Alf was part of the team, although he had no real interest in IT and so would deal with more DIY-oriented technical matters – it was privately acknowledged that he was working his time until retirement in two years. They were known as the TT team, although nobody could remember why. As a team the four of them had been together for five years and had become quite close over that time.

Apart from software and hardware upgrades which they instigated, they tended to be fairly reactive in how they operated. A wide range of head office staff would contact them through a range of communication channels and in a variety of emotional states. A member of the TT team would then go and sort out the problem as best he or she could.

Bill tended to have good days and bad days. Unfortunately, most days were bad days. He was responsible for checking that requests for assistance were dealt with promptly, but he did not take this responsibility very seriously. He was very capable and would help a small number of staff in the head office who he had got to know well over the years. The rest of the time he could be found slumped in his armchair smoking – which was strictly against MLDC policy – and staring into space. Other team members over time had begun to follow this example. The team were even once disciplined for drinking at work, which was also against company policy. Despite these problems effective technical support was provided, although in a very reluctant and reactive manner.

It was the early retirement of Alf on health grounds that presented senior management with an opportunity for change. They were due to introduce an intranet for company communications, and although the development work would be sub-contracted, they wanted the intranet to be run and maintained in-house. Also, they wanted to shake up the technical support function but were aware that lax ways of working had become deeply ingrained.

They used the spare staff establishment post to appoint Felicity. She was not to report to Bill but to report directly to the head of the personnel department. She took over one of the other rooms in the basement. These new arrangements were communicated to the TT team who, although they were initially annoyed, claimed not to care.

There were elements of Felicity's role that were not disclosed to the TT team. Primarily, she represented the new model of IT support – she had an extensive budget and postgraduate qualifications in IT. Her office was refurbished to a high standard, sharing the same corporate livery as the other offices in the building. On the door there was a bold metallic sign proclaiming IT solutions with the slogan underneath 'Here to help'. She was careful to define her role in terms of the newly introduced intranet site. However, more subversively, she began placing practical guides to IT problems onto the intranet. She also established message boards which encouraged people to anonymously post discussions about their IT problems. It was not long before the whole company was reading posts about 'the dreary people who live in the dungeon.' In her role as moderator she would then ask TT team members if they wanted these offensive messages removing.

Over time things began to change in the basement. Jane spent more and more time with Felicity in the IT solutions office and asked if there was any way she could be seconded into the office. Bill left MLDC to study philosophy as a full-time student. When Ted and Jane requested that their office be refurbished, it was suggested that this might be the opportunity to rededicate the whole of the basement to the challenges of IT solutions.

Case study questions

1   In what ways does the TT team meet the criteria of a team?

2   How could the concept of group norms be used to describe the behaviours of the TT team before the arrival of Felicity?

3   How could the concept of group norms be used to describe the behaviours of the TT team after the arrival of Felicity?

4   In what alternative ways could the introduction of the intranet have been managed?

FURTHER READING

Coghlan D. (1994) Managing organisational change through teams and groups, *Leadership and Organization Development Journal*, Vol.15, No.2; pp.18–23.

Although now dated, Coghlan offers an accessible account of debates relating to change through teams and groups. This journal paper provides the reader with references to classic literature in this area and encourages reflection upon the role of groups and teams in change processes, which is too often overlooked.

Buchanan D. and Huczynski A. (2004) *Organizational Behaviour: An introductory text*, 5th edition, Harlow, FT/Prentice Hall.

This particular reading has been chosen due to the emphasis the authors place upon the topic, devoting chapters to group formation, group structure, individuals in groups, and teamworking. These chapters offer relevant and accessible background reading for anyone interested in exploring groups and teams in greater detail.

Cameron E. and Green M. (2004) *Making Sense of Change Management: A complete guide to the models, tools and techniques of organizational change*, London, Kogan Page.

In this applied guide to change management a chapter is devoted to 'Team change'. The strength of this work is that it is very accessible, with many illustrations and an engaging narrative. The downside is that there is a frustrating absence of critical questioning of the theories offered.

King N. and Anderson N. (2002) *Managing Innovation and Change: A critical guide for organizations*, London, Thomson Learning.

King and Anderson devote a chapter to innovation and the social psychology of groups. The chapter is particularly strong in covering psychological theories of groups with special reference to innovation and change.

Leading change

CHAPTER 12

> ## LEARNING OBJECTIVES
>
> To:
>
> - clarify the meanings and theories of leadership
> - review explanations and prescriptions about leading change
> - explore the concept of transformational leadership
> - investigate the dangerous, dysfunctional and devious side of leadership
> - understand the ethical dimensions of leadership
> - critically consider relationships between power and change.

INTRODUCTION

The avoidance of change has been described as the opposite of leadership (Ahn *et al*, 2004: 113), which suggests a close association between leading and changing. There has been enormous interest in the role and significance of 'change leaders' over the last two decades (Caldwell, 2003: 285) that may largely be explained in terms of changes in the environment. Kotter (1996: 27) has provocatively suggested that there has been more academic emphasis upon management than on leadership because management is believed to be easier to teach than leadership. His strong message is that organisations in focusing upon managing change neglect leading change. This is certainly quantitatively apparent in terms of the volume of change management literature in comparison to the change leadership literature.

Leadership has been defined as 'the process of influence, usually by one person, whereby another individual or group is oriented toward setting and achieving certain goals' (Bowditch and Buono, 2005: 195). Ahn *et al* (2004: 112) in acknowledging the increased visibility of business leaders, suggest that we are witnessing a new form of social theatre in which the heroic leader is a central actor.

APPROACHES TO LEADING CHANGE

The following discussion clarifies what is meant by leadership. The main theoretical approaches to leadership are identified before the discussion focuses upon leading change and transformational leadership.

The meanings and theories of leadership

In beginning to understand the meanings of leadership, it is useful to consider a common differentiation between management and leadership. Ahn *et al* (2004: 114) differentiate between process-based management and prospective leadership. Similarly, Kotter (1996: 25) writes about management as 'a set of processes that can keep a complicated system of people and technology running smoothly', whereas 'leadership defines what the future should look like, aligns people with that vision and inspires them to make it happen despite the obstacles.' This differentiation is not purely semantic, as it can form the basis for differentiating between managing change and leading change (see, for example, Bruhn, 2004: 133). Kotter (1996: 26), a great advocate of leadership, uses this differentiation when he asserts that 'successful transformation is 70 to 90 per cent leadership and only 10 to 30 per cent management.'

The norm in management and organisational textbooks is to devote a chapter to the competing theories of leadership. The detail of these theories – which is well documented – will not be discussed here (see, for example, Buchanan and Huczynski, 2005; Mullins, 2005; and Thompson and McHugh, 2002, for effective overviews of the leadership literature). However, a brief summary of major approaches is pertinent to subsequent discussions of leading change.

Rickards (1999: 119) traces historical eras of leadership research in terms of early theories of leadership, modern trait theories, style/skill theories, situational or contingency theories and transformational and other new-leader theories. In a similar manner, Mullins (2005: 286) establishes a framework for studying managerial leadership, incorporating the different approaches listed in Box 14. Each approach is illustrated by means of a hypothetical comment by a change leader, signposted through the use of italics.

Qualities or traits approach *In my experience tall women are always the most effective leaders of change.*

The functional or group approach *A key element of leading change is facilitating teamworking.*

Leadership as a behavioural category *Assertiveness is an integral element of change leadership.*

Styles of leadership *My approach to leading change emphasises working with people.*

The situational approach and contingency models *Leading the accountants through change is a different proposition from leading the canteen staff through change.*

Transformational leadership *Every working day in every workplace interaction I promote the new vision of a new way of working together.*

Box 14 – Approaches to understanding leadership

There is no consensus in terms of the most effective theory of leadership. However, as with many theories of management and organisational behaviour, theories have evolved historically. That is not to say that earlier theories are not revisited – as, for example, reflected in recent interest in transformational leadership. The danger with this overview of the meaning of leadership is that it implies a certainty about our understanding of leadership which does not exist. Grint (2005: 1), a respected authority on leadership, while acknowledging the increase in leadership research, has written 'We have yet to establish what it is, never mind whether we can teach it or predict its importance.' He (2005: 1) identifies four quite different ways of understanding what leadership is:

- *person*: is it WHO 'leaders' are that makes them leaders?
- *result*: is it WHAT 'leaders' achieve that makes them leaders?

- *position*: is it WHERE 'leaders' operate that makes them leaders?
- *process*: is it HOW 'leaders' get things done that makes them leaders?

Although not as succinct as earlier definitions, this fourfold typology may prove to be more realistic.

Leading change

Caldwell (2003: 286) specifically attributes the resurgence of interest in change leadership since the early 1980s to the severe challenges in managing innovation and culture change faced by large US corporations. Special kinds of leadership are critical during times of strategic organisational change (Nadler and Tushman, 1990: 566). However, although strategic change and change leadership are closely associated, it is important to remember that leading change in essence will be concerned with influencing groups and individuals. Morrison (1994: 353) has argued that leaders of change need to understand people rather than change (see also Marshall and Conner, 2000, and Woodward and Hendry, 2004).

RESEARCH CASES IN JOURNALS NO.9 – PILKINGTON (AUSTRALASIA)

The author undertook qualitative research into change leadership in three organisations – Pilkington Australasia, Ford Plastics and Ericsson Australia. Pilkington was operating in an increasingly hostile environment. A team approach to the task of leading change was adopted, although the managing director was not directly involved in selling the need for change. At the time of writing the case study, it remained to be seen whether the lack of involvement of the managing director would be detrimental to transforming Pilkington.

Sector: Manufacturing
Research methods: Qualitative case based upon interviewing and documentary research.
Authors: Graetz, F.
Paper title: Strategic change leadership
Journal details: *Management Decision*, Vol.38, No.8, 2000; pp.550–62

Galpin (1996: 71) is typical of popular approaches to understanding change leadership, believing that effective leaders possess six attributes for leading change (creativity, team orientation, listening skills, coaching skills, accountability, and appreciativeness) and have the skills to apply them effectively to create significant and lasting change in their organisations. Despite their prevalence, these attribute-based approaches do not give significant acknowledgement to leading change in different situations and in terms of different contingencies. As Nadler and Tushman (1990: 564) warn, 'Different kinds of organisational changes will require very different kinds of leadership behaviour in initiating, energising and implementing the change.'

However, leading change is concerned with more than matching the leadership to the change and the situation. Woodward and Hendry (2004: 157) acknowledge the difficulties of defining and resolving all eventualities in organisations undergoing change. Commentators emphasise interaction with different environments as an integral element of leading change:

> *The task of discerning external change and translating that discernment into strategies for internal corporate change – in terms of evolving organisational structures, group culture, and styles of personal interaction – stand as one of the most enduring challenges of leadership.*
>
> *(Ahn et al, 2004: 121)*

In this quotation, the overlap between discussions about strategic change (discussed in Chapter 5) and leadership are very apparent. Despite the high profile of popular leadership literature, it is worthwhile seeking out more research-based literature in order to further understand this complex and contradictory topic. For example, Miller (2002: 368) believes that we can learn from what successful change leaders do and how they do it. Woodward and Hendry (2004: 175–6) undertook two descriptive surveys in order to examine leading and coping processes. They were able to suggest three ways in which change management skills may be enhanced. Those leading change must become more aware of their part in the change management process. People like to appear capable and competent in the workplace at all levels. Change leaders in adapting and coping with change may need support.

Caldwell (2003: 285) undertook research in order to establish whether change leaders and change managers' roles were different. The research was based upon a Delphi-style panel of ten change agent experts and enabled Caldwell to draw the following interesting conclusions. As might be expected, change leaders are perceived as executives or senior managers who envision, initiate or sponsor strategic change, whereas change managers are perceived as middle-level managers and functional specialists who carry forward and build support for change. Change leadership is about creating a vision of change, while change management is about translating the vision into agendas and actions. The two challenges are different, yet complementary (Caldwell, 2003: 291).

Although, Caldwell offers many thoughtful caveats about his research, the notion that change leaders and change managers are complementary is intriguing. Earlier in the chapter the concerns of Kotter about an over-emphasis upon management at the expense of leadership were expressed. However, in his conclusions Caldwell suggests that we need both change leadership and change management in order to effectively deliver change. Gill (2003: 310) cites the findings of an American Management Association (1994) survey. In the survey of 259 senior executives in Fortune 500 companies, the following keys to successful change were identified as important.

- leadership, 92 per cent
- corporate values, 84 per cent
- communication, 75 per cent
- team-building, 69 per cent, and
- education and training, 64 per cent.

It is unsurprising that a survey of senior executives found that leadership was viewed as the most important key to successful change. However, the survey does highlight the perceived centrality of leadership in terms of successful change.

Burke (2002: 271) offers thoughtful guidance on the leader's function and role during organisational change in terms of four phases: pre-launch, launch, post-launch, and sustaining the change. At the pre-launch phase, issues that arise include the leadership's establishing the need for change and providing clarity with regard to the vision. At the launch phase, the leadership communicate the need for change and deal with any resistance to change. At the post-launch phase, the type of issues leadership deal with relate to maintaining consistency and repeating the message. At the sustaining change phase, leadership will be dealing with unanticipated consequences and launching new initiatives. Graetz *et al* (2002: 227) describes how the work of Stace and Dunphy (2001) suggests different forms of change leadership dependent upon the scale of change. This may be summarised as follows:

- developmental transitions (constant change) – best led by hands-on people-centred coaches
- task-focused transitions (constant change) – best led by captains with a directive authoritative leadership style
- charismatic transformations (inspirational change) – best led by a charismatic leader able to rally support with his or her inspirational leadership style
- turnarounds (frame-breaking change) – best led by a commander who adopts a tough hard-nosed top-down directive approach.

A literature has developed around the almost mythical transformational leader, and the following discussion explores this aspect of leading change.

Transformational leadership

The idea of transformational leadership was first promoted by Burns (1978) and is best understood in terms of its differentiation from transactional leadership, although transformational leadership does build upon transactional leadership. Transactional leaders are believed to 'guide or motivate their followers in the direction of established goals by clarifying role and task requirements' (Robbins, 2005: 367). Whereas transformational leaders 'change followers' awareness of issues by helping them to look at old problems in new ways, they are able to excite, arouse, and inspire followers to put out extra effort to achieve group goals' (Robbins, 2005: 367). Influential work into transformational leadership has been undertaken by Bass and colleagues (see Bass and Avolio, 1994). Thompson and McHugh (2002: 272) believe that Bass in developing Burns' transformational model has brought back into the managerial literature on leadership the concept of charisma. Nadler and Tushman (1990: 566) describe the 'charismatic leader' as referring to

> *a special quality that enables the leader to mobilise and sustain activity within an organisation through specific personal actions combined with perceived personal characteristics.*

Three major types of behaviour characterise these leaders: envisioning, energising and enabling (Nadler and Tushman, 1990: 566). There is a potential downside to transformational leadership, which is discussed in the *Critical perspective* section.

CRITICAL PERSPECTIVE

The following critical perspective on leading change is organised around three challenges:

- change leaders may be dangerous, dysfunctional and devious
- change leaders may be unethical
- power remains implicit in orthodox accounts of change leadership.

The following discussion elaborates upon each of these challenges.

Leadership as dangerous, dysfunctional and devious

Conger (1990: 250) writes about the dark side of leadership which sometimes eclipses the bright side 'to the detriment of both the leader and the organisation'. In reviewing the literature on leadership there were frequent warnings about the problematical nature of leadership, suggesting an apparently fine line between heroic accounts of leaders and more troubling accounts of leaders as villains.

> *Despite good intentions, 'magic' leaders may become sufficiently captivated by their vision of what is best for the organisation that they unintentionally overlook internal and external signals that their vision might not be appropriate.*
> *(Bowditch and Buono, 2005: 225)*

The message is that within the mystery of charisma and creativity potentially lurks danger and even madness (Rickards, 1999: 126). Charisma has been identified as a quality of effective leaders (Graetz, 2000). However, Nadler and Tushman (1990: 567) identify the following potential problems with charismatic leaders: the creation of unrealistic expectations, the encouragement of either dependency or counter-dependency, an expectation that the magic associated with charisma will continue unabated, and the disenfranchisement of the next level of management.

Bowditch and Buono (2005: 225) warn about the explosive and unpredictable potential of charisma and how the ambiguities of organisational change may further the interests of narcissistic leaders. A famous study in this area was undertaken by Kets de Vries (1989), who highlighted dispositions of neurotic leaders – aggressive, paranoid, histrionic, detached, controlling, passive-aggressive, narcissistic, dependent and masochistic.

Major potential limitations of transformational leadership include misuse of power, ineffectiveness and unethical leadership practices (Weiss, 2001: 210). Tourish and Pinnington (2002: 157), writing with specific reference to transformational leadership and cults, state that 'If the leader succeeds in altering the psyches of the organisation's members, one person's vision (or delusion) becomes that of many.' In concluding their review of transformational leadership, Tourish and Pinnington (2002: 166) warn that transformational leadership theories 'have the potential to encourage authoritarian forms of organisation'.

Ethical dimensions of leadership

In leading change, leaders should set an example of ethical behaviour to their followers. The manner in which leaders function in positions of influence can contribute to the strengthening or the deterioration of the moral behaviour of members of an organisation (McEwan, 2001: 358). Gill (2003: 313) in his discussion of change leadership cites a Nepalese Buddhist mantra: 'Open your arms to change, but don't let go of your values.'

The hidden values in theories of leadership may be traced. Heifetz (1998: 345) argues that although the trait approach appears to be value-free, the values are simply hidden. Heifetz also highlights the values which inform the situational, contingency and transactional approaches to leadership. The terms 'business ethics' and 'moral leadership' may appear to be oxymorons (Gini, 1998: 360). However, McEwan (2001), in citing the characteristics of ethical leadership of Blanchard and Peale (1988), offers some hope. The five Ps of ethical leadership based on virtue theory are: pride, patience, prudence, persistence and perspective. An ethical change leader may require each of these characteristics.

Power and change

An understanding of power informs an understanding of leadership. Theorising about power has been informed by the disciplines of social theory and organisation theory. Although power seems a straightforward concept, defining the concept of power is more difficult than it first appears (Buchanan and Badham, 1999: 47). Power has been defined as the ability to influence various outcomes (Bowditch and Buono, 2005: 195). In this definition, the close relationship between leadership and power is apparent.

Hardy and Clegg (2004: 343) have critically reflected upon the relationship between power and change. They note the logic and inevitability of the use of power by management, given the high risk of change failure, often attributed to employee resistance. Similarly, Bradshaw and Boonstra (2004: 279) suggest that power in organisational change efforts has been recognised as important since the early 1970s, and that 'conceptual thinking about the relationship between the two has continued to evolve and been enriched by different underlying theoretical assumptions.'

Graetz *et al* (2002: 242–3) highlighted one approach in terms of how power bases identified by French and Raven (1959) may be used as part of change management. This is summarised in Box 15.

Reward power – Rewards are commonly used to purchase support and loyalty.
Coercive power – Lack of compliance is associated with suffering of some kind.
Referent power – Personal loyalties and friendship are used in manipulation.
Legitimate power – Change is presented as a necessary condition for success, which can be decided only by senior staff.
Expert power – Specialist knowledge is required to understand the relevance and appropriateness of change attempts.

Box 15 – Power bases (French and Raven) and change

Buchanan and Badham (1999: 56), in reviewing different conceptualisations of power, suggest three different but related concepts of:

- power as a property of individuals
- power as a property of relationships, and
- power as an embedded property.

In a similar manner, Bradshaw and Boonstra (2004: 279) conceptualise four fundamentally different perspectives of power, suggesting different approaches to organisational change. In Box 16, the essence of these four perspectives has been summarised.

Hardy and Clegg (2004: 360) warn that much of the organisational change management literature assists change management failure due to 'its lack of pragmatism about power'. As Bradshaw and Boonstra (2004: 279) suggest, 'Transformational change in organisations can be more fully understood and enabled through the simultaneous recognition of the tensions between different perspectives on power.' The argument here is that power merits greater recognition as an integral component of our understanding of change management, although once again this is not the orthodoxy.

> **Manifest – Personal power**
> Power explained in terms of person 'A' having more or less power than person 'B'
> **Manifest – Structural power**
> Power explained as resting in a position or location
> **Latent – Cultural power**
> Power explained as the creation and reproduction of largely latent or unconscious shared meanings
> **Latent – Personal power**
> Power explained in terms of how individuals limit themselves and unquestioningly obey

Box 16 – Bradshaw and Boonstra's perspectives on power

Empowerment has been viewed positively by some commentators: 'Empowered individuals have a sense of trust, energy, commitment, responsibility, and pride in their work...' (Weiss, 2001: 255). However, Hales (2000: 516) draws upon an extensive literature review, as well as his own empirical work, noting the increasingly documented divergence between the widespread rhetoric of empowerment and lack of evidence of substantively empowered workers.

SYNOPSIS

A common differentiation was between process-based management and prospective leadership. A problem identified was the voluminous, confusing and contradictory nature of the leadership literature. Rather than a single approach to leadership, there was a series of competing approaches, including the qualities or traits approach, the functional or group approach, leadership as a behavioural category, styles of leadership, the situational approach and contingency models, and transformational leadership.

Grint warned that in terms of leadership we have yet to establish what it is, never mind whether we can teach it or predict its importance.

Although strategic change and change leadership are closely associated, it was important to remember that leading change in essence will be concerned with leading people. Leading change was concerned with more than matching the leadership to the change and the situation. Woodward and Hendry suggested ways in which change management skills could be enhanced, noting that change leaders who have to adapt and cope with change may themselves need support.

A useful means of differentiation was by establishing whether change leaders' and change managers' roles were different.

Transformational leadership was best understood in terms of its differentiation from transactional leadership. Transactional leaders were believed to guide or motivate through the clarification of role and task requirements, whereas transformational leaders were believed to inspire followers. Influential research undertaken by Bass and colleagues was acknowledged.

The literature on leadership contained frequent warnings about the problematic nature of leadership. Potential problems with charismatic leaders included the creation of unrealistic expectations, the encouragement of dependency or counter-dependency, and people's becoming hesitant to disagree or come into conflict with the leader. Major potential limitations of transformational leadership included the misuse of power, ineffectiveness and unethical leadership practices.

Leaders were identified as making a contribution to the strengthening or the deterioration of the moral behaviour of members of an organisation.

Leadership was seen as value-laden. Despite scholars' choosing to study leadership as if it was value-free, hidden values were present in theories of leadership.

In order to understand leadership it was necessary to understand power. Bowditch and Buono defined power as the ability to influence various outcomes. French and Raven in an early study of power identified the following power bases: reward power, coercive power, referent power, legitimate power and expert power. In a more recent and sophisticated analysis, Bradshaw and Boonstra identified four perspectives on power: personal power (manifest), structural power (manifest), cultural power (latent), and personal power (latent).

DISCUSSION QUESTIONS

1 What is different about leading change and managing change?
2 Bruhn has suggested that leading change is more art than science and managing change more science than art – what are the implications of this view for understanding leadership?
3 What would potentially motivate senior management interest in the concept of transformational leadership?
4 Why might a 'good' leader turn 'bad'?
5 How can power inform a more sophisticated understanding of leading change?
6 Why does empowerment capture the imagination of both employees and managers?

Case study – Leading change in Crusty Bakeries

Crusty Bakeries Limited (CB Ltd) is one of the largest producers of bread and bread-based products in Britain. Despite fierce competition in the sector, CB Ltd products remains popular with customers and the company is also popular with institutional investors. The main operation is based in the Midlands, with satellite distribution centres radiating out from this operational hub. The Midlands site is huge and as well as producing bakery products is the location for the head office.

Jayne County as head of human resources is responsible for running the senior manager development programme. One element of her role has been to develop operational managers with a view to their subsequently joining the senior management team that runs CB Ltd. She has drawn up a short list of three potential candidates for the next place on the highly coveted senior manager development programme. Her private summary notes about each manager read as follows.

Pete Wylie (Transport manager)

Pete has progressed from driving delivery vans to a highly influential position in CB Ltd. As transport manager he is responsible for ensuring that products are delivered daily over a wide geographical area. If anything goes wrong, it is very evident very quickly. He runs the operation like clockwork – which is not always how it was before he took over. There was an element of risk in his initial appointment in that he was one of very few managers not to have a university qualification. However, at the appointment interviews five years ago the other graduate candidates were perceived as being rather 'green'. The role required a manager who could deal effectively with confrontation. Pete appears to thrive on confrontation – in his regular dealings with the wagon drivers much of his communications have been non-verbal. He has a huge physical frame and when he becomes annoyed he tends to clench his fists. Occasionally, when he feels a wagon driver has been shirking he asks the driver for his keys and drives the wagon himself, even if this means driving many hundreds of miles. These stories of Pete's trips have become folklore in the depot – yet the most frequently-told story relates to Project Shake.

Pete has always used his 'thick wagon driver' reputation to good effect. Those who know him well – and that is a relatively small grouping – know he is extremely intelligent and has a natural ability for logistics. He rapidly transformed the transport department and this was recognised. However, everything almost came unstuck when the petrol companies experienced a series of strikes centred upon major oil terminals. In a short space of time television news stories started featuring pictures of empty supermarket shelves. However, throughout the dispute CB Ltd products were distributed as normal. It was a long time before it finally emerged that Pete had been warned about the strikes by a friend who drove the tankers, which had enabled him to stockpile fuel at a local aircraft base. Project Shake would have caused the transport department to go into deficit if the strike had not then taken place, but as it turned out it allowed CB Ltd to gain competitive advantage over major competitors.

Kevin Coyne (Research and development manager)

Kevin is usually seen wearing his lab coat and spectacles. Kevin gained his PhD in America and appears to enjoy leading a team of scientists. They work on a surprisingly wide range of products with customers' health and safety of paramount importance. Kevin facilitates the weekly 'coffee club' meetings at which he updates colleagues on developments and encourages them to air any grievances. The grievances are few and far between. Most of the scientists joined because of Kevin's reputation for innovation amongst the scientific community. Kevin hates administration and bureaucracy and has delegated all this work to a very capable assistant. He is not popular with senior management because of his failure to attend the monthly management meetings. However, he rarely leaves the labs and has been known to work 24-hour days, driven solely by his fascination with science.

A few months ago he took eight of the top scientists out to a local pub and treated them all to a ploughman's lunch. At this lunch he made the 'Dog and Duck challenge', to the effect that in 12 months' time they would return to the pub again, but that then there would be half the salt there currently was in the bread rolls. This dramatic challenge caught the imagination of the fairly staid scientists, and great advances have already been made towards meeting this goal.

Mark Smith (Senior management accountant)

Mr Smith is the longest-serving member of staff of the three short-listed candidates. He is a professionally-qualified management accountant who provides financial and other information for management within CB Ltd which may be used for planning, control and decision-making purposes. He runs the management accounting department very efficiently, requiring all staff to adhere to strict (some might say overly formal) dress codes. He also insists that all staff sign in and sign out each day. These idiosyncratic requirements have caused conflict with the human resource department, but Mr Smith has remained steadfast in demanding adherence to his standards.

He claims to champion the development of younger people, but there is a suspicion that he prefers less qualified staff because this maintains the gap between his and their levels of expertise. His expertise is considerable, and his financial knowledge is trusted and appreciated in CB Ltd. However, his own department suffers from a high turnover of staff and he is referred to behind his back as 'Dr Death'. He has a public persona of being charming yet a tendency to be cruel to people. This is most tangible when he gathers budgetary information. He often uses this exercise to humiliate other managers, particularly in his references to how they are perceived by the senior management team.

In recent months he has again come into conflict with the personnel department. In analysing his spreadsheets he identified labour costs as being a significant outgoing in many departments. He has proposed to senior management that more agency staff are appointed on different terms and conditions as a means of lowering labour costs. He has additionally tabled a paper suggesting a reduction in pension benefits for new staff.

Case study questions

1 In respect of the three candidates, is it possible to differentiate between their work in terms of their roles as managers and leaders?
2 Explain the leadership of each manager in terms of the person, result, position and process, as described by Grint.
3 Explain the actions of each leader in terms of power.

FURTHER READING

BRADSHAW P. and BOONSTRA J. (2004) Power dynamics in organizational change: a multi-perspective approach, in J. J. BOONSTRA (ed.) *Dynamics of Organizational Change and Learning*, Chichester, John Wiley & Sons.

The Bradshaw and Boonstra chapter is located in a comprehensive book of change readings edited by Boonstra. The chapter benefits from being rigorously researched in order to advance a critical perspective. Although the chapter is quite complex, it is particularly recommended for its treatment of power with regard to change.

BUCHANAN D. and BADHAM R. (1999) *Power, Politics and Organizational Change: Winning the turf game*, London, Sage Publications.

Although intuitively you would imagine a large quantity of literature that would relate organisational change to power and politics, serious discussions of the relationships between these concepts are limited in number. Buchanan and Badham are frequently cited by academics studying and researching change. This book benefits from drawing upon relevant social theory yet also contains many illustrations of the exercise of power and politics in the workplace.

GRINT K. (2005) *Leadership: Limits and possibilities*, Houndmills, Palgrave Macmillan.

This book is recommended for anyone familiar with general textbook discussions of leadership who wants to read more deeply on the subject. Through drawing upon social theory, Grint encourages new ways of understanding leadership.

HICKMAN G. R. (ed.) (1998) *Leading Organizations: Perspectives for a new era*, Thousand Oaks, California, Sage Publications.

This reader on leadership has contributions from more than 50 authors. Although some contributions are taken from business magazines rather than academic journals, the strengths of the book are the diversity of perspectives on leadership and the way the book encourages reflection upon the processes of leadership.

Communicating change

LEARNING OBJECTIVES

To:

- understand organisational communications in terms of processes, content and barriers

- understand change communications in terms of processes, content and barriers

- consider the rhetoric of change communications

- introduce the concept of organisational silence.

INTRODUCTION

It is easy to take communication for granted due to its prevalence and relevance to organisational life. As Clegg *et al* (2005) suggest, organisations are first and foremost communicating entities. Communication may play an integral role in change management, some commentators going as far as to suggest that 'without effective employee communication, change is impossible and change management fails' (Barrett, 2002: 219). Despite the centrality – or possibly because of the centrality – of communication, the field of study tends to be highly applied, with an emphasis upon the practicalities of communicating at the expense of empirical work (Goodman and Truss, 2004: 218). Communication may be defined as 'the transference and understanding of meaning' (Robbins, 2005: 299). The pilot research of Daly *et al* (2003: 157) illustrates the type of change management programmes being communicated:

- the integration of an acquired company
- being acquired as a company
- the introduction of new technologies, and
- organisational re-engineering.

Each of these change management programmes is unique, and the 'it depends' maxim is particularly applicable to change communications. Quirke (1995: 87) has suggested that change communications strategy will be dependent upon the type of change, the degree of urgency, the speed of change, and reactions to the change. However, as Balogun and Hope Hailey (2004: 181) state, in change situations:

The question everyone wants an answer to is, what is going to happen to me?

Although this question appears crass, it is likely to be the norm and may relate to a human desire for self-preservation in the face of adversity. The question signposts the need to consider not just sending messages but also receiving messages. Against the potential backdrop of greater job insecurity, the end of jobs for life and a proliferation of change initiatives, this question becomes increasingly relevant. The contemporary challenge for corporate communications is to motivate employees 'who have priorities vastly different from the priorities of the company' (Goodman, 2001: 122). This has been expressed more profoundly by Finstad (1998: 717), who encourages members of an organisation to examine the existential questions:

Who are we, what do we want, and where are we going?

These questions suggest that change communications are never as neutral as functional explanations of communications may imply. This chapter focuses upon internal organisational communications and how changes are communicated within organisations. It is acknowledged that organisations are involved in communicating changes with many other groups – for example, customers or clients, shareholders and government agencies. (Ihator, 2004, offers an interesting historical perspective on corporate communications with groups external to the organisation.)

The *Approaches* section of the chapter is organised around communication processes, communication content and communication barriers. In the *Critical perspective* section the rhetoric of change, as well as the concept of organisational silence, are discussed.

APPROACHES TO CHANGE COMMUNICATIONS

This section is organised around three communication concepts: processes, content and barriers. Although in organisations these concepts are unlikely to be so neatly compartmentalised, in terms of understanding it is helpful to consider each concept separately. Each concept is introduced in terms of organisational communication in general before moving to change communications in particular.

Any specific quantification of communications with employees is suspect. However, Kotter (1996: 89) has calculated 'the total amount of communication going to an employee in three months = 2,300,000 words or numbers.' Every individual and every organisation has to communicate in order to progress, which may explain why change and communication are often closely related. Manning (1992: 4) offers an eloquent argument for studying communication:

Communication – ambiguous, paradoxical, and equivocal – should be seen as a defining feature of human beings, and an appreciation of its vagaries a valuable step toward a sensitivity to the diversity and sensibilities of people.

In this quotation, Manning is suggesting that although the study of communication may be problematical, it is integral to understanding individuals. Communications are integral to organisations – ranging from communicating a choice of meal in the canteen to one person to attempting to communicate the strategic plan to a whole organisation. Understanding organisational communications has to acknowledge the diversity of contexts as well as the breadth of communication choices. The internal and external context of organisational communications has to be understood (see discussion of context in Chapter 4).

Communication processes

Aspects of organisational functioning for which effective communication is regarded as crucial are co-ordination, control and human factors (Rollinson, 2005: 577). Organisational communications are often understood in terms of communication channels and/or communication networks. The 'grapevine' is a well-known informal communication network (McKenna, 2000: 168). However, in terms of formal communication networks, the wheel, Y, chain, circle and all channel networks have all been highlighted.

Communications can flow vertically or laterally – 'vertical' communications are classified as either upward or downward communications (Robbins, 2005: 301). Hayes (2002: 116) summarises the main communication channels as: written communication via hard copy, electronic communication via email, video conferencing, telephone, face-to-face communication on a one–to-one, one-to-group or group-to-group basis.

Hayes (2002: 114) regards the management of change as often a top-down process. He acknowledges nonetheless that senior management do receive upward communication that provides information 'in order to clarify the need for change, and develop and implement a change programme'. A range of questions emerge, such as when to communicate change. Guidelines on the timing of change communications with employees may be summarised as follows (Balogun and Hope Hailey, 2004: 173):

- Employees prefer hearing about change from management rather than as rumour.
- Early communications allow employees time to understand and adjust.
- Employees prefer honest and even incomplete announcements to cover-ups.
- Employees learn about changes despite policies of silence.

Another question relates to the perceived importance of communications in change management. The CIPD (2004) Organising for Success research programme offered useful empirical insights into the centrality of communications skills in the context of reorganisation. The skills of a reorganising team seen as major enablers of success were ranked as follows (the figures represent the percentages of reorganisations):

- skills in people management, 71 per cent
- communication skills, 68 per cent
- skills in managing organisational culture, 55 per cent.

These findings suggest that communications are perceived as an important aspect of change management within organisations. Quirke (1995: 125) uses the metaphor of a communication escalator when communicating change. The degree of change and the degree of involvement determine which of the following steps is most appropriate: awareness, understanding, support, involvement or commitment. These steps may be matched to different employees – for example, agents and suppliers may require awareness of a change whereas the sales force and customer service staff may require involvement in a change. Similarly, different communication channels may be utilised – for example, a newsletter may generate awareness about a change whereas a team meeting may create involvement in a change.

The communication of a major change provides an 'MoT' for organisational communication processes: 'Companies cannot afford not to improve the current communication practices if they find them lacking' (Barrett, 2002: 222). Although not empirically tested or supported, this is an interesting proposition. A failure to effectively communicate a change may reflect a failure of the broader organisational communication processes. Barrett (2002: 224) advocates an assessment of current communication practices as a necessary precursor to communicating a major change.

One dilemma in much of this discussion is the assumption that change is planned rather than emergent, with the implication that planned change requires planned communications. However, the existence of emergent change challenges traditional emphasis upon planned change approaches to communicating change.

Communication content

Goodman and Truss (2004: 219) offer a definition of the meaning of communication content:

> *The content of communication concerns what information is conveyed to employees before, during and after the change initiative, as well as what information is sought from employees.*

Communication content will be very dependent upon the messages being communicated, the sender and receiver of the messages, and the wider context of communications. Weiss (2001: 168) suggests the type of questions managers and employees must ask themselves before sending messages.

- What is the nature of the information/message being sent?
- What medium is most appropriate for acceptance of this message?
- What are the likely consequences if the message is transmitted through an inappropriate medium?

In the literature there is a tendency to offer practical guidance on the content of change communications. A good example of this tendency is Galpin (1996: 39), who offers fundamental principles of a communications plan, including that messages should be linked to the strategic purpose of the change initiative, communications should be realistic and honest, and communications must be proactive rather than reactive. In these principles there is an emphasis upon communication content as well as upon communication processes. Similarly, Paton and McCalman (2000) offer guidelines to follow when communicating change events, including setting the appropriate tone and building in feedback. However, importantly, they acknowledge the need to customise the message, because understanding change communications in terms of generic principles will never reflect the complexity and diversity of organisational life.

In terms of communicating change, there are many choices for organising communications involving dimensions that include style, focus, participation, contribution and level. Despite a great many choices, 'as yet, there are few hard and fast rules on the subject'(Caluwe and Vermaak, 2003: 92). One expectation would be that organisations might subcontract the creation of communication message content to external experts. However, Goodman (2001: 120) found, in a review of corporate communication trends based on research with Fortune 1000 companies, that the creation of messages was carried out within organisations. External help was provided with regard to communications in terms of technology, production, distribution, and execution. Bowditch and Buono (2005: 127) regarded the content of change communications as a powerful tool shaping images of organisational change and mindsets accompanying change. 'It is a statement of an organisational dream – an attempt to stretch the imagination and to motivate people to rethink organisational possibilities.' This quotation shifts the emphasis away from mechanistic approaches which refer to communication processes towards interpreting the content of change messages. Barrett (2002: 225) emphasises in terms of change communications the need for 'a clearly stated, believed in, understood, and meaningful vision statement, which management should be involved in developing and communicating'. Although this appears to be good advice, there are many potential barriers to effective communications.

Communications barriers

Despite the amount and frequency of organisational communication, barriers to communication exist which may lead to communication breakdowns. In Box 17 examples of communications barriers are highlighted.

Judging, criticising, sending solutions and avoiding another's concerns. (Weiss, 2001: 170)
Inability to think clearly, encoding difficulties, noise, selectivity, the bruised ego, environmental factors, incomplete feedback and rumour. (McKenna, 2000: 172)
Mechanical, psychological, semantic, organisational barriers. (Beck *et al*, 2002: 55)
Barriers in sending messages, barriers to reception, barriers to understanding, barriers to acceptance, and barriers to action. (Torrington *et al*, 2002: 105)

Box 17 – Communications barriers

The wide range of barriers reflects the communication choices available and the variety of different communication contexts. One specific communications barrier highlighted by Robbins (2005: 317) is the concept of communication apprehension, defined as 'undue tension and anxiety about oral communication, written communication, or both'. This concept appears particularly applicable when considering the communication of major changes to individuals in terms of the question expressed earlier in the chapter – about what is going to happen to *me*?

The danger is that a communications breakdown may not merely be a failure to communicate but a failure to change. This may explain why Balogun and Hope Hailey (2004: 170) advocate message repetition as part of change communications, and Nadler and Tushman (1997) even advocate over-communicating. They suggest that extreme anxiety at times of change means that people do not effectively receive messages the first time, requiring messages to be repeated through various media. Burnes (2004a: 480) believes that 'Anything from management has to be stated at least six times in six different ways before people start giving it credence.' Or this may be restated as 'I know you think you understand what you thought I said. But I am not sure that what you heard is what I meant' (Robbins and Finley, 1998: 52).

RESEARCH CASES IN JOURNALS NO.10 – UNIVERSITY SERVICES + 3

The paper presents four case studies of implementing quality programmes. All four case studies are based in the United States – university services, outreach education, veterans' hospital and messaging technology. The case studies provide empirical evidence of communication problems. The key themes that are believed to emerge from the cases are creating and communicating vision, sense-making and feedback, establishing legitimacy, and communicating goal achievements.

Sector: Various
Research methods: Observations, document analysis, interviews and questionnaires.
Authors: Lewis, L. K.
Paper title: Communicating change: four cases of quality programs
Journal details: The *Journal of Business Communication*, Vol.37, No.2, 2000; pp.128–55.

Lewis (2000: 151) found that failures in communication contributed to stalled and/or failed programmes of change. His case-study-based conclusions suggest that communications failures may lead to change failures. The findings are similar to the research conclusions of Daly *et al* (2003: 161), 'that internal communication had a role in the successful implementation of change management programmes'. Effective communications are an important (possibly integral) ingredient in successful change management. Caluwe and Vermaak (2003: 90) cite authors (Kotter, 1990; Beckhard and Pritchard, 1992; Kotter and Schlesinger, 1979; Beer, 1980) all emphasising communication as a tool deployed to increase the feasibility of change processes (see also Goodman and Truss, 2004, for further discussion of communications in terms of change management success).

CRITICAL PERSPECTIVE

The following critical perspective on communicating change as part of organisational change is organised around two challenges:

- employees may not trust change communications
- negative responses of employees to change may not be communicated.

The following discussion elaborates upon each of these challenges.

The rhetoric of change communications

Caluwe and Vermaak (2003: 91) offer an enlightening definition of the change process as 'a process whereby people collectively create a new reality through language'. Similarly, Johnson *et al* (2005: 529) have explained the symbolic significance of language in relation to change: 'Either consciously or unconsciously, change agents may employ language and metaphor to galvanise change.' These quotations capture the diversity of meaning which language possesses, and emphasise the functions language can perform.

One way of understanding the language of change is in terms of its rhetorical construction. Collins (2000: 386) writes that the lexicon of management is based upon fads and buzzwords. The study of rhetoric has a long history and may be defined as follows:

> *Rhetoric is the art or the discipline that deals with the use of discourse, either spoken or written, to perform or persuade or motivate an audience, whether that audience is made up of one person or a group of persons.*
>
> *(Corbett, 1990: 3)*

However, rhetoric is often regarded as something of a red flag, Eccles and Nohria (1992: 9) and Watson (1995: 8) noting that rhetoric is often dismissed as 'mere rhetoric'. Often an attempt is made to differentiate the rhetoric of change from the reality of change. Such a dualism has, for example, proved persuasive for HRM researchers (see, for instance, Poole and Mansfield, 1992).

Eccles and Nohria (1992: 9) state that in order to gain a fresh perspective on management it is nonetheless necessary to take language and hence rhetoric seriously. This view has been echoed by other commentators, suggesting that rhetoric merits particular attention (McKenna and Beech, 1995: 16; and Tyson, 1995: 29).

Finstad (1998) identified four forms of rhetoric with specific reference to organisational change in municipal services in Norway – monocratic, opportunistic, anarchical and professional. Many of the accounts of change communications in the *Approaches* section depicted communications as something neutral and apolitical. However, change communications are inevitably politicised. 'The choice of what, when and how to communicate as well as the release of disconfirming information are often political issues' (Dawson, 2003: 174). Bowditch and Buono (2005: 128) warn that 'Once trust and confidence are undermined, they are exceedingly difficult to restore.' They cite research (Hosmer, 1995) suggesting that trust is based on the components of integrity, competence, consistency, loyalty and openness. Dawson (2003: 166) uses the illustration of employees' questioning total quality management:

> *If the rhetoric of change does not align with the substance of change, then employees who find themselves having to do more with less resources are likely to become cynical about management change initiatives and to view TQM as a totally questionable method.*

A very real dilemma with regards the rhetorical nature of change communications is how much these communications are trusted. Knights and Collinson (1987), in their case study organisation referred to as Slavs, offer fascinating insights into the effects of different communications, specifically in terms of a human relations strategy and financial accounting information. Shopfloor workers ridiculed the new human relations strategy as presented to them in the glossy in-house magazine, regarding these communications as management propaganda (a form of rhetoric). However, shopfloor workers appeared to accept the discipline of financial accounting information. Knights and Collinson (1987: 471) note that 'It was in principle possible to query the accounts which justified this large-scale redundancy – stewards were unable to muster any significant shopfloor opposition to the audit.' These findings are all the more surprising given these shopfloor workers' mistrust of other management communications and poor job prospects in the region. In a similar manner, Goodman and Truss (2004: 224) draw the following critical conclusion from their case-study-based research:

> *In general, employees in both organisations felt that they had been informed of changes after, rather than before, the event, that management were out of touch with employee concerns, that others were better informed than they were about the changes, and that they did not understand how the changes would affect them.*

Although their findings were based upon only two case study organisations, they suggest that despite all the prescriptions relating to how to effectively communicate change, individuals may still feel poorly informed about change.

Organisational silence

This chapter has been concerned with both the process and content of change communications. However, there appears to be merit in considering almost the opposite of communication – silence. Quirke (1995: 75) in his functionalist account of communicating change captures the potential dilemma. Senior managers are frustrated at the slowness with which employees respond to change: 'Their people nod in all the right places, make all the right noises, then go off and do something quite different.' According to Morrison and Milliken (2000: 706) the apparent paradox in organisations is that 'most employees know the truth about certain issues and problems within the organisations yet dare not speak that truth.' They (2000: 707) introduce the concept of organisational silence in an intriguing *Academy of Management Review* paper:

> *The possibility that the dominant choice within many organisations is for employees to withhold their opinions and concerns about organisational problems – a collective phenomenon that we have termed organisational silence – is one that we believe deserves serious research attention.*

Organisational silence is perceived as a dangerous impediment to organisational change and development (2000: 707). In a similar manner, Daly *et al* (2003: 161) cite a manager who pointed out: 'Change initiatives will disappear into the cracks if management are not careful...' This notion of change initiatives disappearing, rather than being explicitly resisted, speaks to many of the debates in this textbook. However, it may prove to be easier to diagnose organisational silence than to rectify it.

> *Effectively creating systems that encourage voice, however, requires an understanding of the complex dynamics within many organisational systems that maintain and reinforce silence instead.*
>
> *(Morrison and Milliken, 2000: 721)*

Although Morrison and Milliken are cited here as part of a critical perspective on change communications, their work suggests that senior managers may gain from transferring some of their energies into managing organisational silence, rather than managing change communications. Also, the practical implication is that managing evident resistance may be easier than managing intangible silence.

SYNOPSIS

Organisational communications were often understood in terms of communication channels and/or communication networks. In terms of formal communication networks, the wheel, Y, chain, circle and all channel networks have been identified. The main communication channels included written communication via hard copy, electronic communication via email, video conferencing and telephone. Quirke used the metaphor of a communications escalator when communicating change.

The content of communications concerned information conveyed to employees. In the literature there was a tendency to offer practical guidance on change communications. Paton and McCalman offered guidelines to follow when communicating change events, including setting the appropriate tone and building in feedback. Importantly, they acknowledged the need to customise the message. King and Anderson warned about the inevitability of differences in perspective about change processes that affect large numbers of individuals and work groups.

Despite the amount and frequency of organisational communication, barriers to communication existed which may lead to communications breakdowns. Barriers to communication were many and varied, and included judging, criticising, sending solutions and avoiding another's concerns. The range of barriers reflects communication choices available and the variety of communication contexts. The danger is that a communications breakdown is not merely a failure to communicate but a failure to change.

The symbolic significance of language in relation to change was acknowledged, in particular the rhetorical construction of change language. Despite rhetoric's often being dismissed as 'mere' rhetoric, rhetoric offered a fresh perspective on management.

There appeared to be merit in considering the opposite of communication – silence. According to Morrison and Milliken, most employees know the truth about certain issues and problems within the organisations yet dare not speak that truth, a collective phenomenon termed 'organisational silence'.

DISCUSSION QUESTIONS

1 What criteria should be used to determine what should and should not be communicated with regard to a particular change?
2 How do you judge the truthfulness of a change communication?
3 Is it possible for an organisation to remove all communications barriers?
4 Are there any occasions when a dishonest change message is acceptable?
5 Is there a need to take the rhetoric of change seriously, and if so, why?
6 Why might individuals remain silent in the face of change?

Case study – Communications about a new job evaluation scheme

Organisational context

The Office of Qualitative Social Science – affectionately abbreviated to OOqSS – provides qualitative economic, social and political data for government departments in the civil service. Invariably, it has been overshadowed by its sister office which gathers quantitative social science data, although its staff quite enjoy the anonymity of being the office nobody has heard about. The staff are highly qualified social scientists who in most instances have chosen to work in public service rather than the private sector. One such member of staff is Robert Wyatt who after completing his university studies in social theory joined OOqSS over 20 years ago. Staff in OOqSS have done their best to avoid radical change, but in a manner similar to the rest of the civil service have recently had to respond to a series of government-driven changes. One of these changes was the implementation of a job evaluation scheme, which may be explained in terms of four communication events.

Event 1: trade union meeting

Robert has been a trade unionist all his working life and attended union branch meetings out of both a sense of duty and a sense of loyalty. However, he is prone to daydreaming, and when the branch official announced the piloting of a job evaluation scheme in OOqSS, his mind was on the previous night's TV documentary about shipbuilding. He slowly began to tune back into what was being said as the official impressed upon members that this job evaluation scheme had implications for all civil service employees. In particular, there was a strong belief in the joint trade union co-ordinating group that job evaluation might lead to better pay for low-paid workers in the civil service. This was why the union was participating in the pilot, and this rationale appealed to Robert's socialist beliefs. However, the branch official warned that there was a tendency with job evaluation schemes for employees to 'talk up' what they did, which had implications for other employees. The official emphasised that it was imperative that in the pilot interviews members did not 'talk up' their work. The meeting concluded, and although Robert was not a statistician he felt the odds were good that he would not be invited to the pilot interviews. He returned to the Poverty in Schools Project feeling that he had done his duty, but that he was not that much wiser about job evaluation.

Event 2: meeting with personnel representatives

Robert was disappointed when he learned that he was to be one of the pilot interviewees for the job evaluation scheme. He was invited to attend a briefing event organised by the personnel department, although there would also be presentations from the relevant trade unions. He enjoyed the free buffet lunch that was provided before sitting down to a very professional PowerPoint presentation on CSJE. CSJE was the unimaginative label given to the civil service job evaluation scheme. On one slide there was a definition of job evaluation:

> *Job evaluation offers a means to measure and evaluate jobs relative to one another. It involves a thorough analysis of the role based on information about the job. This information is then presented in a consistent format to ensure that all jobs are compared and evaluated logically and fairly.*

So that is what they mean, he thought, and wondered if it would be perceived as cheeky if he went and helped himself to some more sandwiches. The personnel department spokesperson was explaining that CSJE was being introduced into the civil service in order to introduce real-world accountability into civil service work. CSJE was an integral element of the conservative minister's modernisation crusade. Robert decided to opt for another sandwich.

Event 3: job evaluation interview

It had been agreed that a trade union representative would sit alongside each interviewee at the job evaluation interviews in order to ensure that the process was fair. It had even been jokingly suggested that the union representative would kick the interviewee under the table if he or she 'talked up' the job. Robert met the union representative in the canteen in order to ensure that he would say the right things. They then jointly went over to the personnel department. CSJE required Robert to do some preparatory work answering a series of generic questions such as the following.

■ Do you have to plan, prioritise and organise work or resources to achieve agreed goals?

- What knowledge and experience, however gained, do you need to carry out your basic day-to-day responsibilities?
- Are you required to lift, carry or handle large or heavy objects routinely?

The questions went on and on and although Robert understood that the questions had to be sufficiently generic to apply to all civil service employees, he was quickly losing faith in the methodology. The interview required him to answer the questions in person and give specific illustrations with reference to the work that he did. He had feared that the process would somehow reveal that he was an incompetent social scientist, but it seemed that the methodology never enabled anything more than a superficial analysis. Also, as a good trade unionist he made sure that he did not oversell himself in any way. The interviewer explained at the end of the interview that the interview would be typed up and he would have a chance to check what had been said and the transcript would be verified by the head of OOqSS.

Event 4: conversation with head of OOqSS
About a month later, one evening Robert's boss drifted into his office. Robert was typing up the final report for the Poverty in Schools Project. His boss sat on a desk and they chatted both as colleagues and as friends. His boss commented that he had to sign off the CSJE transcript but it was difficult to recognise that it was meant to be an account of the work that Robert did for OOqSS. Robert believed he had a good rapport with his boss and explained that as a trade unionist he had been instructed not to 'talk up' his work. His boss cautioned that the transcript should be honest and suggested three enhancements based upon his knowledge of the work Robert did, which Robert agreed to. They then spent two hours talking about the pros and cons of research interviewing on different projects they had worked on, before the caretakers threw them out of the building.

Reflections
This case may be atypical in terms of organisational life in that everyone appears to have been a winner. Robert stayed fairly true to his trade union beliefs. The trade union protected the interests of members. The personnel department effectively carried out the CSJE interview. The head of OOqSS effectively verified the transcript – and in time the government minister had large amounts of qualitative and quantitative job evaluation information to peruse.

Case study questions
1   Identify the communication processes for each of the communication events.
2   Identify the communication content for each of the communication events.
3   Identify the communications barriers for each of the communication events.
4   Is this case study a rare case of everybody winning?

FURTHER READING

BARRETT D. J. (2002) Change communication: using strategic employee communication to facilitate major change, *Corporate Communications: An International Journal*, Vol.7, No.4; pp.219–31.

This journal paper is recommended as further reading because it brings together the areas of change and communications, which are often dealt with separately. A model is proposed based upon the desk research of the author into selected Fortune 500 companies. The paper has an applied feel and is a good resource for encouraging consideration of the practicalities of change through communication.

BOWDITCH J. L. and BUONO A. F. (2005) *A Primer on Organizational Behavior*, 6th edition, Chichester, John Wiley & Sons.

Bowditch and Buono devote a chapter to communication which is recommended reading for anyone who seeks an overview of the general organisational communications literature. The strengths of the chapter are the coverage of the major theories relating to communication and the particular emphasis upon organisational communication. Their discussions of envisioning and communicating organisational change and ethics and communications are particularly relevant to issues raised in this chapter.

CLEGG S, KORNBERGER M, and PITSIS T. (2005) *Managing and Organizations: An introduction to theory and practice*, London, Sage Publications.

Clegg *et al* devote a chapter to managing communications in their thought-provoking management textbook. It is recommended here because in a balanced chapter the authors cover the major theories as well as exploring more critical perspectives on communications.

QUIRKE B. (1996) *Communicating Corporate Change: A practical guide to communication and corporate strategy*, London, McGraw-Hill.

This book achieves what it sets out to achieve in the title. It offers the reader practical guidance on communicating change in an organisational context. Quirke appears to have considerable relevant experience of change communications; it would have been good if there had been more references to theoretical/empirical work in this highly applied field.

Control and change

INTRODUCTION

Haberberg and Rieple (2001: 375) believe the challenge for most organisations is to find an appropriate balance between control and anarchy. Being in control of change appears to be a desirable aspiration, although as this chapter suggests, controlling change may prove as illusory as controlling nature. However, as with nature there may be merit in at least attempting control. Child (2005: 111) has written about control as an 'elusive concept', neglected by many writers on organisations. Possible reasons are that managing is regarded as encompassing control, or that it is perceived in a sinister fashion as too closely related to power and manipulation. In the first part of this chapter, approaches to control are introduced in terms of the meanings and theories of control in general, and specifically of controlling change. In the *Critical perspective*, the compatibility of organisational change and control will be questioned; control in organisations is related to broader control in society and increased surveillance.

APPROACHES TO CONTROL IN ORGANISATIONS

In understanding control in an organisational context it is necessary to acknowledge that different control mechanisms and processes co-exist (Johnson and Gill, 1993: 14). As with many change management topics, no single perspective dominates – instead, there are competing perspectives (Rollinson, 2005: 512):

■ *managerialist perspective*: how managers can best maintain control

■ *open systems perspective*: modelling control systems for design and analysis purposes

■ *political perspective*: understanding the internal dynamics of control – eg how control is exercised, and whether it gives rise to resistance or counter-control.

The following discussion focuses upon managerialist explanations of control, whereas more social and political explanations will be offered in the *Critical perspective*.

The meanings and theories of control

Control in organisations is not as straightforward as it initially appears. It can only ever partly be achieved, yet it is something that managers are employed to strive for (Watson, 2002: 222). This is not to say that there is not a need for management control.

> *In fact, there are few differences between organisational behaviour writers and managers on this central issue: the point of studying behaviour for both groups is to contribute to its control.*
>
> *(Ackroyd and Thompson, 1999: 4)*

Theories of control in organisations may be based upon assumptions about rational and unambiguous organisational behaviour, although ambiguity, doubt and uncertainty are key features of organisations (Manning, 1992: 4). In defining 'control', Child (2005: 112) initially offers the following thought:

> *Control may be defined as a process whereby management or other groups are able to initiate and regulate the conduct of activities such that their results accord with the goals and expectations held by those groups.*

This definition of control will be used for this chapter, although Child subsequently makes links between control and power. The definition above helps to illustrate the centrality of control in broader processes of managing. In understanding control it is necessary to acknowledge that control is an ongoing process rather than a single event. This process includes monitoring what is achieved, comparing what is achieved with what should have been achieved, and making provision for remedial action to be taken where a discrepancy appears.

A major challenge in understanding management control is the diversity of controls, both implicit and explicit, that exist in organisations. A useful starting point is to identify three different types of control: administrative control, social control and self-control (Johnson and Gill, 1993: 20). These types of control may be illustrated by examples – of administrative control, a wage payment system; of social control, group norms; and of self-control, personal motives. Although management control implies administrative control, it is apparent that other forms of control are at work. This form of classification has been developed further by Child (2005: 119), who has identified six significant categories of control in organisations:

- personal centralised control
- bureaucratic control
- output control
- control through electronic surveillance
- HRM control
- cultural control.

RESEARCH CASES IN JOURNALS NO.11 – CONSULTANCY CO.

The authors present Consultancy Co. as an intriguing case study of company culture being used as a means of management control. A strength of this research case is in its access to organisational information. The case forms part of a larger research project concerned with employment practices in small and medium-sized enterprises. Consultancy Co. was a consultancy specialising in software for telephony, IT and security services and employing some 150 workers. In this organisation company culture was believed to be used as a means of management control. A finding which emerges from the research was that in exchange for freedoms in work time, employees had to accept regulation of their social time. The reader gains an appreciation of both the potential advantages of achieving control through culture as well as some of the less tangible disadvantages.

Sector: Management services
Research methods: Observations, in-depth interviews and documentation.
Authors: Grugulis I., Dundon T., Wilkinson A.
Paper title: Cultural control and the 'culture manager': employment practices in a consultancy
Journal details: *Work, Employment and Society*, Vol.14, No.1, 2000; pp.97–116

Child acknowledges that more than one category can be adopted in a single organisation, and also that the final three categorisations of control are compatible with newer forms of organisation. These categorisations may be gathered together under the umbrella of official control apparatus which Watson (2003: 85) has concisely defined as:

> *The set of roles, rules, structures, value statements, cultural symbols, rituals and procedures managerially designed to co-ordinate and control work activities.*

This definition captures the wide range of controls that may be at work in any one organisation at any one time.

Controlling change

Collins (1998: 24), writing with reference to organisational change, regards management as primarily about control, whereas work is about co-operation. This suggests that an element of change management must address the control of change. Similarly, Wilson (1992: 7) described the essence of the managerial task as establishing rationality or predictability out of the chaos that characterises change processes.

There are parallels between senior management's desire to control change and the desire of individuals to control change. If we are going through a major change in, for example, a personal relationship or moving home, there may be occasions when the situation is out of control, but overall we will probably want to maintain as much control as possible over a constantly changing situation. Conner (1998: 70) neatly captures this human desire to control change: 'Change is not perceived as negative because of its unwanted effect as much as because of our inability to predict and control it.'

It was noted earlier that the concept of control in mainstream writing on organisations remains elusive, an implication of which is the absence of coverage of control in mainstream change management literature (see, for example, Burnes, 2004a; Paton and McCalman, 2000; and Senior and Fleming, 2006). Although the omission of coverage of control may suggest that control is not relevant to change management, another explanation is that different approaches to change management place different emphases upon control. Rickards (1999: 141) differentiates between hard systems' concerns with control and prediction of systems performance, and 'soft systems [that] have been more concerned with the capacity of human actions in systems to adapt and modify the system's characteristics.'

Hayes (2002: 166) believes that 'Every stage of the change process raises issues of control...' He favours a practical/functional approach, suggesting seven steps a change manager can take to maintain control during transition:

- develop and communicate a clear vision of the future state
- appoint a transition manager
- develop a transition plan
- provide the resources for the transition
- reward transition behaviours
- use multiple and consistent leverage points for change, and
- develop feedback mechanisms.

Such step models are a common feature of the change management literature (see Mento *et al*, 2002, for a discussion of three exemplars of step models), although change management step models have attracted criticisms (Collins, 1998). In terms of change management literature, control is often introduced as a response to apparently irrational resistance to change.

> *Hence, when management seek to change the work-content of a job or to increase control over employees in order to improve productivity or otherwise increase efficiency, such developments – especially if they involve a loss of autonomy or extra effort from employees for no additional reward – are often resisted.*
> *(Keenoy, 1992: 95)*

In Chapter 10 resistance was discussed in detail, and those discussions particularly with reference to managing resistance may be regarded as management attempts to gain control over the change process. In recent years cultural control has become increasingly relevant as a potential means of both changing organisations and controlling change. Rollinson (2005: 530) identifies potential reasons for cultural control, including: it increases acceptability of surveillance practices, encourages greater effort of employees, and decreases dissent and discontent among employees. Cultural change was the focus of Chapter 7, and such forms of change may be related to increasing management control. Often such controls are much less obvious than, for example, financial control and may redefine areas of management control. Carnall (2003: 64), in his discussion of control in the context of change, revisits the work of Walton (1985), highlighting three management models which are potentially applicable to change management:

- the control model
- the transitional model, and
- the commitment model.

171

The seven-step approach (Hayes, 2002) discussed earlier was a good illustration of the transitional model. It is informative to differentiate between the control model and the commitment model as different means of controlling change. Carnall (2003: 65) regards the control model as producing reliable but not outstanding performance. There has been a shift towards seeking competitive advantage out of high performance, with commitment believed to help deliver high performance.

However, despite the above discussion of the practicalities of controlling change, there remains a potential contradiction between organisational change and control which is developed further in the following *Critical perspective*.

CRITICAL PERSPECTIVE

Thompson and McHugh (2002: 101) are sceptical about the treatment of control in mainstream writing, regarding it as 'ambiguous at best, marginal at worst'. The following critical perspective on control as part of organisational change is organised around three challenges:

- increased control may hinder organisational change
- organisational change may increase conformity, and
- organisational change may increase surveillance.

The following discussion elaborates upon each of these closely interrelated challenges.

Organisational change and control

Thompson (1989: 151) warned that 'no one has convincingly demonstrated that a particular form of control is necessary or inevitable for capitalism to function successfully.' Control may even be an impediment to organisational change. Tight control may destroy commitment, produce poor quality, and instigate poor industrial relations and high absenteeism (Salaman and Asch, 2003: 12).

Although the concept of change implies uncertainty, mainstream literature and senior managers appear to favour the certainty that control promises. Burnes (1996: 11) noted a tendency 'to replace choice with certainty and preference with prescription...' as a fundamental tenet of the organisational change literature.

However, in seeking to control change something may be lost. Argyris (2001: 199) describes the change professional as being 'caught in the middle of the battle between autonomy and control...' Issues of creativity, innovation and empowerment – all potentially part of a change agenda – may be stifled through the pursuit of control (see Amabile, 2001, for further discussion).

There is a dilemma about the potential certainty of control and the very real uncertainty of change. King and Anderson (2002: 224) have questioned the manageability of organisational change, including the illusion of control. Writing with specific reference to practising managers they warn that 'There will almost always be influences which are unanticipated and beyond the manager's direct control.' The theoretical explanations of control in the previous section may be regarded as largely managerialist attempts to design solutions to management problems of control. However, the goal of achieving control over the processes of organisational change may prove illusory:

Control can never be absolute and in the space provided by the indeterminacy of labour, employees will constantly find ways of evading and subverting managerial organisation and direction of work. This tendency is a major source of the dynamism in the workplace.

(Ackroyd and Thompson, 1999: 47)

This quotation intriguingly hints at human potential that is an integral element of all organisations. The downside of increased control may be to lessen the contribution individuals are able to make to an organisation. Organisations may change through the process of individuals' bending rules, suggesting that organisations may benefit from less management control in certain areas – for example, creativity and design. Ackroyd and Thompson (1999: 1) wrote their fascinating book *Organizational Misbehaviour* because they believed the literature tended to depict people almost exclusively as conforming and dutiful, and that there was a normative bias in the study of organisational behaviour.

It is our conviction that both managers and organisation behaviour specialists alike not only underestimate the extent of organisational misbehaviour but that they also exaggerate the extent to which organisational behaviour can be changed by them.

(Ackroyd and Thompson, 1999: 1)

Managers and social scientists overlook organisational misbehaviour, bracketing it off as somehow peripheral or inessential (Ackroyd and Thompson, 1999: 14). Instead, the authors argue for a greater appreciation of self-organisation – the tendency of groups to form interests and establish identities and develop autonomy based on these activities (1999: 54). They (1999: 5) believe that during the current period of significant organisational change, the alteration of organisational structures is helping to reconstruct the conventional forms in which misbehaviour finds expression. This is an intriguing proposition although very difficult to empirically substantiate.

Control and society

Control in organisations may be explained in terms of broader changes in control identified in society. Commentators such as Ritzer (2004) and Bryman (2004) have highlighted an increased emphasis upon control in society with reference to the concepts of 'McDonaldisation' and 'Disneyisation'.

Ritzer(2004: 1) originally identified the McDonaldisation phenomenon in 1993, defining this wide-ranging process as: 'the process by which the principles of the fast-food restaurant are coming to dominate more and more sectors of American society as well as of the rest of the world'. He (2004: 12) identified four alluring dimensions which explained the success of McDonalds in offering consumers, workers and managers efficiency, calculability, predictability and control. Although Ritzer offers McDonaldisation as an explanation of contemporary management and organisational behaviour, he remains critical of such trends. In a similar manner, Bryman (2004: 1) has defined Disneyisation as:

The process by which the principles of the Disney theme parks are coming to dominate more and more sectors of American society as well as the rest of the world.

Bryman (2004: 13) acknowledges that 'Disneyisation and McDondaldisation can be thought of as parallel processes rather than in any sense competing.'

One commonality in these parallel processes pertinent to this chapter is the increasing emphasis upon control in organisations. The change management implications of such developments are that senior management in changing organisations are increasing control over both employees and customers, and that this increased control may not be beneficial for employees or customers.

Control and surveillance

Bryman (2004: 131) closely relates control and surveillance in his discussions of Disneyisation, and in earlier discussions Child identified control though electronic surveillance as one potential control strategy. A consequence of organisational change may be increased control through surveillance.

Management writers such as Townley (1994) have utilised the work of Foucault (1979) to offer new perspectives on management. In particular, the metaphor of the panopticon is helpful in explaining increased surveillance in organisations and society. The idea of the panopticon was developed by Jeremy Bentham as a revolutionary form of prison, and the metaphor was more recently promoted by Michel Foucault. Foucault (1979: 302) described the architecture of the prison as follows:

> *At the periphery, an annular building; at the centre, a tower; this tower is pierced with wide windows that open onto the inner side of the ring; the peripheric building is divided into cells, each of which extends the whole width of the building; they have two windows, one on the inside, corresponding to the windows of the tower; the other on the outside, allows the light to cross the cell from one end to another.*

Foucault explains how this architecture allows a supervisor to be located in the tower whereas the prisoners are located in their cells. The prisoners are made visible whereas the supervisors cannot be seen. In the purview of the central tower inmates never know when they are being watched, so through internalising this process they control themselves. The metaphor is applicable to contemporary organisations in that through the process of surveillance managers are able to control employees.

An applied illustration of panopticonism is evident in 'mystery shopping'. Mystery shoppers are increasingly used in service organisations such as banks, shops and hotels in order to monitor service quality. The information is gathered anonymously by the mystery shopper who either poses as a shopper or is a shopper. The information gathered may help senior management understand their own organisations from the perspective of a customer. However, if employees are aware that mystery shopping is taking place but not who the mystery shoppers are, they may begin to alter their interactions with all customers. In a manner similar to the panopticon the employees are made visible while being unable to see their observers. In this illustration it is apparent how changes in surveillance may increase control.

The above discussion has highlighted the potential for organisational change to increase control through surveillance. Arguments could be offered for and against surveillance. However, concerns have been raised by groups such as the Institute of Employment Rights (Ford, 1998) about surveillance at work – in particular, the consequences of increased surveillance for the privacy and autonomy of employees.

SYNOPSIS

The competing perspectives of managerialist, open systems and political approaches to control were identified. The *Approaches* section focused upon managerialist explanations of control. Six significant categories of control in organisations were identified: personal centralised control, bureaucratic control, output control, control through electronic surveillance, HRM control and cultural control.

The essence of the managerial task was described as establishing rationality or predictability out of the chaos that characterises change processes. However, there was an absence of coverage of control in mainstream change management literature. Three management models were potentially applicable: the control model, the transitional model and the commitment model.

Control may prove to be an impediment to organisational change, tight control potentially destroying commitment, producing poor quality, and instigating poor industrial relations and high absenteeism. Although the concept of change implied uncertainty, mainstream literature and senior managers appeared to favour the certainty that control promises. Argyris described the change professional as being caught in the middle of the battle between autonomy and control, and King and Anderson questioned the illusion of control.

Control in organisations was explained in terms of broader changes in control identified in society. Commentators such as Ritzer (2004) and Bryman (2004) highlighted an increased emphasis upon control in society in terms of the concepts of 'McDonaldisation' and 'Disneyisation'.

A consequence of organisational change may be increased control through surveillance. Management writers have utilised the work of Foucault to offer new perspectives on management. In particular, the metaphor of the panopticon helped to explain increased surveillance in organisations and society.

DISCUSSION QUESTIONS

1   Is it possible to have successful organisational change without control?

2   Which is more important – creativity or conformity? (Think in terms of a specific type of organisation)

3   Why is management control a goal in organisations?

4   What are the implications for management of acknowledging the existence of organisational misbehaviour?

5   Would you personally prefer to work in an organisation with or without surprises, and why?

6   What elements of the official apparatus of control are likely to increase and decline in the future?

Case study – Controlling the archaeology department

The archaeology department of Midchester University has a prestigious reputation for its world-class research. Academics regularly speak at international conferences and some have even become minor celebrities through their appearances on TV archaeology shows. The department has a relaxed atmosphere and most of the 35 academics and five administrators enjoy working in the department.

The appointment of Steve Diggle as head of department one year ago surprised everyone. His research track record did not compare favourably with some of the professors in the department. However, because no internal candidates had applied for the position, senior management found itself presented with an opportunity to introduce a 'new broom'. On appointing Steve, senior management informed him of the apparent anarchy that pervaded the department. His task was to replace this chaos with effective management and organisation – and with this in mind, he dreaded his first day at work.

However, his experience of running the department proved to be unexpectedly positive. When he met academics they greeted him in a cheerful manner and voluntarily offered their assistance. They would talk at length about their latest research and moan about students getting in the way of the real work. They would invariably at some point make reference to the top-quality award for research that the department had achieved at the last assessment. Also, the implication was that with hard work they could repeat their research assessment success. Their work rate could not be faulted – every week an academic presented a staff seminar paper on his or her latest research findings. At these seminars staff spoke with such passion and enthusiasm that it was a joy to behold. Steve had a similar experience with the administration team, who were one of the most professional groups of administrators he had ever encountered. There would regularly be students in the administration office chatting with the administrators. As he reported to a colleague from his old university, 'I was ready for war – but everything is so peaceful!'

As part of his role he had to countersign travel and expenses forms before they were submitted to the finance department. A number of the claims occasionally appeared to be rather imaginative, but it was when he received a claim for one month's five-star hotel accommodation in Sydney that he challenged the claimant. It proved to be very difficult to make contact with the claimant, who was apparently on a 'dig' in a remote part of the world. When he made contact, the professor apologised for his oversight, explaining that he had stayed on in Sydney after a very successful conference. The claim was corrected, but a similar pattern became evident in other claims.

The senior management of the university requested management information in respect of teaching as part of an institutional quality assessment. At the briefing meeting it was impressed upon Mr Diggle that this information was important to the institution, and that it had to be gathered quickly and effectively. He prioritised this task that afternoon and drew up a list of the course leaders who were best placed to provide the information. The following morning he met with the administration team and impressed upon them the importance of gathering this information. They were helpful, but frowned when he showed them the list of course leaders they were required to contact. They explained that in the past the administrators had always gathered the information and ghost-written the reports on behalf of the course leaders because the academics did not like being troubled with such bureaucracy.

Steve decided that it was time for decisive intervention. He sent out a strongly-worded memo to relevant course leaders requesting specific information to be supplied within 10 days. In those instances where he met individuals he reinforced the importance of this information in person. Everyone he met responded positively and although acknowledging their heavy workloads also acknowledged the importance of gathering information. After 10 days Steve reviewed progress. Not one single course leader had submitted anything.

Case study questions

1   Explain the problems presented in this case study in terms of theories of management control.

2   Design a change strategy to rectify these problems, with specific reference to the problems of management control.

FURTHER READING

CHILD J. (2005) *Organization: Contemporary principles and practice*, Oxford, Blackwell.

The writings of John Child about organisational behaviour are highly respected, and in this textbook he devotes a chapter to what he regards as the elusive concept of control. His discussion of control is informed by a comprehensive knowledge of relevant literature, which is discussed in a very accessible and engaging manner.

JOHNSON P. and GILL J. (1993) *Management Control and Organizational Behaviour*, London, Paul Chapman.

As the title suggests, this book maintains a focus upon management control. The book offers a helpful overview of the different theoretical approaches to management control and their origins. Specific chapters benefit from being related to areas such as culture and control and leadership and control.

STREATFIELD P. J. (2001) *The Paradox of Control in Organizations*, London, Routledge.

This is an unusual and thought-provoking book, which as the title suggests is organised around the perceived paradox of control. The paradoxical position which managers find themselves in is that they are both 'in control' and 'not in control' at the same time. This concept is developed throughout the book, which challenges mainstream thinking about control. Issues that emerge in the book are illustrated with reference to the author's own experiences of working as a manager in SmithKline-Beecham.

THOMPSON P. and MCHUGH D. (2002) *Work Organisations: A critical introduction*, Basingstoke, Palgrave.

Thompson and McHugh in their critical introductory textbook on work organisations offer an interesting overview of debates relating to control. In particular, they devote a chapter to control concepts and strategies. Their writing favours more radical accounts of control, which balance functionalist/managerialist accounts found in the mainstream management and organisational behaviour literature.

Learning and change

LEARNING OBJECTIVES

To:

- review the concepts and theories of organisational learning

- identify learning from change management success

- identify learning from change management failure

- critically review the claims made for organisational learning.

INTRODUCTION

The title of this chapter is more of an aspiration than a statement of reality, as Thorne (2000: 306) highlights in the following quotation:

> *A crucial difference between writers on change and writers on organisational learning is how the latter group actively embraces failure as a valuable and positive part of learning and development. In contrast, change writers, if they mention failure, almost invariably describe it negatively as lack of success.*

The quotation suggests two camps of writers – those writing about learning and those writing about change. This chapter seeks to inform understanding about change management through explaining connections between learning and change. We are still learning about the complex inter-relationships between learning and change: some of the concepts, particularly in terms of their ambiguity, confuse rather than clarify understanding. Although history implies learning, extracting learning from the past can never be guaranteed. Abrahamson (2000: 79) warns that 'companies that forget the past are condemned to relive it...' However, Van der Bent *et al* (1999: 395), in concluding their paper on organisational learning and change processes, remind us that 'remembering is an important prerequisite to learning.'

Many senior managers claim that their organisations are 'learning organisations' and by association do remember. However, this chapter will challenge popular rhetoric surrounding the proliferation of dubious recipes for success and fashionable notions of learning organisations.

This chapter is organised in terms of clarifying the meanings and theories of organisational learning, and accounts of change management success are reviewed. However, Sorge and Van Witteloostuijn (2004: 1212) have warned that 'organisational change has an undeniable tendency to produce failure.' The *Critical perspective* section highlights the potential of learning from change management failure rather than attempting to replicate the successes of other organisations, and organisational learning is critically reviewed.

APPROACHES TO ORGANISATIONAL LEARNING

The concepts of learning and change are closely related – organisations undergoing change will find it difficult, if not impossible, to define and resolve all eventualities (Woodward and Hendry, 2004: 157). Eventualities that any change of status quo raises may be regarded as opportunities for organisational learning.

The meanings and theories of organisational learning

In this section, the intention is to focus upon organisational learning and learning organisations in terms of their different meanings and the theories that exist. Argyris (1999: 1), one of the leading protagonists in debates about organisational learning, offered a helpful although polarised distinction between the learning organisation and organisational learning:

> *We divide the literature that pays serious attention to organisational learning into two main categories: the practice-oriented, prescriptive literature of the 'learning organisation', promulgated mainly by consultants and practioners, and the predominantly sceptical scholarly literature of 'organisational learning', produced by academics.*

In reality the distinction is not this precise, as Argyris subsequently acknowledges – however, it offers a helpful starting point. Interest in organisational learning has grown over the past decade, although influential writers such as Argyris have been writing about organisational learning for over 40 years. Thompson and McHugh (2002: 247) suggest that 'much of the discussion of learning in organisations nowadays comes under the heading of organisational learning...' Hayes (2002: 39) explains why organisational learning has become so important in the context of change. The collective nature of learning is especially important in complex and turbulent environments because in such circumstances senior managers may not be the best-placed individuals to identify opportunities and threats. The idea that organisations have an ongoing capability to learn about change appears admirable and essential given that 'the idea of change itself is changing' (Abrahamson, 2000: 79).

Antonacopoulou and Gabriel (2001: 439) describe learning as 'a dynamic transformational process, continuously extended and redefined in response to the context in which it takes place'. In this particular definition it is apparent why learning and change are often related. A diversity of viewpoints regarding organisational learning exists (Van der Bent *et al*, 1999: 377). Burnes *et al* (2003: 457) cite the work of Probst and Buchel (1997) identifying at least four different approaches to learning – by developing a strategy, developing a structure, developing a culture and developing human resources.

Argyris (1999: 7), reviewing the scholarly literature on organisational learning, believes that it is 'intentionally distant from practice, non-prescriptive, and value-neutral...' Theories of organisational learning have been identified in the disciplines of social psychology, management theory, sociology, information theory, anthropology and political theory (Argyris and Schon, 1978). Many definitions of organisational learning have been put forward, although there is no widespread consensus definition of organisational learning (Denton, 1998: 16). However, Burnes *et al* (2003: 453) define organisational learning in terms of four common propositions that underpin the concept, which may be summarised as follows. Organisations must learn at least as fast as the environment changes. Movement away from traditional forms of learning to organisational learning will be dependent upon the amount of instability in the environment. Maintaining alignment with the organisation's environment is no longer solely the responsibility of senior management. The whole workforce must be involved in the identification of the need for change, implementing change and learning.

Another consistent theme in the organisational learning literature has been an ongoing interest in single-loop and double-loop learning.

> *Single-loop learning occurs when matches are created, or when mismatches are corrected by changing actions. Double-loop learning occurs when mismatches are corrected by first examining and altering the governing variables and then the actions.*
>
> *(Argyris, 1999: 68)*

The easiest way to understand these two forms of learning is in terms of their origins, relating back to the electrical engineering of a central heating system. A thermostat (single-loop learner) may be programmed to detect states of 'too cold' or 'too hot' and correct this by turning the heat on or off. If the thermostat asked itself why it was set at 68 degrees Fahrenheit, or why it was programmed as it was, then it would be a double-loop learner (Argyris, 1999: 68).

Argyris (1999: 69) believes that single-loop and double-loop learning are required by all organisations. However, in terms of organisational changes, single-loop learning is the norm. Also, in terms of 'unfreezing', introducing new values and behaviour and 'refreezing'-type change models (Lewin, 1951), such models are useful for single-loop learning, but gaps exist when attempting to produce double-loop learning using such models. The importance of this distinction as part of our understanding of organisational learning is that it signposts a potential need for individuals in organisations to move from single-loop to double-loop learning. Potentially, individual learning about change could then help individuals deal with change.

As Argyris (1999: 1) stated, as well as the scholarly literature about organisational learning there is the more practice-oriented, prescriptive literature of the 'learning organisation'. The concept of the 'learning organisation' was popularised by the publication of a book by Peter Senge (1990), *The Fifth Discipline*. Although Senge has become closely associated with the learning organisation, Pedler *et al* (1997) identify writers who contributed to shaping the idea of the learning organisation (these include Argyris and Schon, 1978; Peters and Waterman, 1982; Deming, 1986; Harrison, 1995; Dixon 1994). Jackson (2001: 121) in his review of Senge and the learning organisation highlights variants which have included 'the learning company' (Pedler, Burgoyne and Boydell, 1991), 'the knowledge-creating company' (Nonaka, 1991) and 'the living company' (De Geus, 1997).

In *The Fifth Discipline*, Senge (1990: 4) uses a simple yet persuasive rhetoric to promote the learning organisation. 'Learning organisations are possible because, deep down, we are all learners... Learning organisations are possible because not only is it our nature to learn but we love to learn.' He (1990: 6–10) identifies the five component technologies or disciplines of a learning organisation, which may be summarised as follows:

- systems thinking – thinking in terms of systems
- personal mastery – defined as high levels of proficiency
- mental models – understanding the mental models at work
- building a shared vision – developed by people working together
- team learning – team intelligence exceeds that of the individuals.

The fifth discipline which gives the book its title is systems thinking: 'Without a systemic orientation, there is no motivation to look at how the disciplines interrelate' (Senge, 1990: 12).

Learning from change management successes

The goal of success is embedded in societies and individuals (Paton and McCalman, 2000: 2), and this goal is very evident in the change management literature. Understandably, senior managers want their change management initiatives to be perceived by all interested parties as successful, as illustrated by Brown (1998: 157) in his book on organisational culture. Brown features an interesting case study of change in the Post Office. As part of the write-up he includes a letter from the then Chief Executive of the Post Office about publishing the research-based case study in the textbook. The following extract is taken from the published letter:

> *On a first reading I was left strongly with the impression that your chapter described an organisation in crisis and unsuccessfully trying to implement change.*

The letter counters this impression with details of the positive advances that had been made in the Post Office. However, the letter concisely conveys the very real human desire of the Chief Executive to be associated with success rather than failure. It may be regarded as human nature to strive towards success, rather than failure.

Carnall (2003: 225) warns that 'achieving change is one thing – learning from the process of change is an entirely different thing.' An optimistic starting point for such learning would be to consider occasions on which senior managers appear to have successfully accomplished change. In considering change management success it is worthwhile acknowledging larger ongoing debates about how we assess an organisation's strategic performance. For example, Haberberg and Rieple (2001: 119) identified measures including financial performance, stakeholder satisfaction, profit margin, asset utilisation, and unit sales value, operational and financial strength. It is very conceivable that a change could be successfully managed, yet be unsuccessful in terms of such measures. Clegg and Walsh (2004: 231) have written about examples of latent functions of change management, such as continuing rhetoric and education on organisational competitiveness and demonstrating to the City that a company is taking an issue seriously.

An important consideration in any discussion of change management success is the criteria used to determine success – and the inevitability that any specific change management initiative is unlikely to meet all the criteria of success. Iles and Sutherland (2001: 13) identified three problems with judging the efficacy of change programmes. These relate to:

- the multidimensional nature of the impact
- analysis of the causes of the underlying problem, and
- the perceptions of different people involved in the change.

Peters and Waterman (1982) are regarded as the initiators of the recipe approach to successful change management. They identify eight attributes of successful companies. Inevitably, businesses attempted to develop these attributes in their own searches for excellence. Despite many criticisms (see, for example, Pascale, 1990, and Guest, 1992) their work encouraged a burgeoning literature on how to successfully manage change. Many potential success factors for change have been generated based upon a mix of research, business experience and personal anecdote. Mento *et al* (2002: 45) suggest that 'three of the most well known are Kotter's strategic eight-step model for transforming organisations, Jick's tactical ten-step model for implementing change, and General Electric's (GE's) seven-step change acceleration process model.' Interestingly, each of these models implies that following the steps prescribed will lead to successful change management. In terms of learning about change, senior managers believe that they can learn from previous success through adopting these n-step approaches (see Collins, 1998, for an effective challenge to the n-step approach to change management). Many ingredients have been suggested in the recipes for successful change management – for example, culture by Smith (2003) and teams by West *et al* (2004).

In reviewing the change management literature over the past decade, a more systematic and reasoned search for change management success factors is evident, which goes beyond simple n-step guides. Clarke and Manton (1997), in seeking to develop a benchmarking tool – a best practice model for change – identified the following key success factors: commitment, social and cultural communication, tools and methodology and interactions. The idea of a benchmarking tool is likely to appeal to senior managers in allowing the acknowledgement of contingencies relevant to specific organisations. Smith (2003) surveyed 210 managers across North America about major change efforts in the previous two years. One of the interesting asides arising out of this paper was the data cited by the survey respondents to describe the degree of success of their change efforts.

sales data

revenue data

cost data

financials

operations data

what insiders think

measurement of customer satisfaction

informal customer comments

progress against schedule

regulatory decisions

unanticipated consequences, and

other

This range of data highlights how success in different organisational contexts is being defined and how success means different things to different people. The implication is that even within the same organisation, different definitions of success may co-exist. For example, a change may result in an increase in customer satisfaction, but simultaneously increase costs. The forward-looking desire to improve performance of strategists (Stacey, 2003: 1) may help to explain the preoccupation of looking for change management success factors which can be copied. The CIPD (2004) research programme Organising for Success offered empirical insights into change management successes and failures based upon a questionnaire survey of senior mangers involved in change initiatives. The survey identified six key characteristics typically associated with successful reorganisations:

- organisation-wide holistic change
- project management
- employee involvement

- effective leadership
- communication with external stakeholders
- internal and external experience.

Boonstra (2004: 463), in drawing conclusions from a rigorous and thorough collection of readings about the dynamics of organisational change and learning, identifies the following principles relating to success factors in organisational change: there is no one best way in organising and changing; human beings are motivated by meaningful work; and organisation is a process of interaction. In such principles there is far less emphasis upon prescription evident in n-step approaches to change and much more acknowledgement of the ambiguities and contradictions of change. Miller (2002: 359) in his discussion about successful change leadership warns against leaders' declaring victory too early, as may be explained under the pressures of the stock market. At what point can a change be declared successful?

> *The most general lesson to be learned from the more successful cases is that the change process goes through a series of phases that, in total, usually require a considerable length of time.*
>
> *(Kotter, 1995: 59)*

Change is dynamic and can be ambiguous, and even a change that is declared to be successful may with hindsight prove to have been unsuccessful. There are many dependent contingencies rippling through the above discussion which, unfortunately, the change management success recipe books choose to overlook.

CRITICAL PERSPECTIVE

The following critical perspective on learning and change as part of organisational change is organised around two challenges:

- that change management failure may be more informative that success
- that theories and concepts of organisational learning have shortcomings.

The following discussion elaborates upon each of these challenges.

Learning from change management failure

Although the previous discussion acknowledged human preferences for success over failure, failure may ironically offer a better opportunity to learn about change management. Argyris (1999: 123) draws from his notes on 32 major reorganisations in large organisations in which he was involved in a consulting and research role the following conclusion:

> *I did not find one that could be labelled as fully completed and integrated three years after the change had been announced (and in many cases had gone through several revisions). That is, after three years there were still many people fighting, ignoring, questioning, resisting, and/or blaming, the reorganisation without feeling a strong obligation personally to correct the situation.*

Understanding of change management may be furthered through learning from such messy situations as depicted by Argyris, rather than through searching for standardised recipes and steps to achieve successful change management.

For example, the Clarke and Manton (1997) change management key success factors benchmarking tool (discussed earlier) is appealing in many ways, bringing certainty to the uncertain world of change management and in being normative, suggesting success for the person using the tool. However, Stacey (2003: 414) sceptically notes that the validity for particular tools comes from 'pointing to how organisations that use particular tools and techniques, or have particular attributes, are successful while those that that do not use, or possess, them fail'. Success may be a consequence of using a particular change management tool; equally, success may be a consequence of the competitive environment or a particular style of leadership.

The high failure rate of change initiatives in general has been commented upon by many writers (Kotter, 1995: 59; Guimaraes and Armstrong, 1998: 74; Burke, 2002: 1; De Caluwe and Vermaak, 2004: 197). In earlier chapters, research evidence was cited suggesting, despite positive rhetoric, that there was empirical evidence of high failure rates of change initiatives such as TQM, BPR and downsizing. These failures are ironic when set against the plethora of best practice guidance on how to manage change (Hamlin, 2001: 19). Academic commentators have to share some of the responsibility for change management failure. Despite managers and consultants having access to literature on organisational change, a large number of change management programmes still fail (Woodward and Hendry, 2004: 155).

A recurrent theme of this textbook has been the importance of avoiding universal solutions. The literature will not provide any universal solutions to the problems of change management failure. Frequent warnings about change management failure raise questions about what we can learn from change failure – in particular, the many competing explanations for change management failure (see, for example, Redman and Grieves' discussion of TQM failure featured in Chapter 7). However, despite the potential learning opportunities of exploring change management failure, talking and writing about failure is engaging with an organisational taboo (Thorne, 2000: 305; Sennett, 2001: 203). Fortunately, more serious accounts of change management have sought to break this taboo, 'because ignoring failure can limit our understanding of the theory and practice of organisational change' (Thorne, 2000: 305).

Kotter's (1995) eight-step model was developed after a study of over 100 organisations varying in size and industry type. After learning that the majority of major change efforts failed, Kotter couched his model as a way of avoiding errors in the change process (Mento *et al*, 2002: 45). As a consequence of the many different contexts in which change management takes place and the competing explanations of change management, inevitably there are competing explanations for change management failure. In considering specific change management failures, a number of factors are likely to be at work. Buchanan and Badham (1999: 157) identify explanations of change management failure that exist:

- methods are not properly understood or are only partly applied
- quality programmes are criticised by their designers for implementing bureaucratic quality controls rather than encouraging commitment to quality and the customer
- business process re-engineering projects fail due to being partial, incremental, focused upon cost-cutting, rather than strategic and/or radical restructuring.

Buchanan and Badham (1999: 157) acknowledge that a combination of personal and local factors are blamed by those directly responsible for change implementation. However, there is 'an alternative explanation that does not rely on individual and organisational failings, but which attributes high failure rates to the political difficulties inherent in major change initiatives'. The politics of organisational change was discussed in Chapter 10. Dawson (2003: 168) warns about 'recipes for success' which tend to ignore change contradictions and ambiguities, which view conflict and resistance as obstacles, and which overlook the complex boundaries of change that continuously shift and re-form. These warnings include the problematical nature of basing current changes upon retrospective evaluations of past 'successful' change strategies. Senior managers must consider and critically reflect on change rather than simply adopt the latest fashion or fad.

Also, the need for and the possibility of bringing about revolutionary change is believed to be a common misconception. Burke (2002: 1) offers three explanations for why large-scale fundamental organisation change rarely works:

- deep organisational change, particularly cultural change, is very difficult
- it may be difficult to make a case for change, particularly when an organisation appears to be doing well, and
- our knowledge of planning and implementing change is limited.

In reviewing the literature, different explanations of change management failure were apparent, as summarised in Box 18.

Strategic perspective – implementation problems, lack of sufficient support and technical and political factors
Structural perspective – difficulties in terms of technologies and division of labour
Power and politics perspective – defence of existing power relations, interests and positions
Cultural perspective – existing rules, habits, institutional arrangements and values
Psychological perspective – problems encountered in change processes

Box 18 – Different perspectives on change failure

In Box 18 Boonstra (2004: 461) offers a summary of explanations for organisational change failures, differentiating between explanations from different perspectives. These competing explanations inevitably reflect the academic discipline interests of different academics.

Hamlin (2001: 21) has suggested that some of the responsibility for change management failures rests with change managers, which is a similar position to his co-authors (Keep and Ash, 2001: 301) when they suggest that 'often, management puts the responsibility for change onto the "change" itself' (see also Griffith, 2002). There has been a functionalist tendency in explanations of failure offered so far. The implication is that if the way in which change is managed is altered, the outcome will change from failure to success. However, the challenge of delivering future success dependent upon how change is managed is considerable.

> *Business firms remain incapable of predicting accurately the technical and commercial outcomes of their own (and others') innovative activities.*
> *(Pavitt and Steinmueller, 2002: 351)*

There is a literature questioning the whole premise of change management. Griffith (2002: 298) warns that 'there can be no such things as successful change management programmes, actions or skills. In short, the whole industry is a fraud.' More philosophically, King and Anderson (1995: 125) have questioned the manageability of organisational change, arguing that the 'general illusion of manageability is composed of three sets of second-order illusory beliefs – the illusion of linearity, the illusion of predictability, and the illusion of control.' These illusions may be posed as questions:

- Does change proceed through stages?
- Are change processes predictable?
- Can managers control change?

If your answers to these questions are negative, change management failure becomes more of an inevitability than the taboo described earlier in this discussion. The argument can be taken to a logical if pessimistic conclusion by drawing upon theories of population ecology.

Organisations do not adapt to changed conditions – they die and are replaced by other organisations that are better aligned with the requirements of the environment. Thus death, not change, is critical because organisations rarely, if ever, change sufficiently enough to remain alive under changing conditions.

(Grint, 1998: 136)

This perspective on organisational change is very different from orthodox thinking. The underlying premise of the industry that has grown up around researching and managing organisational change and the premise for this textbook are challenged. No organisation exists for ever, although as Levine (2001: 1251) has remarked, there is a 'fantasy that an organisation must exist...' Pedler *et al* (1997: 234) in reflecting upon organisation ecology bring together the learning and change themes of this chapter.

Death does not figure greatly in the theories of organisational development, which may account in part for their tendency to 'look on the bright side', but contemporary evidence suggests that the ecologists' assumption is the likely fate, sooner or later, of all companies.

Senior managers through learning may limit change management failures and even achieve change management successes. However, the quotation raises awkward questions about organisational learning leading to immortality or to a good death (Pedler *et al*, 1997: 237).

Critically reviewing organisational learning

In the Understanding section of this chapter the meanings and theories of organisational learning and learning organisation were introduced. The intention here is to critically review these popular concepts.

Most theories of learning in general – and organisational learning, in particular – begin from a starting point of individual learning. However, individual learning is rarely encouraged in organisations except within very narrow parameters (Denton, 1998: 160). Conceptual concerns may be raised about whether we are concerned with an object called organisation learning or with learning on the part of individual members of an organisation. Van der Bent *et al* (1999) raise the question whether organisations as entities can do anything in their own right.

Argyris (1999: 7) identified challenges to organisational learning that arose from the literature – organisational learning is contradictory, organisational learning is a meaningful notion but not always beneficent, and do real-world organisations learn productively? These challenges may be explained as follows. The potentially contradictory nature of organisational learning relates to the belief that individuals rather than organisations learn. Although organisational learning is regarded as a neutral term, organisational learning may not always be used for good purposes. Argyris cites the emotive example of Nazi learning about carrying out evil. Also, the ability of organisations to remember past events, analyse alternatives, conduct experiments and evaluate the results of action may be questioned.

Burnes *et al* (2003: 457) highlight three reservations which have been raised about organisational learning: firstly, the lack of any consensus definition of the abstract concept of organisational learning; secondly, the scarcity of rigorous research in the area; and thirdly, the problems of generalising theories across different contexts, particularly in terms of generalising from studies of organisational learning undertaken in different countries.

Argyris (1999: 6) with his sustained interest in organisational learning is well placed to evaluate the learning organisation, and as might be imagined, he offers both bouquets and brickbats. He believes that the prescriptions that the likes of Schein and Senge offer are useful 'as guides to the kinds of organisational structures, processes and conditions that may function as enablers of productive organisational learning'. However, his concerns include ignoring analytical difficulties posed by organisational learning, no serious attention paid to processes that threaten the validity and utility of organisational learning, and the short shrift given to implementation difficulties.

Jackson (2001: 144–8) has drawn together the major criticisms of the learning organisation, which include:

- the learning organisation is ambiguous, amorphous and ill-defined
- Senge's books are based on the author's consulting experience rather than on systematic or rigorous research, and
- questions remain about the ethical and moral basis of the rhetorical vision of the learning organisation.

Thompson and McHugh (2002: 249) are sceptical about the learning organisation, believing that 'it has little respect for the learning theory from which it claims descent…' Watson (2002: 196) challenges the influential writing of Senge because it 'is explicitly rooted in systems thinking with both the naïve idealism and the unitary assumptions about organisations of his approach being apparent in the characterisation of learning organisations'. The above criticisms of the learning organisation tend to be at a conceptual level. However, given that the learning organisation is believed to have been driven by practioners, it is worthwhile considering examples of its application (see Research cases in Journals No.12).

RESEARCH CASES IN JOURNALS NO.12 – BANKS A, B, C, D AND E

The cases featured in this paper address learning on new technology projects in five anonymous banks referred to as Banks A to E. The cases were based upon interviews with 42 bank managers and industry consultants over 18 months. The author was also able to draw upon ten years' experience in the industry. The projects in Banks A, B and C were categorised by the participants as failures. The projects in Banks D and E by contrast were regarded as successful. The author believes that the case studies provide evidence that learning from past mistakes or past successes continues to be the exception rather than the rule.

Sector: UK retail banking
Research methods: Interviews.
Authors: Harris, L.
Paper title: The learning organisation – myth and reality? Examples from the UK retail banking industry
Journal details: *The Learning Organisation*, Vol.9, No.2, 2000; pp.78–88

Burnes *et al* (2003: 454) suggest that the term 'learning organisation' is used much less frequently now than in the late 1980s and early 1990s.

SYNOPSIS

Influential writers such as Argyris have been writing about organisational learning for over 40 years. Organisational learning was concisely defined as enhancing the collective ability to act more effectively. There is a more practice-oriented, prescriptive literature on the 'learning organisation' popularised by the publication of a book by Peter Senge, *The Fifth Discipline*. Senge identified the five component technologies or disciplines of a learning organisation as: systems thinking, personal mastery, mental models, building a shared vision, and team learning.

In considering change management success, ongoing larger debates about assessing an organisation's strategic performance were acknowledged. An important consideration in any discussion of change management success was the criteria used to determine success. The goal of success is embedded in societies and individuals, and this goal was very evident in the change management literature. Peters and Waterman were regarded as the initiators of the recipe approach to successful change management. Subsequently, many potential success factors for change have been generated, based upon a mix of research, business experience and anecdote.

Understanding about change management may be furthered through learning from change management failures, rather than searching for standardised recipes/steps to achieving successful change management. The high failure rate of change initiatives was acknowledged. However, exploring change management failure was regarded as engaging with an organisational taboo. Kotter, after learning that the majority of major change efforts failed, couched his model as a way to avoid making major errors in the change process.

Organisational learning and learning organisations were critically questioned in terms of their organisational relevance. There were conceptual concerns about whether we are concerned with an object called organisation learning or the learning of individual members of an organisation. Argyris identified challenges to organisational learning arising out of the literature – organisational learning is contradictory, organisational learning is a meaningful notion but not always beneficent, and do real-world organisations learn productively? Jackson drew together criticisms of the learning organisation which included: that the vision of the learning organisation was ambiguous, amorphous and ill-defined, and that Senge's books tend to be based on the author's consulting experience rather than on systematic or rigorous research.

DISCUSSION QUESTIONS

1 What have been the major learning points about change management that senior managements of organisations appear to have tried to make use of?

2 Do you believe that in any one particular organisation or sector more or less is being learned about change management?

3 Why do taboos exist in terms of writing and talking about failure?

4 What form would the opposite of a learning organisation take?

5 When should senior management encourage organisational learning?

6 Which is the more persuasive concept – organisational learning or the learning organisation?

FURTHER READING

BURNES B., COOPER C. and WEST P. (2003) Organisational learning: the new management paradigm? *Management Decision*, Vol.41, No.5; pp.452–64.

This paper provides the reader with an informative overview of the complex and often contradictory subject of organisational learning. The authors acknowledge the existence of the concept of the learning organisation but choose to major upon organisational learning. The authors do not offer new empirical material but do draw upon an extensive review of the more academic literature. They maintain a balance between explaining the appeal of organisational learning, while also challenging sweeping claims made for organisational learning.

CHILD J. (2005) *Organization: Contemporary Principles and Practices*, Oxford, Blackwell.

Child devotes a very informative chapter to 'organising for learning'. A strength of the chapter is that Child balances extensive theoretical knowledge of organisational learning with discussion of the operationalisation of the concept inside organisations.

KRANSDORFF A. (1998) *Corporate Amnesia: Keeping know-how in the company*, London, Butterworth-Heinemann.

In a book which should interest both academics and practioners Kransdorff establishes the concept of organisational memory in times of change. His fear is that if organisational memory is not facilitated, organisations will experience corporate amnesia. Although this sounds rather populist, the book is written in a thoughtful, reflective manner and is very compatible with debates about organisational learning introduced in this chapter.

SENGE P. (1990) *The Fifth Discipline: The art and practice of the learning organisation*, New York, Doubleday.

One of those influential books which gave considerable impetus to the learning organisation as a concept. As this chapter has demonstrated, the views of Senge have attracted bouquets as well as brickbats. However, in encouraging debates about learning organisations, the book made a significant contribution.

Conclusions

INTRODUCTION

This textbook has responded to the challenges of change management in a theoretical rather than a practical manner. The intention in this chapter is to draw upon earlier discussions in order to identify major emergent themes. The literature cited in this chapter is largely literature already cited. In terms of drawing upon previous chapters, synopses of the main themes discussed in previous chapters are available towards the end of each chapter. The aims of this textbook were to:

- advance understanding about change management from a critical perspective
- encourage an appreciation of the centrality of individuals in organisational change processes
- provoke debate in terms of the past, present and future understanding of change management.

These aims have guided discussions throughout this textbook, and it may be useful to bear them in mind when reading the conclusions. It is hoped that the reader will draw his or her own conclusions from what has been a wide-ranging textbook. However, the following conclusions about change management understanding may be drawn from the process of writing this textbook.

An understanding of change management:
- always benefits from classifying what is changing
- must recognise and address the different levels of analysis informing change management
- is predicated upon an acknowledgement of the ambiguities of change
- is informed by the past, the present and the future
- requires an understanding of individual learning, group learning and organisational learning about change
- must acknowledge the problematic nature of managing change
- involves understanding relationships between change and stability
- requires an improved understanding of the concept of hope.

Box 19 – Conclusions about understanding change management

The following discussion explores each of these conclusions in more detail and cross-references the conclusions to earlier discussions in the textbook about relevant theories and concepts.

THE CLASSIFICATIONS OF CHANGE

In Chapter 3 the change classifications framework was introduced, offering a complicated answer to a simple question – what is change? Although the change classifications framework was developed primarily as an academic classification tool, it was believed to have potential to be applied to change inside organisations in terms of the past, present and future. The framework encouraged understanding of change management, moving from the general to the particular and through a process of inquisitive questioning. The emphasis upon understanding change in specific contexts rather than generalisations about change has been a theme of this textbook.

The whole textbook has emphasised classification as a means of clarifying understanding about change management. Each chapter in introducing theories and concepts has sought through classification to clarify the meanings of different change management concepts. Invariably, there are competing classifications of change, and in Chapter 3 classifications by Paton and McCalman (2000), Burke (2002), Dawson (2003) and Balogun and Hope Hailey (2004) were cited as illustrative examples of competing change classifications. However, the existence of competing explanations allows comparisons of similarities and differences between change management in different situations. Dunphy (1996) argued for the existence of competing theories and empirical investigation to substantiate their claims. It is through such classifications and subsequent original research that it is possible to begin to challenge the generalisations and all-pervasive hyperbole of change management and to advance understanding about change management.

> Understanding change management always benefits from classifying what is changing.

CHANGE MANAGEMENT AND LEVELS OF ANALYSIS

Diverse sources of literature inform understanding about change. Collins (1998), for example, identifies hero-manager reflections, biographies, guru works, student-oriented texts, critical monographs and research studies. There are differences between these sources, but there are also similarities. One similarity which became apparent was a frequent failure to address different levels of analysis either in the theories of change management or in the practice of change management. At its crudest this involved theorising about generalised organisational change with no apparent appreciation of either the wider context in which organisations operated or of the individuals and groups which comprised organisations. In a similar manner there was a danger that senior managers in attempting to change their organisations may not have been addressing the need for individuals and groups to change. Woodward and Hendry (2004) in their survey found that one third of senior managers acknowledged that people aspects were ignored in their change programmes. However, this apparent lack of appreciation of individual involvement in organisational change is not a purely academic concern.

> *Change doesn't happen because a chief executive or other top management figure says it should; change happens because the majority of people involved willingly or unwillingly agree to change their behaviour.*
>
> *(Conner, 1998)*

The quotation equates with many of the arguments in this textbook. However, the practical realisation of what Conner is proposing may be more difficult to achieve.

As an antidote Box 2 highlighted a range of change management writers who urge a greater appreciation of individual change as part of organisational change processes. Randall (2004) believed that 'writers may conflate the process of change at the different levels of individual, group and organisation learning into one seamless series of events.' The explanation of why such conflation has occurred is more difficult to assert. One explanation offered in Chapter 9 was that 'there is little information on individual change in organisations because approaches to managing change have been developed at a group or systems level' (French and Delahaye, 1996). This explanation would certainly fit with discussions in Chapter 2 about the origins of the concept of change management. It was suggested that the concept may have originated with the writings of Kurt Lewin, or organisational development, or the activities of the management consultancies.

Also, the literature that seeks to inform change management understanding has often appeared to be preoccupied with a particular level. Economic analyses were preoccupied with national and sectoral analysis, strategic analyses were preoccupied with sectoral and organisation-wide analyses, group analyses were preoccupied with group norms, and group dynamics and individual-level analysis was preoccupied with the idiosyncrasies of individuals. Each level of analysis has strengths and weaknesses, and change management understanding has been advanced by analysis at each level, the academic disciplines making different contributions at different levels. However, any overall understanding requires a synthesis of understanding at all levels. This may prove challenging for authors because it suggests crossing traditional academic discipline boundaries.

> Understanding change management must recognise and address the different levels of analysis informing change management.

THE AMBIGUITIES OF CHANGE MANAGEMENT

The strength of change management may be that it can be whatever you want it to be. In earlier chapters, the slipperiness of the concept of change was emphasised. Dawson (1994) warned that changes in organisations are never clearly defined, and Dunphy (1996) warned that there is no agreed theory of change. Although clarifying meaning is an important principle of academic work, there may be benefits arising out of ambiguity for both organisations and academics.

In terms of change management practice, the rhetoric of change may be used to persuade employees. The ambiguity of change communications may reflect the ambiguities of change processes. Senior management may use ambiguous rhetoric as a part of the change management process. Johnson et al (2005) suggested that 'change agents may employ language and metaphor to galvanise change.'

Academics benefit from the ambiguities of change management through the lack of precision of the concept, which thus includes rather than excludes competing explanations. For example, a change management conference or journal may receive contributions from a wide range of academics on areas such as operations management, psychology, sociology and economics. In this way the term becomes an umbrella term for a range of contributions to the central goal of advancing understanding about change management. The pluralism arising out of the ambiguity of change management is believed to be positive.

More troublingly, an understanding of change management may remain ambiguous because of limited understanding of change management. Dawson (2003), while acknowledging the emergence of a large body of knowledge about change management over the past 100 years, does not believe that this work has provided any lasting answers. Similarly, Grey (2000) has described the organisational change literature as almost entirely appalling.

> Understanding change management is predicated upon an acknowledgement of the ambiguities of change.

CHANGE MANAGEMENT – THE PAST, THE PRESENT AND THE FUTURE

The dynamic nature of change suggests that an appreciation of time must always be an integral ingredient in understanding change management. 'Change involves a movement to some future state that comprises a context and time that remain unknown' (Dawson, 2003). Change management has to be understood in terms of the past, present and future, and the different contexts of change have to be understood in terms of the past, present and future (Dawson, 2003).

History offers a perspective on change management. At first glance history traces the evolution of understanding about change management from the early and simplistic attempts of Taylor (1911) to classify management through to quite sophisticated accounts of strategic change, such as Darwin *et al* (2002). However, nothing is as it seems. The concept of historiography (Cooke, 1999) explained how our understanding of change management is a product of how history has been written. In Chapter 2, this was illustrated by Cooke (1999) in terms of the contribution of women being written into French and Bell's OD textbook only in the 1996 edition.

In a similar manner the apparent linearity of change management must be questioned. Salaman and Asch (2003) were not alone in regarding organisational change as not being linear: 'If it has any direction, it is very often cyclical.' Burrell (1992) looked at change with specific reference to time, leading him to challenge notions of linearity and chronarchy and to promote the notion of spiral time (depicted pictorially as a coiled serpent). Similarly, Cummings (2002) challenged assumptions about the linearity of change, instead arguing for 'a vision of time not as a straight line but as a spiral, with past, present and future intermingled.'

> Understanding change management is informed by the past, the present and the future.

CHANGE THROUGH LEARNING AND LEARNING THROUGH CHANGING

Learning appears to be a prerequisite of changing, and changing a prerequisite of learning. The ability to learn may move individuals away from the anxiety phase of change (French and Delahaye, 1996). In Chapter 15, learning was considered in terms of learning from change management successes and change management failures – although organisational change has an undeniable tendency to produce failure (Sorge and Van Witteloostuijn, 2004). Change writers, if they mention failure, invariably describe it as lack of success (Thorne, 2000). There appears to be potential in learning from change management failure, yet in exploring change management failure, talking and writing about failure is engaging with an organisational taboo (Thorne, 2000; Sennett, 2001).

Earlier discussions about individual-, group- and organisational-level analysis of change are relevant to learning about change. In the previous chapter organisational learning and learning organisations were reviewed with specific reference to change. Although criticisms were raised about these concepts, it was apparent that advances were being made in understanding relationships between organisational learning and change. There is a similar requirement to understand how individuals and groups learn as part of organisational change processes.

> Understanding change management requires an understanding of individual learning, group learning and organisational learning about change.

QUESTIONING THE MANAGEABILITY OF CHANGE

This textbook has focused upon understanding change management rather than the practice of change management. However, change management is an applied concept, suggesting that change could and should be managed. The textbook has highlighted the problematic nature of managing change. Early writings (Lewin, 1951) were concerned with planned change, and the management of planned change has been a major theme of organisational development (Cummings and Worley, 2000). However, in recent times a greater appreciation of change as emergent has been fuelled by criticisms of planned change (Burnes, 1996). The emergent model of change raises questions about the manageability of change management.

King and Anderson (2002: 163) described the illusory nature of the manageability of organisational change in term of illusions of linearity, predictability and control. Linearity has already been discussed in terms of time. Predictability may be the Achilles' heel of specifically planned change and, more generally, strategic planning. Despite the existence of increasingly sophisticated tools to forecast the future, nobody can predict the future with certainty. Firms remain incapable of accurately predicting the outcomes of their own (and others') innovative activities (Pavitt and Steinmueller, 2002). This is the biggest challenge for the manageability of change management – at times change management writing and practice implies a science of soothsaying. In Chapter 14 the contradictory nature of control and change was discussed. In a manner similar to the illusions of linearity and predictability there remains a question mark over the ability of management to control change. On one level, change must be controlled; on another level, are notions of control realistic?

> Understanding change management is predicated upon an acknowledgement of the problematic nature of managing change.

CHANGE MANAGEMENT AND STABILITY MANAGEMENT

Despite the strong human preference for stability (De Wit and Meyer, 2004), change continues to be encouraged in organisations. Eccles and Nohria (1992) found that arguments for maintaining the status quo were hard to find and even harder to defend. Matheny (1998) warned that maintaining an organisation's status quo could be equivalent to self-destruction, and only the absence of change appears to be regarded as deficiency (Sorge and Van Witteloostuijn, 2004).

However, there were signs that the critical change literature was becoming more circumspect about the case for constant change. 'With all the hype these days about change, we desperately need more messages about some good old-fashioned stability' (Mintzberg *et al*, 1998). As well as understanding change management in terms of stability and change, there is a need to recognise continuity as part of change. Cummings (2002) insightfully highlighted the paradox that managing change requires continuity and that the presence of traditions enables a connection between past, present and future. Sturdy and Grey (2003) adopted a similar perspective on continuity: 'Change and continuity are not alternative objective states: they are not alternatives because they are typically co-existent and coterminous...' The writings of Cummings and Sturdy and Grey are atypical of mainstream change management literature. However, they signpost more radical thinking about change which will inform thinking about change management in the future.

> Understanding change management involves understanding relationships between change and stability.

THE HOPE WITHIN CHANGE MANAGEMENT

In this textbook a critical perspective has been favoured in order to further understanding about change management. This appears pertinent given shortcomings in what is known about change management. However, the study of change management revealed hope as an unacknowledged theme running throughout both the practice and study of change management.

Hope is the fuel of progress and fear is the prison in which you put yourself.
(Tony Benn, quoted in Younge, 2002)

This textbook would not have happened without the 'fuel of progress', and its biggest challenge was the 'fear' of failure. In writing this textbook many change management initiatives were reviewed. These initiatives attracted both bouquets and brickbats, however; the commonality in each one was that their instigators must have hoped that their implementation would make a beneficial difference. As Harung (1997) suggests, 'We act in order to change one state of affairs into one that is more desirable. This is the only worthwhile direction of change.' The conclusion drawn here is that hope is an important ingredient in any understanding of the practice of change management.

What is surprising is that hope is an underdeveloped concept in terms of academic study. Even a critical theorist must hope that his or her writing will influence readers. In subjects such as strategy, mission statements and organisational values are the subject of academic study – and in organisational behaviour, motivation and commitment are the subject of academic study – yet hope appears to remain neglected in the context of change management. In attempting to understand change management and hope, hope is likely to be evident at an individual, group and organisational level.

Burnes (1996) credited Lewin as the originator of change management through his work on planned change. Lewin's work has been both praised and criticised. What cannot be questioned is that his writing has informed debates about change management. What is ironic is that Lewin was writing about hope over 60 years ago, in this instance with specific reference to unemployment.

An analysis of this behavior shows the importance of that psychological factor which commonly is called 'hope'... Hope means that 'sometime in the future, the real situation will be changed so that it will equal my wishes.'

(Lewin, 1942: 80)

Lewin suggests that seldom does the 'psychological future' correspond with what actually happens. In this instance, however, in reflecting upon hope he may have offered a clue to the way forward in terms of change management. Hope is an integral element of any change either at an organisational level or an individual level. This textbook has attempted always to maintain a balance between hopeful progress and critical understanding.

> Understanding change management requires an improved understanding of the concept of hope.

CONCLUDING COMMENTS

Sorge and Van Witteloostuijn (2004) argued for change management through effective management rather than specialised change management, believing that well-established organisation theories are readily applicable in the practice of organisational change. Change management does not necessarily require new theories as much as the effective application of existing theories of management and organisational behaviour. In this textbook, for example, theories relating to communication, leadership and control would be equally relevant in a general management and organisational behaviour textbook. The challenge has been the application of such theories in order to advance change management understanding.

The fascination of studying change management is both that it involves the study of a dynamic aspect of organisational life and also that the process of understanding change management itself is dynamic. The following two quotations highlight the dynamic nature of change management.

Change has been with us forever, and it always will be – but the idea of change itself is changing.

(Abrahamson, 2000)

Change is not an entity to be conquered, outwitted, or prevented. It is an ongoing process that is never completed.

(Bruhn, 2004)

It is just over half a century since Lewin (1951) encouraged interest in the study of change in organisations. In that time theorists have argued for change as something planned and something emergent; they have argued for change as something rational and something irrational. What is certain is that in the future there will be more theories, more debates ... and more change.

References

ABRAHAMSON E. (2000) Change without pain, *Harvard Business Review*, Vol.78, Issue 4, July-August; pp.75–9.

ACKROYD S. and THOMPSON P. (1999) *Organizational Misbehaviour*, London, Sage Publications.

ACKROYD S. (2002) *The Organization of Business: Applying organizational theory to contemporary change*, Oxford, Oxford University Press.

AHN M. J., ADAMSON J. S. A. and DORNBUSCH D. (2004) From leaders to leadership: managing change, *The Journal of Leadership and Organizational Studies*, Vol.10, No.4; pp.112–23.

ALVESSON M. and BILLING Y. D. (1997) *Understanding Gender and Organizations*, London, Sage Publications.

ALVESSON M. and WILLMOTT H. (1996) *Making Sense of Management: A critical introduction*, London, Sage Publications.

AMABILE T. (2001) How to kill creativity, in J. HENRY (ed.) *Creative Management*, London, Open University in association with Sage Publications.

AMBROSINI V., with JOHNSON G. and SCHOLES K. (1998) *Exploring Techniques of Analysis and Evaluation in Strategic Management*, Harlow, FT/Prentice Hall.

AMERICAN MANAGEMENT ASSOCIATION (1994) *Survey on Change Management*, New York, American Management Association.

ANTONACOPOULOU E. P. and GABRIEL Y. (2001) Emotion, learning and organizational change: towards an integration of psychoanalytic and other perspectives, *Journal of Organizational Change Management*, Vol.14, No.5; pp.435–51.

ARGYRIS C. and SCHON D. (1978) *Organizational Learning: A theory of action perspective*, Reading MA, Addison-Wesley.

ARGYRIS C. (2001) Empowerment: the emperor's new clothes, in J. HENRY (ed.) *Creative Management*, London, Open University in association with Sage Publications.

ARGYRIS C. (1971) *Management and Organizational Development*, New York, McGraw-Hill.

ARGYRIS C. (1999) *On Organizational Learning*, Oxford, Blackwell Business.

ARNOLD J. (2005) *Work Psychology: Understanding human behaviour in the workplace*, Harlow, FT/Prentice Hall.

ASCH S. E. (1952) Effects of group pressure upon the modification and distortion of judgements, in C. E. SWANSON, T. M. NEWCOMBE and E. L. HARTLEY (eds) *Readings in Social Psychology*, New York, Holt, Rinehart & Winston.

ASH K., HAMLIN B. and KEEP J. (2001) Introduction, in B. HAMLIN., J. KEEP and K. ASH (eds) *Organizational Change and Development: A reflective guide for managers, trainers and developers*, Harlow, FT/Prentice Hall.

BALOGUN J. and HOPE HAILEY V. (2004) *Exploring Strategic Change*, 2nd edition Harlow, FT/Prentice Hall.

BARRETT D. J. (2002) Change communication: using strategic employee communication to facilitate major change, *Corporate Communications: An International Journal*, Vol.7, No.4; pp.219–31.

BARTLETT C. A. and GHOSHAL S. (1995) *Transnational Management: Texts, cases and readings in cross-border management*, Homewood IL, R. D. Irwin Inc.

BARTOL K. and MARTIN D. (1994) *Management*, New York, McGraw-Hill.

BASS B. M. and AVOLIO B. J. (1994) *Improving Organisational Effectiveness Through Transformational Leadership*, Thousand Oaks, California, Sage Publications.

BECK A., BENNETT P. and WALL P. (2002) *Communication Studies: The essential introduction*, London, Routledge.

BECKHARD R. and PRITCHARD W. (1992) *Changing the Essence: The art of creating and leading fundamental change in organizations*, San Francisco, Jossey Bass.

BECKHARD R. (1969) *Organization Development: Strategies and models*, Reading MA, Addison-Wesley.

BEEKUN R. (1989) Assessing the effectiveness of sociotechnical interventions: antidote or fad? *Human Relations*, Vol.42; pp.877–97.

BEER M. (1980) *Organization Change and Development: A systems view*, Dallas, Scott Foresman.

BEER M., EISENSTAT R. A. and SPENCER B. (1990) Why change programs don't produce change, *Harvard Business Review*, Vol.68, Issue 6, November-December; pp.158–66.

BELBIN R. M. (1981) *Management Teams*, London, Heinemann Educational.

BION W. R. (1961) *Experience in Groups*, New York, Basic Books.

BLANCHARD K. and PEALE N. (1988) *The Power of Ethical Management*, New York, Fawcett Crest.

BOONSTRA J. J. (2004) Conclusions, in J. J. BOONSTRA (ed.) *Dynamics of Organizational Change and Learning*, Chichester, John Wiley & Sons.

BOWDITCH J. L. and BUONO A. F. (2005) *A Primer on Organizational Behaviour*, 6th edition, Hoboken, John Wiley & Sons.

BRADSHAW P. and BOONSTRA J. (2004) Power dynamics in organizational change: a multi-perspective approach, in J. J. BOONSTRA (ed.) *Dynamics of Organizational Change and Learning*, Chichester, John Wiley & Sons.

BRAVERMAN H. (1974) *Labour and Monopoly Capital: The degradation of work in the twentieth century*, New York, Monthly Review Press.

BREHM J. W. (1966) *A Theory of Psychological Resistance*, New York, Academic Press.

BRIDGES W. (1995) *Managing Transitions: Making the most of change*, London, Nicholas Brearly.

BROOKS I. (1999) *Organisational Behaviour: Individuals, groups and the organisation*, Harlow, FT/Pitman Publishing.

BROWN A. (1998) *Organisational Culture*, 2nd edition, London, FT/Pitman Publishing.

BRUHN J. G. (2004) Leaders who create change and those who manage it: how leaders limit success, *The Health Care Manager*, Vol.23, No.2; pp.132–40.

BRYMAN A. (2004) *The Disneyization of Society*, London, Sage Publications.

BUCHANAN D. and BADHAM R. (1999) *Power, Politics and Organizational Change: Winning the turf game*, London, Sage Publications.

BUCHANAN D. and HUCZYNSKI A. (2004) *Organizational Behaviour: An introductory text*, 5th edition, Harlow, FT/Prentice Hall.

BURKE W. (2002) *Organization Change: Theory and practice*, Thousand Oaks, California, Sage Publications.

BURNES B. (2004a) *Managing Change*, 4th edition, Harlow, FT/Prentice Hall.

BURNES B. (2004b) Kurt Lewin and the planned approach to change: a re-appraisal, *Journal of Management Studies*, Vol.41, No.6; pp.977–1002.

BURNES B. (1996) No such thing as...a 'one best way' to manage organizational change, *Management Decision*, Vol.34, No.10; pp.11–18.

BURNES B., COOPER C. and WEST P. (2003) Organisational learning: the new management paradigm? *Management Decision*, Vol.41, No.5; pp.452–64.

BURNS J. M. (1978) *Leadership*, New York, Harper & Row.

BURNS T. and STALKER G. M. (1961) *The Management of Innovation*, London, Tavistock Publications.

BURRELL G. (1992) Back to the future: time and organization, in M. REED and M. HUGHES (eds) *Rethinking Organization: New directions in organization theory and analysis*, London, Sage Publications.

CALAS M. B. and SMIRCICH L. (1996) From the 'woman's' point of view: feminist approaches to organization studies, in S. CLEGG and C. HARDY (eds) *Handbook on Organisations*, London, Sage Publications.

CALDWELL R. (2003) Change leaders and change managers: different or complementary? *Leadership and Organization Development Journal*, Vol.24, No.5; pp.285–93.

CALUWE L. DE and VERMAAK H. (2003) *Learning to Change: A guide for organization change agents*, Thousand Oaks, California, Sage Publications.

CAMERON E. and GREEN M. (2004) *Making Sense of Change Management: A complete guide to the models, tools and techniques of organizational change*, London, Kogan Page.

CAPON C. (2004) *Understanding Organisational Context: Inside and outside organisations*, 2nd edition, Harlow, FT/Prentice Hall.

CARNALL C. A. (2003) *Managing Change in Organizations*, 4th edition, Harlow, FT/Prentice Hall.

CHARTERED INSTITUTE OF PERSONNEL AND DEVELOPMENT (2004) *Reorganising for success: a survey of HR's role in change*, www.cipd.cp.uk/surveys, London, CIPD.

CHILD J. (1972) Organisation structure, environment and performance: the role of strategic choice, *Sociology*, Vol.6, No.1; pp.1–22.

CHILD J. (2005) *Organization: Contemporary principles and practices*, Oxford, Blackwell.

CLARK K. B. and WHEELRIGHT S. C. (2004) Organizing and leading heavyweight development teams (1992), in M. L. TUSHMAN and P. ANDERSON (eds) *Managing Strategic Innovation and Change: A collection of readings*, Oxford, Oxford University Press.

CLARK T. and FINCHAM R. (eds) (2002) *Critical Consulting: New perspectives on the management advice industry*, Oxford, Blackwell.

CLARKE A. and MANTON S. (1997) A benchmarking tool for change management, *Business Process Management*, Vol.3, No.3; pp.248–55.

CLEGG C. and WALSH S. (2004) Change management: Time for a change! *European Journal of Work and Organizational Psychology*, Vol.13, No.2; pp.217–39.

CLEGG S., KORNBERGER M. and PITSIS T. (2005) *Managing and Organizations: An introduction to theory and practice*, London, Sage Publications.

COBB A. T., WOOTEN K. C. and FOLGER R. (1995) Justice in the making: toward understanding the theory and practice of justice in organizational change and development, in R. WOODMAN and W. PASMORE (eds) *Research in Organizational Change and Development*, Vol.8, Greenwich CT, JAI Press; pp.243–95.

COCH L. and FRENCH J. R. P (jnr) (1948) Overcoming resistance to change, *Human Relations*, Vol.11; pp.512–32.

COGHLAN D. (1994) Managing organizational change through teams and groups, *Leadership and Organization Development Journal*, Vol.15, No.2; pp.18–23.

COLLINS D. (2000) *Management Fads and Buzzwords: Critical-practical perspectives*, London, Routledge.

COLLINS D. (1998) *Organizational Change: A sociological perspective*, London, Routledge.

CONGER J. A. (1998) The dark side of leadership (1990), in G. R. HICKMAN (ed.) *Leading Organizations: Perspectives for a new era*, Thousand Oaks, Sage Publications.

CONNER D. R. (1998) *Managing at the Speed of Change*, Chichester, John Wiley & Sons.

COOKE B. (1999) Writing the left out of management theory: the historiography of the management of change, *Organization*, Vol.6, No.1; pp.81–105.

COPELAND T., ROLLER T. and MURRIN J. (1993) *Valuation Measuring and Managing the Value of Companies*, New York, John Wiley & Sons.

CORBETT E. P. J. (1990) *Classical Rhetoric for the Modern Student*, Oxford, Oxford University Press.

CROM S. and BERTELS T. (1999) Change leadership: the virtues of deviance, *Leadership and Organization Development Journal*, Vol.20, No.3; pp.162–7.

CUMMINGS S. (2002) *Recreating Strategy*, London, Sage Publications.

CUMMINGS T. and MOLLOY E. (1977) *Improving Productivity and the Quality of Work Life*, New York, Praeger.

CUMMINGS T. (2004) Organization development and change: foundations and applications, in J. J. BOONSTRA (ed.) *Dynamics of Organizational Change and Learning*, Chichester, John Wiley & Sons.

CUMMINGS T. G. and WORLEY C. G. (2005) *Organization Development and Change*, 8th edition, Ohio, Thomson South-Western.

DAFT R. L. (1995) *Organisation Theory and Design*, Minneapolis/St Paul, West Publishing.

DALY F., TEAGUE P. and KITCHEN P. (2003) Exploring the role of internal communication during organisational change, *Corporate Communications: An International Journal*, Vol.8, No.3; pp.153–62.

DARWIN J., JOHNSON P. and McCAULEY J. (2002) *Developing Strategies for Change*, Harlow, FT/Prentice Hall.

DAWSON P. (1994) *Organizational Change: A processual approach*, London, Paul Chapman.

DAWSON P. (2003) *Understanding Organizational Change: The contemporary experience of people at work*, London, Sage Publications.

Dawson S. (1996) *Analysing Organisations*, Houndmills, Macmillan Business.

De Caluwe L. and Vermaak H. (2003) *Learning to Change: A guide for organization change agents*, London, Sage Publications.

De Caluwe L. and Vermaak H. (2004) Thinking about change in different colours: multiplicity in change processes, in J. J. Boonstra (ed.) *Dynamics of Organizational Change and Learning*, Chichester, John Wiley & Sons.

De Geus A. (1997) The living company, *Harvard Business Review*, Vol.75, Issue 2, March/April; pp.51–9.

De Wit B. and Meyer R. (2004) *Strategy: Process, content and context*, London, Thomson Learning.

Deal T. E. and Kennedy A. A. (1982) *Corporate Cultures: The rites and rituals of corporate life*, Reading MA, Addison-Wesley.

Deal T. E. and Kennedy A. A. (1999) *The New Corporate Cultures: Revitalizing the workplace after downsizing, mergers and reengineering*, London, Orion Business.

Deming W. E. (1986) *Out of the Crisis*, Cambridge, Cambridge University Press.

Dent E. B. and Goldberg S. G. (2000) Challenging 'resistance to change', *Journal of Applied Behavioral Sciences*, Vol.35, No.1; pp.25–41.

Denton J. (1998) *Organisational Learning and Effectiveness*, London, Routledge.

DiGeorgio R. M. (2002) Making mergers and acquisitions work: what we know and don't know – Part I, *Journal of Change Management*, Vol.3, No.2; pp.134–48.

DiGeorgio R. M. (2003) Making mergers and acquisitions work: what we know and don't know – Part II, *Journal of Change Management*, Vol.3, No.3; pp.259–74.

DiMaggio P. and Powell W. W. (eds) (1991) *The New Institutionalism in Organisational Analysis*, London, University of Chicago Press.

Dixon N. M. (1994) *The Organizational Learning Cycle: How we can learn collectively*, London, McGraw-Hill.

Dubrin A. J. (1974) *Fundamentals of Organizational Behavior: An applied perspective*, New York, Pergammon Press.

Duck J. D. (1998) Managing change: the art of balancing (1993), reprinted in *Harvard Business Review on Change*, Harvard, Harvard Business Review Paperback.

Dunkerley D. (2001) Work organizations, managerial strategies and control, in G. Salaman (ed.) *Understanding Business Organisations*, London, Routledge.

Dunphy D. and Stace D. (1993) The strategic management of corporate change, *Human Relations*, Vol.46, No.8; pp.905–20.

Dunphy D. (1996) Organizational change in corporate settings, *Human Relations*, Vol.49, No.5; pp.541–52.

Eccles R. G. and Nohria N. (1992) *Beyond the Hype: Rediscovering the essence of management*, Harvard, Harvard Business School Press.

Eisenhardt K. M. (2000) Paradox, spirals, ambivalence: the new language of change and pluralism, *Academy of Management Review*, Vol.25, No.4; pp.703–5.

Elmuti D. (1997) Self–managed work teams approach: creative management tool or a fad? *Management Decision*, Vol.35, No.3; pp.233–9.

ERNECQ J. (1992) Planned and unplanned organizational change: consequences and implications, in D. M. HOSKING and N. ANDERSON (eds) *Organizational Change and Innovation: Psychological perspectives and practices in Europe*, London, Routledge.

EZZAMEL M., GREEN C., LILLEY S. and WILLMOTT H. (1995) *Changing Managers and Managing Change*, London, Chartered Institute of Management Accountants.

FARIAS G. and JOHNSON H. (2000) Organizational development and change management: setting the record straight, *The Journal of Applied Behavioral Science*, Vol.36, No.3, September; pp.376–9.

FAYOL H. (1916) *General and Industrial Management*, (translated by C. Storrs in 1946), London, Pitman.

FINCHAM R. and EVANS M. (1999) The consultants' offensive: re-engineering – from fad to technique, *New Technology, Work and Employment*, Vol.14, No.1; pp.32–44.

FINCHAM R. and RHODES P. (2005) *Principles of Organizational Behaviour*, Oxford, Oxford University Press.

FINSTAD N. (1998) The rhetoric of organizational change, *Human Relations*, Vol.51, No.6; pp.717–40.

FLYNN F. J. and CHATMAN J. A. (2004) Strong cultures and innovation: oxymoron or opportunity? (2001), in M. L. TUSHMAN and P. ANDERSON (eds) *Managing Strategic Innovation and Change: A collection of readings*, Oxford, Oxford University Press.

FORD J. D., FORD L. W and MCNAMARA R. T. (2002) Resistance and the background conversations of change, *Journal of Organizational Change Management*, Vol.15, No.2; pp.105–21.

FORD M. (1998) *Surveillance and Privacy at Work*, London, the Institute of Employment Rights.

FOREMAN J. (2001) Organizational change, in E. WILSON (ed.) *Organizational Behaviour Reassessed: The impact of gender*, London, Sage Publications.

FOUCAULT M. (2004) Panopticonism (1979), in F. WEBSTER, R. BLOM, E. KARVONEN, H. MELIN, K. NORDENSTRENG and others (eds) *The Information Society Reader*, London, Routledge.

FRANCIS D. and BESSANT J. (2005) Targeting innovation and implications for capability development, *Technovation*, Vol.25, No.3; pp.171–83.

FRANSELLA F. (1975) *Need to Change?* London, Methuen Essential Psychology Series.

FRENCH E. and DELAHAYE B. (1996) Individual change transition: moving in circles can be good for you, *Leadership and Organization Development Journal*, Vol.17, No.7; pp.22–8.

FRENCH J. R. P. and RAVEN B. H. (1959) The social bases of power, in D. CARTWRIGHT (ed.) *Studies in Social Power*, Ann Arbor, University of Michigan Press.

FRENCH W. L. and BELL C. H. (1973) *Organisation Development: Behavioural science interventions for organisational improvement*, Englewood Cliffs NJ, Prentice Hall.

FROST P. J., MOORE L. F., LOUIS M. R., LUNDBERG C. C. and MARTIN J. (1991) *Reframing Organizational Culture*, Beverly Hills, Sage Publications.

FURNHAM A. (1997) *The Psychology of Behaviour at Work: The individual in the organization*, Hove, Psychology Press.

GABRIEL Y. (2001) The state of critique in organizational theory, *Human Relations*, Vol.54, No.1; pp.23–30.

GALPIN T. J. (1996) *The Human Side of Change: A practical guide to organization redesign*, San Francisco, Jossey Bass.

GAUGHAN P. A. (2002) *Mergers, Acquisitions and Corporate Restructurings*, New York, John Wiley & Sons.

GENUS A. (1998) *The Management of Change: Perspectives and practice*, London, International Thomson Business Press.

GEORGE J. M. and JONES G. R. (2001) Towards a process model of individual change in organizations, *Human Relations*, Vol.54. No.4; pp.419–44.

GHAYE T. (2005) Reflection as a catalyst for change, Editorial, *Reflective Practice*, Vol.6, No.2; pp.177–87.

GILL R. (2003) Change management – or change leadership? *Journal of Change Management*, Vol.3, No.4; pp.307–18.

GINI A. (1998) Moral leadership and business ethics, in G. R. HICKMAN (ed.) *Leading Organizations: Perspectives for a new era*, Thousand Oaks, California, Sage Publications.

GOLEMBIEWSKI R., PROEHL C. and SINK D. (1982) Estimating success of OD applications, *Training and Development Journal*, No.72; pp.86–95.

GOODMAN J. and TRUSS C. (2004) The medium and the message: communicating effectively during a major change initiative, *Journal of Change Management*, Vol.4, No.3; pp.217–28.

GOODMAN M. B. (2001) Current trends in corporate communication, *Corporate Communications: An International Journal*, Vol.6, No.3; pp.117–23.

GRAETZ F. (2000) Strategic change leadership, *Management Decision*, Vol.38, No.8; pp.550–62.

GRAETZ F., RIMMER M., LAWRENCE A. and SMITH A. (2002) *Managing Organisational Change*, Chichester, John Wiley & Sons.

GRAVENHORST K. B and IN 'T VELD R. (2004) Power and collaboration: methodologies for working together in change, in J. J. BOONSTRA (ed.) *Dynamics of Organizational Change and Learning*, Chichester, John Wiley & Sons.

GRIFFIN M. A., RAFFERTY A. A. and MASON C. M. (2004) Who started this? Investigating different sources of organizational change, *Journal of Business and Psychology*, Vol.18, No.4; pp.555–70.

GRIFFITH J. (2002) Why change management fails, *Journal of Change Management*, Vol.2, No.4; pp.297–304.

GRIGGS H. E. and HYLAND P. (2003) Strategic downsizing and learning organisations, *Journal of European Industrial Training*, Vol.27, Issue 2–4; pp.177–87.

GRINT K. and CASE P. (1998) The violent rhetoric of re-engineering: management consultancy on the offensive, *Journal of Management Studies*, Vol.35, No.5; pp.557–77.

GRINT K. and WILLCOCKS L. (1995) Business process re-engineering in theory and practice: business paradise regained? *New Technology, Work and Employment*, Vol.10, No.2; pp.99–109.

GRINT K. and WOOLGAR S. (1997) *The Machine at Work: Technology, work and organization*, Cambridge, Polity Press.

GRINT K. (2005) *Leadership: Limits and possibilities*, Houndmills, Palgrave Macmillan.

GRINT K. (1998) *The Sociology of Work: An introduction*, Cambridge, Polity Press.

Guest D. (1992) Right enough to be dangerously wrong: an analysis in search of the excellence phenomenon, in G. Salaman (ed.) *Human Resource Strategies*, London, Sage Publications.

Guimaraes T. and Armstrong C. (1998) Empirically testing the impact of change management effectiveness on company performance, *European Journal of Innovation Management*, Vol.1, No.2; pp.74–84.

Haberberg A. and Rieple A. (2001) *The Strategic Management of Organisations*, Harlow, FT/Prentice Hall.

Haddad C. J. (2002) *Managing Technological Change: A strategic partnership approach*, Thousand Oaks, California, Sage Publications.

Hales C. (2000) Management and empowerment programmes, *Work, Employment and Society*, Vol.14, No.3; pp.501–19.

Hambrick D. C. and Cannella A. A.(jnr) (1989) Strategy implementation as substance and selling, *Academy of Management Executive*, Vol.3, No.4; pp.278–85.

Hamlin B. (2001) A review and synthesis of context and practice, in B. Hamlin, J. Keep and K. Ash (eds) *Organizational Change and Development: A reflective guide for managers, trainers and developers*, Harlow, FT/Prentice Hall.

Hammer M. and Champy J. (1993) *Reengineering the Corporation: A manifesto for business revolution*, London, Nicholas Brearly.

Hammer M. and Stanton S. A. (1995) *The Reengineering Revolution: A handbook*, New York, Harper Business.

Hammer M. (1990) Reengineering work: don't automate – obliterate, *Harvard Business Review*, Vol.68, Issue 4, July-August; pp.104–12.

Handy C. B. (1978) *The Gods of Management*, Harmondsworth, Penguin.

Hardy C. and Clegg S. (2004) Power and change: a critical reflection, in J. J. Boonstra (ed.) *Dynamics of Organizational Change and Learning*, Chichester, John Wiley & Sons.

Harris L. (2002) The learning organisation – myth or reality? Examples from the UK retail banking industry, *The Learning Organization*, Vol.9, No.2; pp.78–88.

Harrison R. (1995) *The Collected Papers of Roger Harrison*, London and New York, McGraw-Hill.

Harrison R. (1972) Understanding your organization's character, *Harvard Business Review*, Vol.50, Issue 3, May-June; pp.119–28.

Harung H. S. (1997) Enhanced learning and performance through a synergy of objective and subjective modes of change, *The Learning Organization*, Vol.4, No.5; pp.193–210.

Harvey Jones J. (1988) *Making it Happen*, Glasgow, Collins.

Hatcher T. (2002) *Ethics and HRD*, Cambridge MA, Perseus.

Hayes J. (2002) *The Theory and Practice of Change Management*, Houndmills, Palgrave.

Heifetz R. A. (1998) Values in leadership (1994), in G. R. Hickman (ed.) *Leading Organizations: Perspectives for a new era*, Thousand Oaks, California, Sage Publications.

Hickman G. R. (ed.) (1998) *Leading Organizations: Perspectives for a new era*, Thousand Oaks, California, Sage Publications.

HODGETTS R. M. (1991) *Organisational Behaviour: Theory and practice*, New York, Macmillan.

HOFSTEDE G. (1991) *Cultures and Organizations, Software of the Mind*, Maidenhead, McGraw-Hill.

HOLMES T. H and RAHE R. H. (1967) The social readjustment rating scale, *Journal of Psychometric Research*, Vol.11; pp.213–18.

HORNSTEIN H. (2001) Organizational development and change management: don't throw the baby out with the bath water, *Journal of Applied Behavioral Science*, Vol.37, No.2, June; pp.223–6.

HOSMER L. T. (1995) Trust: the connecting link between organizational theory and philosophical ethics, *Academy of Management Review*, Vol.20, No.2; pp.379–403.

HUCZYNSKI A. A. (1996) *Management Gurus*, London, International Thomson Business Press.

IACOCCA L. and NOVAK W. (1986) *Iacocca: An Autobiography*, London, Bantam Books.

IHATOR A. S. (2004) Corporate communication: reflections on twentieth-century change, *Corporate Communications: An International Journal*, Vol.9, No.3; pp.243–53.

ILES V. and SUTHERLAND K. (2001) *Managing Change in the NHS: Organisational change*, London, NHS Service Delivery and Organisation R&D Programme (for further details see www.sdo.lshtm.ac.uk).

IRS EMPLOYMENT TRENDS (1997) More than nine in ten organizations experience culture change, *Employment Trends* No.634, Industrial Relations Services.

JACKSON B. (2001) *Management Gurus and Management Fashions*, London, Routledge.

JANIS I. L. (1972) *Victims of Groupthink: A psychological study of foreign policy decisions and fiascos*, Boston, Houghton Mifflin.

JARRETT M. (2003) The seven myths of change management, *Business Strategy Review*, Vol.14, Issue 4; pp.22–9.

JOHNSON G., SCHOLES K. and WHITTINGTON R. (2005) *Exploring Corporate Strategy*, 7th edition, Harlow, FT/Prentice Hall.

JOHNSON P. and GILL J. (1993) *Management Control and Organizational Behaviour*, London, Paul Chapman.

JONES M. (1994) Don't emancipate, exaggerate; rhetoric, reality and reengineering, in R. BASKERVILLE, O. NGWENYAMA, S. SMITHSON and J. I. DEGROSS (eds), *Transforming Organizations with Information*, London, North-Holland.

JONES R. A., JIMMIESON N. L. and GRIFFITHS A. (2005) The impact of organizational culture and reshaping capabilities on change implementation success: the mediating role of readinesss for change, *Journal of Management Studies*, Vol.42, No.2; pp.361–86.

KALLIO J., SAARINEN T. and TINNILÄ M. (2002) Efficient change strategies: matching drivers and tracers in change projects, *Business Process Management Journal*, Vol.8, No.1; pp.80–92.

KANTER R. M., STEIN B. A. and JICK T. D. (1992) *The Challenge of Organizational Change*, New York, Free Press.

KAPLAN A. (1964) *The Conduct of Inquiry*, San Francisco, Chandler.

KAPLINSKY R. (1984) *Automation: The Technology and Society*, Harlow, Longman.

KEENOY T. (1992) Constructing control, in J. F. HARTLEY and G. F. STEPHENSON (eds) *Employment Relations: The psychology of influence and control at work*, Oxford, Blackwell.

KEEP J. and ASH K. (2001) Change agency practice – the future, in B. HAMLIN, J. KEEP and K.

ASH (eds) *Organizational Change and Development: A reflective guide for managers, trainers and developers*, Harlow, FT/Prentice Hall.

KEIDEL K. (1994) Rethinking organizational design, *Academy of Management Executive*, Vol.8, No.4; pp.12–27.

KELEMEN M., FORRESTER P. and HASSARD J. (2000) BPR and TQM: divergence or convergence?, in D. KNIGHTS and H. WILLMOTT (eds) *The Reengineering Revolution: Critical studies of corporate change*, London, Sage Publications.

KETS DE VRIES M. F. (1989) *Prisoners of Leadership*, New York, John Wiley & Sons.

KING N. and ANDERSON N. (2002) *Managing Innovation and Change: A critical guide for organizations,* London, Thomson Learning.

KIRTON M. J. (2003) *Adaption-Innovation: In the context of diversity*, Hove, Routledge.

KNIGHTS D. and COLLINSON D. (1987) Disciplining the shopfloor: a comparison of the disciplinary effects of managerial psychology and financial accounting, *Accounting, Organizations and Society*, Vol.12, No.5; pp.457–77.

KNIGHTS D. and WILLMOTT H. (eds) (2000) *The Reengineering Revolution: Critical studies of corporate change*, London, Sage Publications.

KOLB D. A. (1984) *Experiential Learning: Experience as a source of learning and development*, Englewood Cliffs, Prentice Hall.

KOTTER J. (1990) *A Force for Change: How leadership differs from management*, New York, Free Press.

KOTTER J. P. (1995) Leading change: why transformation efforts fail, *Harvard Business Review*, Vol.73, Issue 2, March-April; pp.59–67.

KOTTER J. P. (1996) *Leading Change*, Boston, Harvard Business School Press.

KOTTER J. and SCHLESINGER L. (1979) Choosing strategies for change, *Harvard Business Review*, Vol.57; pp.106–14.

KUBLER-ROSS E. (1973) *On Death and Dying*, London, Tavistock.

LAJOUX A. R. (1998) *The Art of M&A Integration*, New York, McGraw-Hill.

LAWRENCE P. R. (1969) How to deal with resistance to change, *Harvard Business Review*, Vol.47, Issue 1, January-February; pp.115–22.

LEANA C. R. and BARRY B. (2000) Stability and change as simultaneous experiences in organisational life, *Academy of Management Review*, Vol.25, No.4; pp.753–9.

LEAVITT H. J. (1965) Applied organisational change in industry: structural, technological and humanistic approaches, in J. G. MARCH (ed.) *Handbook of Organizations*, Chicago, Rand McNally.

LEAVITT H. J. (1964) Applied organizational change in industry: structural, technical and human approaches, in W. W. COOPER, H. J. LEAVITT and M. W. SHELLY (eds), *New Perspectives in Organization Research*, New York, Wiley.

LEGGE K. (1995) *Human Resource Management: Rhetorics and Realities*, London, Macmillan.

LEONARD P. (1998) Gendering change? Management, masculinity and the dynamics of incorporation, *Gender and Education*, Vol.10, No.1; pp.71–84.

LEVINE C. H. (1980) *Managing Fiscal Stress: The crisis in the public sector*, Chatham NJ, Chatham House.

LEVINE C. H. (1978) Organizational decline and cut-back management, *Public Administration Review*, Vol.38; pp.316–25.

LEVINE D. P. (2001) The fantasy of inevitability in organisations, *Human Relations*, Vol.54, No.10; pp.1251–65.

LEWIN J. E. and JOHNSTON W. J. (2000) The impact of downsizing and restructuring on organizational competitiveness, *Competitiveness Review*, Vol.10, No.1; pp.45–55.

LEWIN K. (1997) Time perspective and morale (1942), in K. LEWIN *Resolving Social Conflicts and Field Theory in Social Science*, Washington, American Psychological Association.

LEWIN K. (1997) Frontiers in group dynamics (1947), in K. LEWIN *Resolving Social Conflicts and Field Theory in Social Science*, Washington, American Psychological Association.

LEWIN K. (1951) *Field Theory in Social Science*, New York, Harper & Row.

LEWIS L. K. (2000) Communicating change: four cases of quality programs, *Journal of Business Communication*, Vol.37, No.2; pp.128–55.

LINES R. (2004) Influence of participation in strategic change: resistance, organizational commitment and change goal achievement, *Journal of Change Management*, Vol.4, No.3, September; pp.193–215.

LITTLER C. R., WEISNER R. and DUNFORD R. (2000) The dynamics of delayering: changing management structures in three countries, *Journal of Management Studies*, Vol.40, No.2; pp.225–56.

MACY B., BLIESE P. and NORTON J. (1994) Organisational change and work innovation: a meta-analysis of 131 North American field experiments 1962–1990, in R. WOODMAN and W. PASMORE (eds) *Research in Organisation Change and Development*, Vol.7, Greenwich CT, JAI Press.

MANNING P. K. (1992) *Organizational Communication*, New York, Aldine De Gruyter.

MARRIS P. (1974) *Loss and Change*, London, Routledge & Kegan Paul.

MARSHALL J. and CONNER D. (2000) Another reason why companies resist change, *Strategy and Business*, August.

MATHENY J. A. (1998) Organizational therapy: relating a psychotherapeutic model of planned personal change to planned organizational change, *Journal of Managerial Psychology*, Vol.13, No.5–6; pp.394–405.

MAYO E. (1933) *The Human Problems of an Industrial Civilization*, Basingstoke, Macmillan.

MCEWAN T. (2001) *Managing Values and Beliefs in Organisations*, Harlow, FT/Prentice Hall.

MCKENNA E. and BEECH N. (1995) *The Essence of Human Resource Management*, London, Prentice Hall.

MCKENNA E. (2000) *Business Psychology and Organisational Behaviour: A student's handbook*, Hove, Psychology Press.

MCKINLEY W., ZHAO J. and RUST K. (2000) A sociological interpretation of organizational downsizing, *Academy of Management Review*, Vol.25, No.1; pp.227–43.

MCLOUGHLIN I. and CLARK J. (1994) *Technological Change at Work*, Buckingham, Open University Press.

MCLOUGHLIN I. (1999) *Creative Technological Change: The shaping of technology and organisations*, London, Routledge.

MENTO A. J., JONES R. M. and DIRNDORFER W. (2002) A change management process:

grounded in both theory and practice, *Journal of Change Management*, Vol.3, No.1; pp.45–69.

MERRON K. (1993) Let's bury the term 'resistance', *Organizational Development Journal*, Vol.11, No.4; pp.77–86.

MILES R. E. and SNOW C. C. (1984) Fit, failure and the hall of fame, *California Management Review*, Vol.26, No.3; pp.36–52.

MILLER D. and FRIESEN P. H. (1984) *Organizations: A quantum view*, Englewood Cliffs NJ, Prentice Hall.

MILLER D. (2002) Successful change leaders: what makes them? What do they do that is different? *Journal of Change Management*, Vol.2, No.4; pp.359–68.

MINTZBERG H. (1983) *Structure in Fives: Designing effective organizations*, New Jersey, Prentice Hall International Editions.

MINTZBERG H., AHLSTRAND B. and LAMPEL J. (1998) *Strategy Safari*, London, FT/Prentice Hall.

MORGAN G. and STURDY A. (2000) *Beyond Organizational Change: Structure, discourse and power in UK financial services*, London, Macmillan.

MORGAN G. (1986) *Images of Organization*, Newbury Park, Sage Publications.

MORRISON D. (1994) Psychological contracts and change, *Human Resource Management*, Vol.33, No.3, Fall; pp.353–72.

MORRISON E. W. and MILLIKEN F. J. (2000) Organizational silence: a barrier to change and development in a pluralistic world, *Academy of Management Review*, Vol.25, No.4; pp.706–25.

MOVVA R. (2003) Myths as a vehicle for transforming organizations, *The Leadership and Organization Development Journal*, Vol.25, No.1; pp.41–57.

MULLINS L. J. (2005) *Management and Organisational Behaviour*, 7th edition, Harlow, FT/Prentice Hall.

NADLER D. A. and TUSHMAN M. L. (2004) Beyond the charismatic leader: leadership and organizational change (1990), in M. L. TUSHMAN and P. ANDERSON *Managing Strategic Innovation and Change: A collection of readings*, New York, Oxford University Press.

NADLER D. A. and TUSHMAN M. L. (1997) *Competing by Design: The power of organizational architecture*, Oxford, Oxford University Press.

NONAKA I. (1991) The knowledge-creating company, *Harvard Business Review*, November/December; pp.96–104.

NUTT P. C. (2004) Organizational de-development, *Journal of Management Studies*, Vol.41, No.7; pp.1083–103.

OGBONNA E. and WILKINSON B. (2003) The false promise of organizational culture change: a case study of middle managers in grocery retailing, *Journal of Management Studies*, Vol.40, No.5; pp.1151–78.

ORLIKOWSKI W. J. and BARLEY S. R. (2001) Technology and institutions: what can research on information technology and research on organizations learn from each other? *MIS Quarterly*, Vol.25, No.2, June; pp.145–65.

OXMAN J. A. and SMITH B. D. (2003) The limits of structural change, *MIT Sloan Management Review*, Fall; pp.77–82.

PAGE T. (1998) *Diary of a Change Agent*, Aldershot, Gower.

PASCALE R. T. (1990) *Managing on the Edge*, New York, Touchstone.

PATON R. and DEMPSTER L. (2002) Managing change from a gender perspective, *European Management Journal*, Vol.20, No.5; pp.539–48.

PATON R. A. and MCCALMAN J. (2000) *Change Management: A guide to effective implementation*, 2nd edition, London, Sage Publications.

PAVITT K. and STEINMUELLER W. E. (2002) Technology in corporate strategy: change, continuity and the information revolution, in A. PETTIGREW, H. THOMAS and R. WHITTINGTON (eds) *Handbook of Strategy and Management*, London, Sage Publications.

PEARCE J. A. II and RAVLIN E. (1987) The design and activation of self-regulating work groups, *Human Relations*, Vol.40; pp.751–82.

PEDLER M., BURGOYNE J. and BOYDELL T. (1991, 1997) *The Learning Company: A strategy for sustainable development*, 1st and 2nd editions, London, McGraw-Hill.

PERREN L. and MEGGINSON D. (1996) Resistance to change as a positive force: its dynamics and issues for management development, *Career Development International*, Vol.1, No.4; pp.24–8.

PETERS T. J. and WATERMAN R. H. (1982) *In Search of Excellence: Lessons from America's best run companies*, New York, Harper & Row.

PETTIGREW A. M. (1973) *The Politics of Organizational Decision-Making*, London, Tavistock.

PETTIGREW A. M. (1977) Strategy formulation as a political process, *International Studies of Management and Organization*, Vol.7, No.2, Summer; pp.78–87.

PETTIGREW A. M. (1979) On studying organizational cultures, *Administrative Science Quarterly*, Vol.24, No.4; pp.570–81.

PETTIGREW A. M. (1985) *The Awakening Giant: Continuity and change in ICI*, Oxford, Blackwell.

PETTIGREW A. M. (1990) Longitudinal field research on change theory and practice, *Organization Science*, Vol.1, No.3; pp.267–92.

PETTIGREW A. M. (1992) The character and significance of strategy process research, *Strategic Management Journal*, Vol.13, Special issue; pp.5–16.

PETTIGREW, A. (1999) Organising to improve company performance, Warwick Business School, *Hot Topics*, Vol.1, No.5; pp.1–7.

PETTIGREW A., FERLIE E. and McKEE L. (1992) *Shaping Strategic Change: Making change in large organizations*, London, Sage Publications.

PETTIGREW A. M. and FENTON E. M. (eds) (2000) *The Innovating Organization*, London, Sage Publications.

PETTIGREW A., THOMAS H., and WHITTINGTON R. (2002) Strategic management: the strengths and limitations of a field, in A. PETTIGREW, H. THOMAS and R. WHITTINGTON (eds) *Handbook of Strategy and Management*, London, Sage Publications.

PIDERIT S. K. (2000) Rethinking resistance and recognizing ambivalence: a multidimensional view of attitudes toward an organizational change, *Academy of Management Review*, Vol.25, No.4; pp.783–94.

PIORE M. J. and SABEL C. F. (1984) *The Second Industrial Divide: Possibilities for prosperity*, New York, Basic Books.

POOLE M. and MANSFIELD R. (1992) Managers' attitudes to human resource management:

rhetoric and reality, in P. BLYTON and P. TURNBULL (eds) *Reassessing Human Resource Management*, London, Sage Publications.

PREECE D. (1995) *Organisations and Technical Change: Strategy, objectives and involvement*, London, Routledge.

PREECE D. (2005) Technology and organisations, in L. J. MULLINS (ed.) *Management and Organisational Behaviour*, Harlow, FT/Prentice Hall.

PROBST G. and BUCHEL B. (1997) *Organizational Learning*, London, Prentice Hall.

PROCHASKA J. O. (1984) *Systems of Psychotherapy*, Homewood IL, Dorsey Press.

PURCELL J. (1987) Mapping management styles in employee relations, *Journal of Management Studies*, Vol.24, No.5; pp.533–48.

QUIRKE B. (1995) *Communicating Change*, London, McGraw-Hill.

QUIRKE B. (1996) *Communicating Corporate Change: A practical guide to communication and corporate strategy*, London, McGraw-Hill.

RANDALL J. (2004) *Managing Change/Changing Managers*, London, Routledge.

REDMAN T. and GRIEVES J. (1999) Managing strategic change through TQM: learning from failure, *New Technology, Work and Employment*, Vol.14, No.1; pp.45–61.

REED P. J. (2001) *Extraordinary Leadership: Creating strategies for change*, London, Kogan Page.

RICKARDS T. (1999) *Creativity and the Management of Change*, Oxford, Blackwell Business.

RITZER G. (2004) *The McDonaldization of Society*, Revised New Century Edition, Thousand Oaks, California, Pine Forge Press.

ROBBINS H. and FINLEY M. (1998) *Why Teams Don't Work*, London, Orion Business.

ROBBINS S. P. (2005) *Organizational Behavior*, 11th edition, New Jersey, Pearson Prentice Hall.

ROBERTSON P. J. and SENEVIRATNE S. J. (1995) Outcomes of planned organisational change in the public sector: a meta analytic comparison to the private sector, *Public Administration Review*, Vol.55, No.6; pp.547–58.

ROLLINSON D. (2005) *Organisational Behaviour and Analysis: An integrated approach*, 3rd edition, Harlow, FT/Prentice Hall.

ROMANELLI E. and TUSHMAN M. L. (1994) Organizational transformation as punctuated equilibrium: an empirical test, *Academy of Management Journal*, Vol.37, No.5; pp.1141–66.

ROSE N. (1989) *Governing the Soul: The shaping of private self*, London, Routledge.

ROSENBROCK H. H. (1989) *Designing Human-Centred Technology*, London, Springer Verlag.

SALAMAN G. and ASCH D. (2003) *Strategy and Capability: Sustaining organizational change*, Oxford, Blackwell.

SALAMAN G. (1997) Culturing production, in P. DU GAY (ed.) *Production of Culture/Cultures of Production*, London, Sage Publications in Association with the Open University.

SALEM M., LAZARUS H. and CULLEN J. (1994) Developing self-managing teams: structure and performance, *Journal of Management Development*, Vol.11, No.3; pp.24–32.

SATHE V. (1985) *Culture and Related Corporate Realities*, Homewood IL, Irwin.

SCARBROUGH H. and CORBETT J. M. (1992) *Technology and Organization: Power, meaning and design*, London, Routledge.

SCHEIN E. H. (1992) *Organizational Culture and Leadership*, San Francisco, Jossey Bass.

SCHNEIDER B., BRIEF A. P. and GUZZO R. A. (1996) Creating a climate and culture for sustainable organizational change, *Organizational Dynamics*, Vol.24, No.4; pp.7–19.

SCHON D. A. (1963) Champions for radical new inventions, *Harvard Business Review*, Vol.46, Issue 2, March-April; pp.77–86.

SENGE P. (1990) *The Fifth Discipline: The art and practice of the learning organisation*, London, Random House Business Books.

SENIOR B. and FLEMING J. (2006) *Organisational Change*, 3rd edition, Harlow, FT/Prentice Hall.

SENNETT R. (2001) Failure, in G. SALAMAN (ed.) *Understanding Business Organisations*, London, Routledge in association with the Open University.

SHAH P. (2000) Network destruction: the structural implications of downsizing, *Academy of Management Journal*, Vol.43, No.1; pp.101–12.

SHEPARD H. A. (1967) Innovation-resisting and innovation-producing organizations, *Journal of Business*, Vol.40; pp.470–7.

SILVERMAN D. (1970) *The Theory of Organisations*, London, Heinemann Educational Books.

SINANGIL H. K. and AVALLONE F. (2001) Organizational development and change, in H. K. SINANGIL and C. VISWESVARAN (eds) *Handbook of Industrial Work and Organizational Psychology*, Vols. I and II, London/New York, Sage Publications.

SMITH M. E. (2003) Changing an organisation's culture: correlates of success and failure, *The Leadership and Organization Development Journal*, Vol.24, No.5; pp.249–61.

SORGE A. and VAN WITTELOOSTUIJN A. (2004) The (non)sense of organizational change: an essay about universal management hypes, sick consultancy metaphors and healthy organization theories, *Organization Studies*, Vol.25, No.7; pp.1205–31.

STACE D. and DUNPHY D. (2001) *Beyond the Boundaries: Leading and recreating the successful enterprise*, Sydney, McGraw-Hill.

STACEY R. D. (2003) *Strategic Management and Organisational Dynamics: The challenge of complexity*, 4th edition, Harlow, FT/Prentice Hall.

STEIN J. R. (1995) Towards a socio-economic framework on technological change, *International Journal of Social Economics*, Vol.22, No.6; pp.38–52.

STICKLAND F. (1998) *The Dynamics of Change*, London, Routledge.

STREATFIELD P. J. (2001) *The Paradox of Control in Organizations*, London, Routledge.

STUART R. (1995) Experiencing organisational change: triggers, processes and outcomes of change journeys, *Personnel Review*, Vol.24, No. 2; pp.3–87.

STURDY A. and GREY C. (2003) Beneath and beyond organizational change management: exploring alternatives, *Organization*, Vol.10, No.4; pp.651–62.

TARAS D. G. and BENNETT J. T. (2002) Technological change and industrial relations, *Journal of Labor Economics*, Volume XXIII, Number 3, Summer; pp.335–8.

TAYLOR F. W. (1911) *Scientific Management*, New York, Wiley.

THOMPSON P. and MCHUGH D. (2001) Studying organisations: an introduction, in G. SALAMAN (ed.) *Understanding Business: Organisations*, London, Routledge in association with the Open University.

THOMPSON P. and MCHUGH D. (2002) *Work Organisations: A critical introduction*, 3rd edition, Basingstoke, Palgrave.

THOMPSON P. and O'CONNELL DAVIDSON J. (1995) The continuity of discontinuity: managerial rhetoric in turbulent times, *Personnel Review*, Vol.24, No.4; pp.17–33.

THOMPSON P. (1989) *The Nature of Work: An introduction to debates on the labour process*, London, Macmillan.

THORNE M. L. (2000) Interpreting corporate transformation through failure, *Management Decision*, Vol.38. No.5; pp.305–14.

THORNHILL A., LEWIS P., MILLMORE M. and SAUNDERS M. (2000) *Managing Change: A human resource strategy approach*, Harlow, FT/Prentice Hall.

TICHY N. M. (1983) *Managing Strategic Change: Technical, political and cultural dynamics*, New York, John Wiley & Sons.

TIDD J., BESSANT J. and PAVITT K. (2005) *Managing Innovation: Integrating technological, market and organizational change*, Chichester, John Wiley & Sons.

TORRINGTON D., HALL L. and TAYLOR S. (2002) *Human Resource Management*, Harlow, FT/Prentice Hall.

TOURISH D. and PINNINGTON A. (2002) Transformational leadership, corporate cultism and the spirituality paradigm: an unholy trinity in the workplace? *Human Relations*, Vol.55, No.2; pp.147–72.

TOWNLEY B. (1994) *Reframing Human Resource Management*, London, Sage Publications.

TRIST E. L. and BAMFORTH K. W. (1951) Some social and psychological consequences of the Longwall method of coal getting, *Human Relations*, Vol.4, No.3; pp.3–38.

TUCKMAN B. W. (1965) Development sequence in small groups, *Psychological Bulletin*, No.63; pp.384–99.

TYSON S. (1995) *Human Resource Strategy: Towards a general theory of human resource management*, London, Pitman.

URWICK L. (1947) *The Elements of Administration*, 2nd edition, London, Pitman.

VAN DER BENT J., PAAUWE J. and WILLIAMS R. (1999) Organizational learning: an exploration of organizational memory and its role in organizational change processes, *Journal of Organizational Change Management*, Vol.12, No.5; pp.377–404.

WALTON E. and RUSSELL M. (2004) Organizational change: strategies and interventions, in J. J. BOONSTRA (ed.) *Dynamics of Organizational Change and Learning*, Chichester, John Wiley & Sons.

WALTON R. E. (1985) From control to commitment: transforming work-force management in the USA, in K. CLARK, R. H. HAYES and C. LORENZ (eds), *The Uneasy Alliance: Managing the productivity- technology dilemma*, Boston MA, Harvard Business School Press.

WATSON G. (1969) Resistance to change, in W. G. BENNIS, K. D. BENNE and R. CHIN (eds) *The Planning of Change*, New York, Holt, Rinehart & Winston.

WATSON T. (2002) *Organising and Managing Work*, Harlow, FT/Prentice Hall.

WATSON T. J. (1995) In search of HRM: beyond the rhetoric and reality distinction, or the case of the dog that didn't bark, *Personnel Review*, Vol.24, No.4; pp.6–16.

WATSON T. J. (2003) *Sociology, Work and Industry*, 4th edition, London, Routledge.

WEBER M. (1947) *The Theory of Social and Economic Organization (trans)*, Glencoe IL, Free Press.

WEISS J. W. (2001) *Organizational Behavior and Change: Managing diversity, cross-cultural dynamics, and ethics*, Cincinnati, Ohio, South-Western College Publishing (a division of Thomson Learning).

WEISS J. W. (2003) *Business Ethics: A stakeholder and issues management approach*, Cincinnati, Ohio, South-Western College Publishing (a division of Thomson Learning).

WEST M. A., HIRST G., RICHTER A. and SHIPTON H. (2004) Twelve steps to heaven: successfully managing change through developing innovative teams, *European Journal of Work and Organizational Psychology*, Vol.13, No.2; pp.269–99.

WHIPP R. (1996) Creative deconstruction: strategy and organization, in S. R. CLEGG, C. HARDY and W. R. NORD (eds) *Handbook of Organization Studies*, London, Sage Publications.

WHITTINGTON R. (2001) *What is Strategy and Does it Matter?* London, Routledge.

WILKINSON A., GODFREY G. and MARCHINGTON M. (1997) Bouquets, brickbats and blinkers: Total Quality Management and employee involvement, *Organization Studies*, Vol.18, No.5; pp.799–819.

WILKINSON A., REDMAN T., SNAPE E. and MARCHINGTON M. (1998) *Managing with Total Quality Management: Theory and practice*, London, Macmillan.

WILKINSON B. (1983) *The Shop Floor Politics of New Technology*, London, Heinemann.

WILLCOCKS L. and MASON D. (1987) *Computerising Work: People, systems design and workplace relations*, London, Paradigm.

WILLMOTT H. (1994) Business process re-engineering and human resource management, *Personnel Review*, Vol.23, No.3; pp.34–46.

WILLMOTT H. (1993) Strength is ignorance; slavery is freedom: managing culture in modern organizations, *Journal of Management Studies*, Vol.30, No.4; pp.515–52.

WILLMOTT H. (1995) The odd couple? Re-engineering business processes: managing human relations, *New Technology, Work and Employment*, Vol.10, No.2; pp.89–98.

WILSON D. (1992) *A Strategy of Change*, London, Routledge.

WILSON E. (ed.) (2001) *Organizational Behaviour Reassessed: The impact of gender*, London, Sage Publications.

WIRTENBERG J., ABRAMS L. and OTT C. (2004) Assessing the field of organization development, *The Journal of Applied Behavioral Science*, Vol.40, No.4; pp.465–79.

WOODD M. (1997) Human resource specialists – guardians of ethical conduct?, *Journal of European Industrial Training*, Vol.21, No.3; pp.110–16.

WOODWARD J. (1958) *Management and Technology*, London, HMSO.

WOODWARD J. (1965) *Industrial Organization: Theory and practice*, London, Oxford University Press.

WOODWARD S. and HENDRY C. (2004) Leading and coping with change, *Journal of Change Management*, Vol.4, No.3; pp.155–83.

WORLEY C. G. and FEYERHERM A. E. (2003) Reflections on the future of organization development, *The Journal of Applied Behavioral Science*, Vol.39, No.1; pp.97–115.

WORREN N. A. M., RUDDLE K. and MOORE K. (1999) From organizational development to change management: the emergence of a new profession, *The Journal of Applied Behavioral Science*, Vol.35, No.3, September; pp.273–86.

WORTHINGTON I. (2003a) Business organisations: the external environment, in I. WORTHINGTON and C. BRITTON (eds) *The Business Environment*, Harlow, FT/Prentice Hall.

WORTHINGTON I. (2003b) Monitoring change, in I. WORTHINGTON and C. BRITTON (eds) *The Business Environment*, Harlow, FT/Prentice Hall.

WREGE C. D. and HODGETTS R. M. (2000) Frederick W. Taylor's 1899 pig iron observations: examining fact, fiction, and lessons for the new millennium, *Academy of Management Journal*, Vol.43, No.6; pp.1283–91.

WRIGHT C. (2005) Critical consulting: new perspectives on the management advice industry (book review), *Journal of Management Studies*, Vol.42, No.2; pp.467–70.

YOUNGE G. (2002) The stirrer, *The Guardian Weekend*, 20 July, pp.37–40.

ZWEIG P. (1995) The case against mergers, *Business Week*, 30 October.

Index

Also from CIPD Publishing . . .

Business Environment:

Managing in a strategic context

John Kew and John Stredwick

Business environment has become an established and growing part of most business courses. Having knowledge of the key environmental influences – economic, social, and legal – is essential to developing an understanding of business strategy at every level.

Written in an easy to use format, for students with little or no prior knowledge of the subject area, practical implications of theories are emphasised and examples clearly set out.

The text also includes chapter objectives, student activities, definitions, case studies, lists of further reading and a tutor support site.

Order your copy now online at www.cipd.co.uk/bookstore or call us on 0870 800 3366

John Kew was Principal Lecturer in Management Studies and Head of the Business School at Harlow College until 1993, teaching Business Environment and Strategic Management on CIPD and DMS programmes. Since 1993 he has been an educational consultant, and has also written Flexible Learning material for the CIPD's Professional Development Scheme.

John Stredwick spent 25 years as a Human Resource Practitioner in publishing and shipbuilding before joining Everest Double Glazing for 11 years as Head of Personnel. In 1992, he joined Luton University as Senior Lecturer and has directed the CIPD programmes since that time. *Business Environment* is his sixth with the CIPD. He is a national moderator for the CIPD and has run several CIPD short courses on reward management.

Published 2005	1 84398 079 7	Paperback	304 pages

The Chartered Institute of Personnel and Development is the leading publisher of books and reports for personnel and training professionals, students and all those concerned with the effective management and development of people at work.

Also from CIPD Publishing . . .

Personal Effectiveness

Diana Winstanley

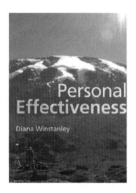

Written by a leading author in this field, this new text on Personal Effectiveness is designed to give students a basic understanding of study skills and management skills, and to give context to other studies.

Suitable for use on a range of undergraduate and postgraduate modules, including those relating to self development, personal skills, learning and development, management skills, study skills and coaching modules, and as part of general business or HR degrees, this text seeks to be both comprehensive and accessible through the use of learning aids.

Each chapter includes:
- learning objectives and a synopsis of content;
- vignette examples to illustrate key points;
- exercises with feedback;
- a self-check exercise and synopsis at the end of the chapter; and
- references and further sources of information.

Order your copy now online at www.cipd.co.uk/bookstore or call us on 0870 800 3366

Diana Winstanley has over 15 years experience of training staff, students and managers in personal effectiveness, as well as in human resource management, and is already a well respected author of a number of books and articles. She has also led, designed and supported a number of PhD and postgraduate programmes in transferable skills and personal effectiveness, and is currently Professor of Management and Director of Postgraduate Programmes at Kingston Business School. Previously she has been Senior Lecturer in Management and Personal Development, Deputy Director of the full-time MBA programme and Senior Tutor at Tanaka Business School, Imperial College London. She also has professional qualifications as a humanistic counsellor.

| Published 2005 | 1 84398 002 9 | Paperback | 256 pages |

The Chartered Institute of Personnel and Development is the leading publisher of books and reports for personnel and training professionals, students and all those concerned with the effective management and development of people at work.

Also from CIPD Publishing . . .

Personnel Practice

4th edition

Malcolm Martin and Tricia Jackson

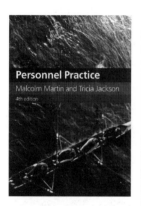

Personnel Practice is widely acclaimed as the definitive introduction to human resource management. It is designed specifically to cater for the CIPD Certificate in Personnel Practice and is invaluable for all students taking the Certificate as well as anyone seeking an overview of the subject area.

This new edition offers an updated look at the subject area, with coverage of up-to-date legislation and information management. Each chapter has a clear overview and concise summary, providing ideal points for revision and reference. The text also contains detailed sources of further information, alongside activities and case studies to test knowledge and link knowledge to practice.

'Personnel Practice should be the standard reference text for all line managers, HR practitioners and undergraduate HR and personnel students developing an interest in and/or responsibility for HR issues who need an understanding of maximising people performance in today's competitive environment.' Alan Lund MCIPD, Programme Manager, East Lancashire Business School

Order your copy now online at www.cipd.co.uk/bookstore or call us on 0870 800 3366

Malcolm Martin BSc, MCMI, FCIPD has been involved in the design and delivery of the Certificate in Personnel Practice programmes for many years, primarily at the training provider, MOL. He has worked for British Steel, Dunlop, Guthrie and the BBA Group, where he held managerial positions in industrial relations, project management and personnel. Since then he has directed numerous CPP courses for corporate clients and for public programmes.

Tricia Jackson BA, MSc (Personnel Management), MInstAM, Chartered FCIPD is a freelance training and personnel consultant, specialising in employment law. Tricia has many years' experience as a generalist practitioner in both the public and private sectors. She is currently involved in tutoring on open-learning and college-based CIPD programmes, competence assessment, identifying and providing training solutions, personnel consultancy and representing clients at employment tribunals.

Published 2004	1 84398 102 5	Paperback	240 pages

The Chartered Institute of Personnel and Development is the leading publisher of books and reports for personnel and training professionals, students and all those concerned with the effective management and development of people at work.

Students

Save 20% when buying direct from the CIPD using the Student Discount Scheme

The Chartered Institute of Personnel and Development (CIPD) is the leading publisher of books and reports for personnel and training professionals, students, and for all those concerned with the effective management and development of people at work.

The CIPD offers ALL students a 20% discount on textbooks and selected practitioner titles.

To claim your discount, and to see a full list of titles available, call 0870 800 3366 quoting 'Student Discount Scheme 1964' – alternatively, visit us online at www.cipd.co.uk/bookstore.

Order online at www.cipd.co.uk/bookstore or call us on 0870 800 3366

NB This offer is exclusive of any other offers from the CIPD and applies to CIPD Publishing textbooks only.